The
Neighbor's Son

Liesel Appel

ISBN 0-7414-2777-X

Published by:

PUBLISHING.COM

1094 New DeHaven Street, Suite 100
West Conshohocken, PA 19428-2713
Info@buybooksontheweb.com
www.buybooksontheweb.com
Toll-free (877) BUY BOOK
Local Phone (610) 941-9999
Fax (610) 941-9959

Printed in the United States of America

Printed on Recycled Paper

Published October 2005

Dedication

With great humbleness I dedicate this book to the forgotten Jews of Bottrop, in particular the Meyer family. And to the German women and men of my generation who rejected their country's past and made the world their home.

... forget your own selves, and turn your eyes towards your neighbor.

Baha'u'llah

I am alone but not lonely
Just my solitary self
With huge strange thoughts
A wanderer on a spiritual quest
With a lifelong feeling of statelessness

No home for my soul
No rest till the end of my quest
Misunderstood and betrayed
Is it too late?
To walk the meadows and hills
Of my childhood again?

Has my country changed?
Nothing stays the same
I have my dead
And must let them go
To hold on is to die myself
And mutilate my soul
But the beautiful and true
We must retain forever
I am who I am.

Part One

Nebulous Womb

Chapter 1

Bottrop - Eigen, Germany 1951

I CAN'T REMEMBER what day of the week or what month, but it was spring around Easter time. Not many trees or flowers blossomed on Gladbecker Strasse, a busy thoroughfare in the gray coal-mining town of Bottrop near Essen north of Cologne.

The day began like most days. My mother fussed over my lack of appetite, coaxed me to eat a little more of my breakfast and drink more of the honey-sweetened, warm milk which always formed a skin on top. I can still see her there on her wooden chair opposite me at the kitchen table; the white and blue cross-stitched linen table cloth with the matching napkin to protect my lap from any spills. Manners and proper eating habits I had been taught early which included sitting upright on the front of my chair, not lean forward or slouch back. My left hand, formed into a fist clenched my thumb and had to remain by the side of my plate. No elbows on the table were tolerated in our home.

I attended the Volkschule (public school) and was already in the third grade. We were on spring vacation. I had asked Mother, whom I called Mutti, if I could play outside after I was done with breakfast.

At nine years old I would have loved the company of other children, but because of class differences to make contact

1

with the little girl who lived opposite us in a small dingy track house on Gladbecker Strasse was not proper. Her father was a coal miner and Mother said "you have nothing in common with her." Still, I knew her name was Erika and we sometimes waved to each other.

At this time of year the heavy, itchy wool stockings I had worn since fall were replaced by cotton knee socks held up with elastic. I hopped in the air to test how much lighter my body felt and Mother said, "Stand still." She buttoned the navy cardigan she had knitted for me right up to under my chin. I was eager to escape my mother's control.

She issued her warnings, as she usually did, about what not to do while outside. "Don't get dirty, don't bother the neighbors and don't cross the street."

In those days and in our neighborhood where everyone knew each other it did not include a caution about strangers. In all likelihood no unknown person would come our way.

I was ready to go outdoors when Frau Lauder, one of our tenants who lived with her ailing husband above us on the third floor, stopped by to speak to Mother. She was in a highly agitated state and I was resigned that she had spied on me again and observed me do something wrong, such as leave the front door of our apartment building open. I was sure to be reprimanded for it later. When my mother ushered Frau Lauder into the living room I took advantage of the moment and ran down the stairs.

On this day rather than play in the shady back garden I decided on the sunny pavement out front. I was good at finding ways to occupy myself. Children like me were called a Nachkoemmling (late descendant). My only sibling, Fritz, was already twenty years old when I was born.

I drew eight large hopscotch squares. Then I skipped on my right leg while I slid a smooth, broken piece of tile around without touching the lines. My game kept me absorbed and I made it more and more complicated for myself by taking bigger jumps.

Then I sensed his presence.

I did not see him approach. He did not arrive by car or on the tram which passed along our street hourly and made a stop near our house. I never looked up until he was very near and stood just outside the perimeter of the white chalk lines of my game.

It was strange that at this moment there was no one else on any part of the street and all the businesses seemed deserted. Our block had a Gasthof (Tavern), Kino (Movie Theater), butcher shop and the Koch's bakery as well as a milliners, grocery store and cigarette shop in the building we owned. Not even the small department store to the left of the Kino had anyone going in or out.

I continued to play hopscotch. Every once in a while I turned my head and looked up at him.

Now the man spoke. "Guten Tag. Kleinest Maedel wo wohnst Du? (Good day. Little girl where do you live?)"

Without my mother's permission I wasn't sure if I should reply. I abandoned my game and backed up towards our front door. Then I pointed to our three-storey brick townhouse behind me.

The stranger was dressed in special occasion or business attire, dark suit, shirt and tie. He looked somewhat like my almost thirty year old brother, but Fritz was taller and fairer.

3

I was surprised, but not frightened by the man. His brown eyes were kind and his face bore a smile. What was in the briefcase he carried? I did't say a word and continued to stare; he was beginning to fascinate me. His complexion had a summer's tan and how curious, a round, black piece of cloth much smaller than a hat was bobby-pinned to his dark, curly hair.

Papa came to my mind. He had worn big felt hats with a crease on top to keep the rain off his face, but this cap was small, barely visible from the front and wouldn't protect him from the weather. Mutti used bobby pins on my hair sometimes to keep my braids in place, but I had never seen them on a man.

After we checked each other out a little longer the man spoke again. "Don't be frightened little girl," he said.

I wondered if I should run inside.

"I'm from Bottrop and lived here before the war." His voice was sad, but he still smiled at me. "You're too young and weren't born yet when my family and I left."

So this is what it was, I felt better. Doctors made house calls and he looked like one. I thought that maybe Frau Lauder's husband was sick again and therefore she had stopped by to get Mutti's advice just before I slipped outside.

"Herr Lauder's upstairs," I said, helpful.

The man still cast his eyes around as I became chattier. "We haven't been here that long, just four and a half years."

He seemed pre-occupied.

"My Oma and Opa are dead. This was their house. Now it's ours. Mutti says we need the rent."

Now he gave me his full attention. "What were their

4

names?"

"Their name was Menken and they had a grocery store."

"Menken," he said. "Fritz and Wilhelmina, nice people, put things on credit if someone couldn't pay for food."

I nodded. Often Mutti told me how benevolent my grandparents had been, especially Oma. Our family joked about certain neighbors who had always come up with ridiculous excuses when it was time to pay. Oma had put necessities like eggs, bread, butter and salt herrings on a handwritten tab for them and Oma was gullible. She believed the hard luck stories and her bookkeeping notes got lost.

"People took advantage of Oma, drove your grandparents almost into bankruptcy," my mother said. "But I sent those freeloaders packing."

"My brother's named after Opa, his name's also Fritz." I now felt more at ease with the stranger because he knew my grandparents and said they were nice.

"Are you by chance the Steffens' daughter?"

"I am."

"Then, tell me what's your name?"

"Liesel, Liesel Steffens. Do you know my parents?"

"Yes, I do."

"How come?"

He put the briefcase down between his legs and pointed at the department store to the left of the Kino.

"We were next door neighbors. 334 Gladbecker Strasse that building and store belonged to us."

5

I frowned. Now he was making up a story and I couldn't let him get away with it. I knew for sure it was the Witke's store and that they resided in the apartment above.

"Nah nah," I said and shook my head. "The Witkes have always lived there."

He became very serious. "No, Kleine," he said, "not always. My family built that store. It was ours until all Jewish property was destroyed."

"Jewish property? What's that?"

"You heard about Kristallnacht, haven't you?"

I thought he said Christmas Nacht (night).

"That's when we were attacked and lost everything."

"You lost everything on Christmas Nacht?"

"They took my father away. My poor mother and dear wife. They were beaten and thrown on the pavement."

"They were beaten, why? What did you do?"

"I couldn't help them. I was unconscious by that time."

He took a handkerchief from his pocket, wiped his eyes, paused and then murmured.

"I don't know why I'm telling you this. They grabbed our infant son from his baby carriage and threw him off the second floor balcony at the back of that building."

"Oh, no, that's awful! Why did they do such a horrible thing?"

"We escaped Bottrop with nothing but our lives. Today is the first time I've come back."

I had never heard anything like it. "Where did you go?"

6

"Another far away country," he said. "Israel. Ich bin ein Jude."

Jude? I had no idea what a Jew was. I had never heard of Israel. What I had just been told was shocking beyond belief. My upbringing taught me politeness towards all adults. Lawyers and doctors were addressed by Herr Doktor and Herr Anwalt.

I said, "Herr Jude if you live faraway why have you come back to Bottrop?"

Now he smiled again. "My son and I are visiting a good friend, a lady, over on Sterckrader Strasse. I came here to look for a special man."

"What kind of man?"

He answered with care. "You see little girl because of this man my son's life was spared. Blessed be God, a miracle happened."

"It did?"

"Yes, it did. In the darkness of the night with all the broken glass a man caught the baby in his arms. He saved our son from certain death, at the time we had no idea."

"You didn't?"

"Gendarmes came and took us away. We thought our son was forever gone."

Tears rolled down my cheeks and I quickly wiped them with the back of my hand.

"Please don't cry," he said. "It took many years, but we were reunited with our son and he's alive and well."

"Danke, danke," I said.

7

"Now little girl comes the important part. I don't know who this man was, only that he lived here. I came to express deep gratitude to him. Do you understand me?"

What a horrible story. A little boy thrown from the balcony. People beaten. I couldn't imagine such awful things had happened in our peaceful neighborhood. But the ending was good and it got even better. I knew the man who must have saved the baby.

"That man was my Papa," I declared.

Now the stranger looked surprised. "Then my search has come to an end," he said.

There was no doubt in my mind that my beloved Father was the person he had come to thank. How many times had I watched Papa bring poor people home from the streets? Give them food and a friendly word even though Mutti protested? There had been countless occasions of my father's generosity. My chest swelled with pride at this moment.

"My Papa," I said again.

"Can you take me to see him, please? I can't wait a minute longer."

"Oh no, that's not possible." My tears flowed again. "Papa's dead. Last summer; that's when he died."

The disappointment in the visitor's voice is something I will never forget. "What a tragedy; should have returned sooner. Your father was a very brave man. He took a great risk that night."

I nodded. "My Papa was the bravest."

"Such a heroic deed and I've come too late."

He looked at me with sorrowful eyes. "How tragic, so young and no father. You loved your Papa very much, didn't you?"

"Oh yes," I said to my new friend to cheer him up. "He was wonderful. I was his favorite, everywhere we went together. I'm a Wunschkind (desired child) you know."

Mother and I had not gotten over the fact that Papa was no longer by our side to guide us with his strength. Mother often said, "Liesel, we have been left to fend for ourselves."

"Good bye, Liesel Steffens." The stranger shook my hand and turned to go. "Great pleasure to meet the daughter of such a brave man, one day I hope to see you again." He picked up his briefcase.

Little did I know that my life was just about to take a drastic turn. "Please, don't leave," I suddenly said, "come inside and meet Mutti."

The man hesitated and seemed to think over my invitation. I reached for his left hand and pulled him through the door. This was the right thing to do and the man said nothing when I hurriedly climbed the two flights of stairs to our apartment with him in tow.

"Kommen Sie schnell (come on quickly). Mutti remembers. She'll be proud that Papa saved your baby. We'll all be happy."

When I remember back, the man might not have wanted to intrude, but I wasn't going to let that stop me. He had lived next door and there was something special about him. Neighbors didn't need an invitation; they always popped in to ask Mutti for advice on one thing or another. He already knew our family and our names. Mutti would recognize him and she would be pleased with me for bringing him to her. Plus he had come a long way from a different country and needed our hospitality. Maybe we could put him up in the guestroom for a day or two. I was eager to hear more of his unbelievable story and wanted to get Mutti's opinion. In my mind Father was always a hero.

Our apartment door was usually locked. Since I must have left it ajar when I rushed out we walked right in. I took the man's hand again and led him down the corridor to the front.

"Mutti look!" I was excited when I burst into the living room with the man behind me. "This visitor tells us something important about Papa."

I was startled by darkness. This morning like every day as soon as I woke up, the heavy lined brocade curtains which Mutti had sewn to keep out the winter cold were pulled back and tied to the side of the three tall windows that faced the street. Now they were closed again and only a small, amber silk shade table lamp on the console behind the sofa gave a little illumination.

Frau Lauder was still here which made me uncomfortable. She and Mother were seated next to each other on the upholstered corner sofa that curved around the big, round oak table. I expected my mother to get up and greet the stranger with a welcoming handshake.

She did stand up, but she remained behind the table and she held on to it as if she needed to steady herself. When she stared past me at the man who was behind me she took in a deep breath. To my great surprise the serious expression on her face changed not to pleasant recognition of a former neighbor. The few times I had seen my mother look upset like this a disaster had soon followed. She was white as a sheet.

10

Something was wrong, very wrong. I began to explain why I had brought the stranger home, but before I could utter another word Mother pointed to me and ordered, "Liesel, to your room." Her voice was emotional and stern, and she glared in a way that told me I had to do as I was told.

I was mystified. My heart beat faster and faster and felt like it was about to jump out of my chest.

"My room? Why?"

"Do as I say," she said.

In my confusion I ignored her command. If only we had more light in the room we could see what was going on.

"Mutti, bitte," I pleaded. I turned to the man who still stood at the threshold of the room. He seemed prepared to leave.

"Frau Lauder, bitte, take Liesel to her room," my mother demanded.

Frau Lauder got up from the sofa and moved towards me. I tried to escape the ironfisted, heavy-set tenant, but she grabbed me by the arm and marched me out past the stranger to my room at the other side of the hall. I tried to shake her off, but she twisted my arm until I cried out in pain. By the time she had pushed me into my room and locked the door I was beside myself with frustration.

"Warum, why?" I kicked and banged the door until every part of my body hurt. I peeped through the keyhole, but the key was in it on the outside. What in the world was going on in the living room? I heard nothing until a short time later our grandfather clock in the corridor ding-donged and I counted, "eins, zwei, drei"....until I reach eleven.

11

A small window in my room faced the street and the window sill was wide enough to support my body so I could lean out.

I caught a glimpse of the man's back as he hurried down the street. "Hello, where're you going? Come back." I shouted. "What's your name? Come back, talk to me."

Either he didn't hear or he didn't want to. He continued toward Sterckrader Strasse and was soon around the corner and out of sight.

I thought of escape from my room and stretched my legs to reach the stone ledge below. I was very agile and often dangled from our balcony in the back which made Mother scream in horror. Should I jump down and catch up with the man?

"Papa," I called. Papa was a hero and had saved the man's son. Mutti didn't understand, but I did and I was proud of Papa even if she wasn't.

I didn't hear Mother unlock the door. "Get down, close the window," she said. "Follow me." I went after her to the living room, scared and chewing my lower lip.

Frau Lauder was gone. It was all her fault I was sure. "Mutti, Frau Lauder's wrong. That man never came to hurt us; he wanted to thank Papa."

Mother trembled and her breathing was fast and heavy when she turned to face me. I saw how angry she still was. "How dare you bring someone like that into our house?" I had never heard this kind of harshness in her voice before. "You are a disgrace to your Papa."

This was beyond my comprehension. Mother's words, her anger, her condemnation of me. Why didn't she see that all

I had wanted was bring her joy? I knew when I deserved punishment and when it was just. Sometimes I was disobedient or made a mistake, but this was different. Why did she say I had disgraced Papa? Never would I do such a thing. I adored my father and had always tried to please him in every way.

"But Mutti," I stamped my foot with the injustice of it all. "You're wrong. Papa knew this man. He even saved his son on Christmas Nacht. That's what the man told me. He came back to thank Papa."

She moved so close now that her hot breath was on me when she tilted my face with both of her hands and forced me to look up at her. Her perspiration dropped on my forehead. I squeezed my eyes shut.

"You ... look at me and pay attention," she demanded. My mother had strong, large hands. She grabbed my shoulders and shook my limp body until I opened my eyes. I saw her take a side glance towards the door. Did she expect someone to eavesdrop or burst in?

"Do not listen to people you don't know," she said. "That's very foolish. Your Papa would never save a Jew. He saved you. He saved us from the Jews. He was a good man."

"But they lived next door where the Witkes live now." I tried to break free from her grip. "Papa saved his son on Christmas Nacht. The man said so."

"Stop it, Liesel. Your father was a good man; he saved many people, but never that man or any of his kind. Not ever a Jew." She stepped back and seemed about to cry. "Good God, why in the world would he have saved a Jew? Why? In God's name, why?" I didn't know the answer.

What could this man--this Jew-- have done that was so

terrible? Then my epiphany! My very own parents might somehow be linked to the stranger's tragedy and not in the way I had imagined. Once I heard Opa tell Mutti about hearsay that Nazis had killed innocent people in the neighborhood, children, even babies. Until this moment I hadn't made the connection and believed Nazis were boogieman.

Now, like a flash my mind replayed my parent's words from way back when I was younger. "We're Nationalist and proud of it and Liesel, you're special and a Nationalist too."

"Papa didn't save the baby?" I probed. "What did we do in the war, Mutti?" I didn't want to hear her answer. I felt giddy, closed my eyes and put my head on my chest. With both hands I grabbed my hair and pulled hard on it.

In my mind's eye I saw the flailing arms of the little boy who was thrown from the balcony. There was no worse horror and crime. "What did we do?" I whimpered.

My mother reached for me again. This time she tried to take me into her arms and comfort me, I her only daughter, her husband's legacy. I shrugged from her. Never before had there been a challenge like this between us. The truth about my own family was just beginning to dawn on me. I was terrified.

We looked into each other's eyes, my mother and I. Neither one of us was able to comprehend that at this very instance our lives had changed forever.

Then I blurted out the terrible, final words that I could never take back to the end of my days.

"You." My voice sounded like it belonged to a different person. "You are murderers. Don't ever touch me again."

She looked as if I had slapped her and she tried to hold me, but I pushed her away. She raised her hands and stood

14

back against the huge, carved bookcase as if she had to hold it up with her body. Nothing mattered to me now. Deep in my chest I felt disgust and hate, unpleasant, painful emotions I had never experienced before.

I ran back to my room and slammed the door shut behind me with such force that a picture fell off the wall. I needed to get away from my mother to be alone and think. Because there was no key on the inside I knocked the books and dolls off the top of my dresser. For a thin nine year old I found enough strength to push the heavy wooden dresser against the door.

Exhausted, I threw myself on my bed and sobbed.

That was the day I found out about my parents. My beloved Papa, who used to sit me on his knee and tell me fairy stories, who laughed with me and who smelled of fresh air and musky earth from his hikes in the woods. My Mutti, who took good care of me and praised every one of my accomplishments; on this day my childhood innocence was gone forever.

Nine-year old Liesel -- 1951

Else and Wilhelm Steffens
Just Married

Opa, Oma & Liesel

Grandfather Steffens

Young Mutti & Oma

Young Wilhelm Steffens

Little Liesel

Registration of Liesel's Birth

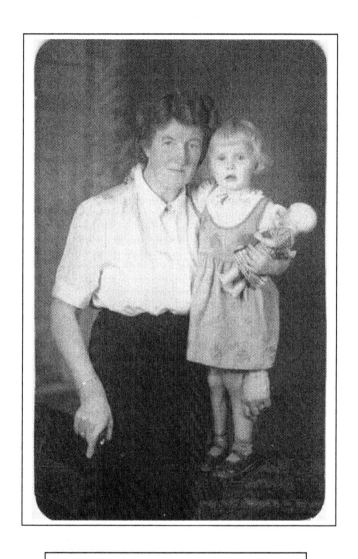

Mutti, Liesel & doll Maritzebill

Chapter 2

The Gift of Life

WHEN I CAME into the world in the autumn of 1941, Germany was already the master of Europe and final victory was in the air. Austria, Czechoslovakia, Poland, Denmark, Norway, Luxembourg, Holland, Belgium, France, Yugoslavia and Greece were all under Nazi domination and the powerful armies of the Third Reich advanced deeper into the Soviet Union day by day.

The Fuehrer kept his promise to create more and new Lebensraum (living space) for his people. The talk in every home was about the brave German soldiers who fought fierce battles on Russian soil and how Hitler was well prepared to wipe Leningrad off the face of the earth before the Russian winter.

It was at this critical and tumultuous time in history I was welcomed into the arms of a family who had deep love for each other and their country.

My birth and the circumstances which surrounded it were related to me so many times throughout my childhood that every detail was etched forever in my mind.

My parents were not young when I arrived. Under normal biological circumstances to give birth so late in life would have been impossible. But the desire for a second child was so strong and meant so much to them that no effort was spared. After many failed attempts and through a family connection in the medical field they found the right fertility expert.

This doctor and professor had helped many other families to heed the Fuehrer's order admonishing all good Germans: "produce more children for the Fatherland." A good German was defined as someone who could not only prove his Aryan ancestry for three generations past, but who was also "desirous and fit to serve faithfully the German people and the Reich." The Reich Citizenship law that encouraged German mothers to produce as many children as possible had been in force since 1935, six years before I was born. In Nazi ideology to bear healthy Aryan children was something a woman was honor bound to do.

There was not the slightest doubt about my family's full qualifications. They were Aryan through and through. A Familienstammbuch (book on family history and ancestry) was always kept in the top drawer of my father's desk and often looked at and shown off to visitors.

I was born on September 14, 1941; a sunny Sunday afternoon, in the small, picturesque town of Klingenberg am Main. We did not stem from this region. My mother's special mysterious operation to get pregnant had taken place in Essen located in the Ruhrgebiet (region around the river Ruhr) to the North not far from Bottrop where she grew up.

Since the beginning of war bombings and attacks by the British could be expected any day on the industrial cities of the Rhein-Ruhr region, especially since the Krupp family had their large metal and ammunition factory in Essen. Not long before that, my father who was a teacher had been promoted to headmaster of his school.

As a precaution and for the protection of Hitler's precious German youth, Father, his staff and all pupils had been evacuated south to continue their schooling in safety. Since my mother was pregnant with me Father didn't want to leave her behind. Besides, she took excellent care of the children's physical needs which was important. She knew how to cook nutritious meals and keep the youngsters clean. Cleanliness was her greatest obsession.

My mother had also many artistic talents. She played the piano and had a nice singing voice. Her hands were never idle. There were always knitting or crocheting projects going on or she was mending someone's socks, patching clothes, or sewing new ones from scratch.

Some of my father's students were quite young, away from their parents for the first time and many felt homesick. Mother nurtured them with warmth and taught them her useful and artistic skills.

My father was proud when she was appointed Leiterin (leader) of the Bund Deutscher Maedel, the female version of the Hitler Youth movement. Even local girls not in Father's school attended her art and handicraft classes.

Besides being the educator in charge of the children's impressionable young minds, Father was also a writer, poet and musician. He loved to fiddle on his gypsy violin and sometimes played duets with my mother on the piano. In the evening a bonfire was lit in the large campground which was surrounded by tall pine trees. Rousing songs about Heimat (homeland) and laughter emanated from the school community and people from several villages around came to listen and applaud.

The makeshift school was hidden away in the forest outside the tiny hamlet of Wort am Main. The nearest hospital for miles around was in Klingenberg (Chiming Mountain) about a half hour train ride away. My mother stayed active and never complained. She worked at her duties with a joyful heart until just before it was time for her labor to begin. Several family members and friends had gathered for the special event like my father's sister Hilda who lived in Northern Germany and arrived by train.

Herr Professor came from Essen to attend my birth, to make sure I arrived safely and nothing went wrong. Even my twenty-year-old brother Fritz was expected on leave from the Navy.

Mother raved to me about my birthplace's scenic beauty. The surrounding mountains were gentle and verdant, not as high and majestic as the Bavarian Alps but just as spectacular. It was wine country which produced some of the headiest and sweetest wines in all of Germany.

Father pondered why the Klingenberg wines were so sweet. His theory was that only after hardships and efforts the best things could be expected. "These grapevines have the rockiest of soils," he would say, "yet they know how to survive, find nourishment and water. Their roots penetrate deep through layers of stone struggling every inch of the way, but this makes them strong and hardy."

Later I wondered if he saw our German people that way.

My father didn't drink wine or any other kind of alcohol, but he had training as a botanist and great fascination with all plant life.

It was through these vineyards that Father escorted his wife up a winding path to the small convent Spital (hospital). My mother spoke often of how the town and Main River stretched through the valley below and how tender their embrace was before they went inside and reported to the Oberin (Mother Superior).

To my mother the professor looked even more distinguished now that he was dressed in his white hospital uniform. A couple of nuns trained as midwives assisted him with my arrival. Mother reminded me countless times that her labor was long and painful and she almost lost her own life. I didn't like to hear this because it made me feel guilty.

Father was not allowed anywhere near the delivery room nor would he have wanted to see his beloved Else suffer. He sat in the waiting room as hour after hour passed.

I was told later that it was one of the nuns who had rushed to him with the news. "Herr Steffens, congratulations. You have a beautiful daughter."

"Heil Hitler," Father is reported to have shouted for everyone to hear. "I'm the happiest man in the world. A miracle child, our gift to the Fuehrer!"

Chapter 3

Wunschkind

FRITZ WAS BORN just nine months after our parents wed. When Fritz teased them that the time frame didn't quite work out and our parents had a "shotgun wedding," Mother blushed and shook her head in denial.

Twenty years earlier my parents had been young, carefree and a most handsome couple. They were tall, blond and fair skinned with healthy, athletic bodies.

By the time I was born they had filled out a little, but still looked imposing. Despite two world wars, they had managed to take good care of themselves and each other.

Special attention was given to Mother during her pregnancy. She told me later how she had eaten ground up eggshells to supply calcium for my strong bones and teeth when I was in her womb. One of Father's many mottos was: "in a healthy body lives a healthy mind."

My parents denounced their previous religion, Lutheran, when my father (41 years old at the time) joined the Nazi party in 1933. Hitler became his deity, the only one worthy of worship. Although Mother was not as convinced right away it was not too long before she came around to my father's point of view. She followed her husband without hesitation in whatever direction he wanted to lead her and the family. Father always knew best.

Only once in a while I witnessed a slight disagreement. The cause was Father's new bible, Hitler's *Mein Kampf.* Mother found it bored her and she couldn't get herself to read it from cover to cover, but Father studied it thoroughly again and again. Although he was in total agreement with its dark doctrines he was not convinced that Hitler's ideals could be transformed into reality and the world could indeed be forever free from the evil and the degenerate beings poisoning what was good and pure in the Germanic race.

At the small convent hospital where I was born anything to do with Hitler was ignored although not denounced. Mother said that soon after my birth the nuns carried me out of her room. I like to believe that they took me to the convent chapel and unbeknown to any member of my family this small order of Franciscan Nuns bestowed on me a secret baptism and God's blessing.

"Du bist ein Wunschkind," I heard my parents say early on.

When I asked what the word meant they told me, "you are a longed for child that fulfills every one of our wishes and dreams Liebling." It was always added right away, "you will bring pride and honor to our great country."

I could never get enough of these words. It always made me smile and feel special. As I grew older I began to feel the weight of responsibility that went with it. I owed a debt to my parents and the Fatherland for my very existence.

Father had wanted a daughter this time and not another son to fight for the Vaterland. He showed his delight in many ways and he wrote a lullaby soon after my birth which both of my parents sang to me:

"Nun schlafe schoen du Kleine

Was weinest Du?

Sanft ists im Mondenscheine

Und suess die Ruh

Sleep my little one

Why are you crying?

The gentle moon shines upon you

When you so sweetly sleep."

*

Mother stayed in the hospital for fourteen days to recover. During this time her beloved first born, Fritz, arrived and looked dashing in his submariner's uniform. He had just been transferred from the Handelsmarine (merchant navy) into the Kriegsmarine (war navy).

War was not my brother's thing, but he kept his thoughts to himself when Father was around. Father would have called him a Feigling (coward) and denounced him. It was Fritz's nature to avoid any kind of confrontation. He was a great practical joker and Mother smiled when she admonished him to behave himself while a guest at the convent. Still, he managed to make the nuns blush and leave the room. No female was safe from my brother's charm and irreverent humor, not even a nun.

All four members of our family were together before Fritz had to depart and was sent into combat. My father arranged to have my Teutonic name-giving ceremony take place right away in the Klingenberg town hall.

31

As told to me many times it was a big and important event for everyone since a new child was being dedicated to the Fuehrer and his cause. My father wanted to have it immortalized by a photograph. This took a while. The stage had to be set just right for this family snapshot of the four of us. Father choreographed the occasion. Many times he got up and studied from a distance what the scene looked like. For him the most important part of this photo session was the huge portrait of Adolf Hitler. He wanted it in the perfect spot placed behind me. So many times it was moved that the photographer began to lose patience. "Willi, that's enough," my mother said.

They considered several names for me, including Dorothea, which was my grandmother's name on Father's side. She had died not long before and the family thought I resembled her. But the name was too long for my father's taste. I ended up not named after anyone with a simple Liesel and no middle name.

In the photo Fritz holds me ever so carefully in his arms and looks curious. What went through his mind? He was a strapping grown man and now he had this tiny infant sister, no bigger than a china doll. My parents on each side of us look delighted and their focus like Fritz's is directed at me. Father's right lapel sports his Nazi Party pin of which he was most proud. He assured it was clearly visible in the photograph.

During the solemn ceremony which for Nationalists served as replacement for baptism, I and my future were dedicated to my father's god, the Fuehrer Adolf Hitler and the Vaterland. No other words would do but Hitler's own, and since the town's Major was present Father asked him to read.

"In my fortress of the Teutonic Order a young generation will grow up, before which the world will tremble. I want the young to be violent, domineering, undismayed, cruel. The young must be all these things. They must be able to bear pain. There must be nothing weak or gentle about them. The free splendid beast of prey must once again flash from their eyes. I want my young people strong and beautiful. This way I can create something new."

As my Papa held my tiny hand he and my mother fought back tears of joy. A new Steffens on this glorious day became part of a generation before which the world was supposed to tremble.

Chapter 4

Aryan Child

I LOVED BOTH my parents, but I had a special bond with my father whom I addressed with great affection as Papa. He exuded such strength and confidence in himself that he transferred it to me. Although there was war and strife outside, inside my world it was secure and safe when he was around. His full name was Heinrich Wilhelm Steffens. Everyone in the family called him Willi.

After we left Klingenberg and the mountains we settled in another small town called Schaale near Muenster in Westphalia. Father was once again headmaster of the only Volksschule which educated children from six to fourteen. We lived in a sprawling apartment above the classrooms. Even though I was just four years old and not of school age yet, on occasions I sat quietly at the back of the class when Father taught.

One time Papa brought me up front and lifted me up to sit on his desk. My legs dangled and all the children stared at me.

"You see," he said and pointed to me, "this is what an Aryan child looks like, blue eyes, high forehead, blond braids." I felt embarrassed to be singled out; I thought all the children looked nice.

Aside from this one never forgotten moment of self-consciousness my early childhood was full of happy memories. My parents lavished so much love and attention on me that it helped me develop in mind, body and spirit.

At the beginning of every month Father made me stand against the doorframe of the living room. He held a ruler over my head, marked the spot and made a notch in the wood with his pocket knife where I had grown. That encouraged me to always stand very straight and tall. As I grew the frame had more and more markings, which mother hated and complained about, but Papa took no notice of her where I and my growth were concerned.

"Do you see this, Else? The child grew another 10 centimeters. She will be taller than any of us; it's time for her to learn to swim."

"Yes, Papa, I want to learn." I was thrilled at the prospect. "Can we go right now?" In no time I was by the door with my towel and swimsuit under my arm and off we went to the municipal swimming pool for my lesson, which turned out to be very short. On the grass Father demonstrated what to do with my arms and legs. Before I had a chance to question him or object he had tied a rope around my waist and plunged me into the cold water.

"Paddle, Liesel, move your arms and legs, go on, you are fine. You are not going to sink."

"Papa, help me."

"Go on, you are fine."

That was how I learned to swim in one afternoon. When my Papa said, "swim," I swam.

At every bedtime I was propped up against my big, soft

pillow filled with down feathers and listened to a fairy story read to me by Mother and sometimes Papa.

The Brothers Grimm tales were my favorite. The story of *The Little Matchstick Girl* who died alone in the snow always got me choked up with tears, as did the *Ugly Duckling* who was really a swan. To cry was frowned upon in our house and not something we did in the open. I remember even at this early age I followed in the Steffens' tradition and turned my face into my pillow so Mother would not see how moved I was and that my face was wet with tears.

I was no more than three years old when I had learned to read simple sentences in children's books. Our house was filled with wonderful literature--Father's treasure--treated with reverence and kept in our best piece of furniture, a huge oak bookcase with stained inlaid glass doors. I knew the assigned spot for all books and kept myself occupied and still when Mother took a nap. After removing some heavy volume, I looked through it and then returned it to its designated place.

In the evenings we played board games like Mensch Argere Dich Nicht (Sorry), which taught me to count, be patient and a good sport when I lost. Mother also invented a card game from which I learned the names of famous German composers and their music.

Every day was interesting and fun, but I was most happy when Papa took me out into the forest. He knew the names of every tree, plant and flower, as well as all the animals.

"Look, Liesel, this birch grows here because the earth is just right for it. Pines thrive only where the soil is sandy. Come and see...look...smell and listen."

When we got home Father would tell Mother, "the child marches like a soldier on the Russian front." I didn't know what the Russian front was or even that there was one, but I knew it was complimentary and I had been good.

I always tried to keep up with Father on those long walks deep into the forest. With my small laced-up leather boots I stamped my feet and swung my arms just like Papa.

He would breathe in the clear, cool air, expand his chest and beat it with his fists. He talked about the strength and beauty of our country and our people. One of his favorite quotes came from a book by the philosopher Paul de Lagarde: "Das Deutschtum liegt nicht im Geblüte, sondern im Gemüte." (Germanness does not lie in descent, but in the soul.)

Then he looked down at me with great tenderness and squeezed my hand. "With you, my Musche Pusche" (his unique, funny name of endearment for me), "your Germanness lies in your blood and in your soul. You are German through and through and have it all--beauty, honor, truth. You are a symbol of our Germanic greatness."

"Yes, Papa." I believed every word he said.

Where his well-being and ours were concerned he followed a nineteenth-century German naturopath by the name of Sebastian Kneipp who had all kinds of theories about how to stay healthy and fight illnesses. Apart from the time Mutti had her operation to conceive me I don't remember any of us having to consult a doctor. Father believed everything could be prevented or cured by us if we followed the Kneipp therapies. He was sure civilization was headed towards disaster unless we went back to nature and a simple living style.

"We have to set an example," he would say. "Kneippen

is the way to go."

Kneippen was a new word used to depict "Hydrotherapie," treatment with water, "Phytotherapie," treatment with plants, and there were nutrition and exercise therapies. Like everything else Father got into and pursued, Mother and I followed and we "kneipped."

A couple of times in my early years I was punished for being too forward and ahead of myself. The first time occurred when I was sent on a day's trial to a kindergarten and I told a group of boys and girls, "there's no Saint Nikolaus (Father Christmas)." The children gasped and told the teacher who told my mother. I was expelled because I had "spoiled" things.

The second time I decided on my own to take an excursion away from home. I walked quite a distance by myself towards the center of town when my frantic mother caught up with me on her bicycle.

"How dare you frighten me like this!" She got off her bike and spanked me right then and there, then lifted me on the backseat and peddled home. I felt some humiliation, but I knew the punishment was just. After all, I was precious to my mother, and she didn't want to lose me.

38

Chapter 5

Pollaken

SOME NEWCOMERS, FAMILIES as well as single people, turned up in Schaale. The community didn't know what to make of them and kept away. They were Germans from the East arriving without possessions; they looked for housing and work. Mother called them Pollaken, which was not a very nice word since it rhymed with Kakerlaken, cockroaches.

During a forest walk with my father we came across a couple of these Pollaken dressed in shabby, torn clothes. They tried to hide in the brush, and hoped we hadn't spotted them but Father flushed them out.

"Heil Hitler," he said and raised his right arm and clicked the heels of his boots. His left hand rested on the walking stick he always carried when we hiked. "Nice day. Where might you be going?"

The two men, one quite old and the other in his late teens, looked dismayed. The older man raised his arm, though not as high as Papa. "Heil Hitler." I looked at the gaunt, dark-eyed boy who stared back at me.

"It's obvious that you are not from here," Papa said.

"No," the old man had a strange accent. "On our way now. Just pass through. Boy's mother is dead. Father too. Was brave soldier on Russian Front. Auf Wiedersehn, we go west now."

I saw a change come over Papa. His face was soft and pleased now and he looked at me. "Liesel, these are Germans."

I nodded and felt relief. "Yes, Papa, they are."

"Well then, what do you think? Shall we take them for one of Mutti's great home cooked meals?" I knew my father had already made the decision.

"Yes, Papa, let's take them," I said.

This was not the first time Father picked up strangers in need of a meal and brought them home. Mutti was always ready to serve food as soon as Father or I came through the door.

"Please friends, follow us to our residence, where a warm meal awaits the two of you."

This sudden friendliness startled the twosome, especially the older man. They tried to decline, but my father wouldn't hear of it.

"Please allow my daughter and me the pleasure of your company at our home; all good Germans are welcome at our table."

"Not proper dressed," the older man said and looked down at his muddy shoes. "Traveled a long way."

"Never mind, that's unimportant. We may even find you something new and clean to wear."

Father never cared or was impressed by the way someone was attired. He didn't care what he wore himself. Mother joked that he had no problem to put on what Fritz had just taken off even though it was dirty.

One time a pupil came to our door and told Mother that Father walked around town with two hats. He had forgotten that one was already on his head and had put the second one on top.

Mutti was the opposite and cared very much about neat appearances. I knew she would look down on the two men's exterior.

The young man didn't say anything. I wanted to find out more about him.

"Come on, let's go," I said. Father smiled at my eagerness and so did the two men who came home with us.

Mother's face showed disapproval when we marched in. The apartment looked and smelled cleaned and disinfected something Mother always did as soon as Father was out of the door. He didn't like noise and fuss around him. A delicious smell of cooking came from the kitchen. Guests were always entertained in the living room. Father invited our visitors to take a seat in Mutti's two best velvet-covered chairs, while he and I sat next to each other on the sofa opposite.

We waited for lunch and Papa made small talk. The boy and I smiled at each other.

"Tell us about yourselves," Father said. "What brought you to these particular parts of the country?"

The two men were not about to open up.

Father kept on. "These are difficult times. Not long before our soldiers prevail in the East. The enemy can never destroy us. This young man and my daughter Liesel are the future of our great homeland. Heil to the Fuehrer!"

Mutti served lunch, the biggest meal of the day, on the

dining table. As always it had a simple but nice setting of china and polished silver cutlery. In the middle was a pretty vase with a bouquet of blue cornflowers, daisies and various grasses. The two strangers looked impressed. They were hungry and ate several plates of potato salad with their vegetable stew which pleased Mother.

"Liesel, please take note. Clean plates like they should be," she said. "Why is it that you can never eat up?" I was shamed into finishing my stew.

When Father asked the boy to tell us about his deceased parents, Mother got upset and raised her hands. I had no specific idea of what war was, but I knew Mother did not like to hear about it. Her son was in it. Father was annoyed with her reaction.

"Else, you know very well that the war is a necessary evil, bound to pass very soon and forgotten. Deutschland will have gained new territories and renewed its strength. Fear does not serve us or our country well, it helps the enemy. Just look at our two Germans guests, they don't complain." He stopped his lecture for Mother and looked at me with a smile.

"My small daughter shows courage. She walks barefoot through cold mountain streams to become strong and to learn how to endure hardship." I was proud that Papa mentioned my achievements and how brave I had been.

His voice grew louder and more passionate. "I am a simple man, but I am an educator and I teach young minds to worship and serve Germanic beauty, to strive towards purity, unspoiled purity and beauty. That's what we live, fight and die for." Our guests remained silent and watched father so fired up.

Mother said "my husband is a very learned man."

But Papa did not want praise. She distracted him from his point. "There is individualistic genius in every German. One German is a good as another."

I nodded. "Yes, Papa, they are."

He didn't hear me. "After this war every last vestige of evil will have been overcome. We are moving forward in the right direction towards our glorious destiny." The more Papa said, the more excited he got. Now he almost shouted and pounded the table with his fists.

"We must honor our humanity, our past and our future. Everything that is non-Germanic must be removed. Even a plant can be purer and more German than some people can ever be and have more substance and soul." He pointed to the potted lily plant which sat in the sun on the windowsill.

"Look at that lily, friends, such an organic existence, such a pure white daughter of a slender mother, raised with tenderness and the morning dew. Just like Liesel, my own daughter."

Everyone looked at me. I didn't understand what Father meant about me and the flower and I stared down at my plate.

Mother tried to change the subject back to her firstborn who was away at sea and might never come home. "Willi, we have a son also."

"Indeed, we have a son." Father was solemn. "And it might be that we will never see him again. A sacrifice we have to make for our Vaterland, no weeping for him, Else, right?"

This was too much for Mother. She got up from the table, covered her face with her hands and retreated to the kitchen.

43

Often it ended this way when we had visitors, unless they were Papa's friends or associates and were just like him. Then they kindled each other's passions with loud speeches or listened on the radio to a broadcast by the Fuehrer. When that was about to happen, Father made sure beforehand Mother and I stayed in the kitchen. I didn't know why.

Father never let an opportunity pass to tell people about our country's great mission and destiny. It all sounded good to me and I felt part of it. Pure, good and noble like my father, that's what I wanted to be.

Chapter 6

Shadows of Darkness and War

IN THE BEGINNING I was unaware of the changes in and all around my home as the result of the shifting fortunes of the war. It was 1945 and my parents did their best to protect me from bad news. The defeats of our armed forces were not spelled out to me like the victories had been.

Nights were less peaceful. My parents stayed up late, and sometimes I woke and saw them huddled together on the sofa in the living room instead of in their beds. I sensed something monumental was about to happen. It made me so anxious that I sucked the ends of my braids and chewed off my fingernails until they bled. At the same time I pacified myself that my Papa would make it right again before long and I asked no questions.

Father went away on trips, which kept him from home for several weeks at a time. Always before he left he lifted me into his arms. "My sweet, dear Musche Pusche," he said, "do not be afraid. Papa will fight to protect you and Mutti. I need you to be strong."

"Will you be a soldier Papa?"

"No, Liebling, your brother is a soldier. Papa has to do other important work."

My girlhood and many years had to pass until as a middle-aged woman I found out the full extent of the "other important work" and where he had done it.

Late during the war, my father and his good friend Erich Koch, whom I knew as "Uncle Erich" and who came to visit us sometimes, worked together in German occupied Poland. When Koch was appointed governor he made my father Minister of Education. Schools were closed so the job was easy. Polish, Jewish and Gypsy children, the population of this region, were no longer entitled to education. German policy, which my father helped implement, was that good resources would be wasted and education was not needed where they were bound to go.

I also learned later that the Germans captured and imprisoned 10,000 Poles, most of them Jews, and sent them to the Treblinka death camp. Only a few escaped; most ended their lives in Treblinka or Majdanek. Two thousand Jews were shot during an uprising in the region. Two hundred Jewish children were transported to the Theresienstadt concentration camp in Czechoslovakia; from there they were shipped to Auschwitz. Koch, my "Uncle Erich," masterminded the mass murder of over 400,000 Jewish and Polish civilians, and the father I adored worked directly alongside him. There were precious little girls like me who did not take walks into the forest with their fathers to pick mushrooms; they were tortured and killed instead.

I don't know to what extent Koch and my father were in contact after the war. In 1951 the Allies captured Koch in Schleswig-Holstein, where he and my father grew up. He was extradited back to Poland for trial and condemned to death by hanging. Due to his failing health the court later commuted his sentence to life imprisonment, and he died in his cell.

*

When Father was away long letters arrived from him. He wrote how much he thought about us and our cozy home and how he lived for the day when he could return.

I asked Mother, "Why has Papa got to be away?"

"He's needed and he does important work for all of us."

"I'm important to Papa."

"Don't act selfish about your father, Liesel," she said.

When I was alone with Mutti my life was more restrictive. She took good care of me, but didn't always allow me to experiment and think for myself as much as my father had. She completed every simple task for me, it was always, "give me that before you drop it, let me open the jar for you, I'll close the buttons on your dress...."

Sometimes I objected, and once when I was still very young, maybe four years old, I gave her a big surprise when I started and completed a project all by myself. It was a piece of needlepoint, a big red rose, which I embroidered with tiny stitches on a piece of canvas. When I offered it to Mother as a gift, she showed joy.

"Thank you, Liebling. I'll turn it into a pillow and treasure it until I die."

I couldn't imagine Mother dead and I longed for my father's return. He and I understood each other and we were "one heart and soul." Mutti was also happier when he was home. Sometimes I saw how my parents necked and kissed in the bedroom.

47

I don't remember all that much about the war because I was so sheltered from it. Nevertheless, looking back, it undermined my childhood happiness over time and turned me from a confident beloved child into one with doubts about her environment and therefore herself.

One evening we heard a huge bang some distance away. My father got his telescope and looked through the window, but when he couldn't spot anything we put on our coats and went outside. My parents held firmly on to my hands as we climbed up the hill behind the school. In the distance we saw a bright orange fire reach for the sky and light the darkness as if it were daytime.

"That was a bomb," Father said.

"Oh Willi, a bomb so close to home! What are we going to do?" Mutti lamented.

The word bomb was new to me. A bomb had hit a nearby town and the smell of smoke stayed in the air for many days.

Chapter 7

Book Burning

NOT LONG AFTER, late one evening, a commotion woke me. I got out of bed and tiptoed on bare feet through the corridor to the door of my father's study. What I saw astounded me. Mutti and Papa emptied the bookcase and stacked books into several large boxes. I hid myself behind a coat rack in the hallway.

My parents didn't detect me when they dragged the heavy load past me to the outside. Our kitchen window faced the garden. That was where I went to look out. And there below were my parents. Mother carried a lantern and showed the way. Father cleared a spot and piled some wood. Mutti gave him a match and he lit paper. Soon I smelled burning and saw that a bonfire had been started.

Papa stood next to the flames and Mutti handed him the books we all loved so much. I watched in disbelief how he held each volume and looked through it as if he wanted to read it one more time and remember every word. Then he threw it into the fire. The flames got higher and higher and sent fragments of paper into the night sky.

I couldn't believe my eyes. My father's books! My parents stood with their arms around each other's waist. Father had a garden rake in his other hand and he poked the cinders. Every single book ended up in the fire and turned to ashes as we watched.

How could this be? Books were such a fundamental part of our lives. We read them almost every single day. They brought us knowledge, joy and beauty. Papa, who didn't care much about material possessions, always talked with pride of his extensive book collection on all kinds of subject matters, many with colorful pictures and illustrations. We had given and received books as birthday gifts. From my youngest days I had held them, looked through them and knew they were valuable. My father had told me over and over, "Liesel, because you are so smart, I want you to inherit my books."

And now they were gone. I fretted what else we would lose. When morning came my parents were pensive and sad. We did not talk about the fire. I stood and stared at the almost empty shelves of the bookcase. A small consolation was that my story books had survived, as well as a handful of father's leather bound volumes. One of them was *The German Genius*, a collection of writings from Germany's past and present by renowned authors like Goethe and Thomas Mann and black and white etchings by Albrecht Duerer. And there were still a couple of thick albums by the famous German cartoonist Wilhelm Busch.

The very next day my parents were busy in the garden again. First they scattered the cindered book remains and dug them into the soil. "Great fertilizer for the roses," Father said. "You'll see Liesel, by summer we'll have most intelligent roses." I nodded, but didn't see his point.

Father handed me the spade. "Come and give me a hand with this shrub." I stood next to him while he ripped and pulled a large bush out of the ground. Mother came over to inspect the size of the hole.

"Willi, hurry up, make it deeper," she said. She looked around to see if anyone was watching. Father dug away, and when Mutti was satisfied, she went inside. She returned to the garden with something wrapped in a blanket. I had no idea what it was, but I saw her bury it carefully in the hole. Father put the rosebush back on top and stamped the earth with his hiking boots.

"Don't you dare tell anyone about this, Liesel," Mother said. I went inside to see what was missing. The spot on the marble console, where my grandmother's blue Peacock vase always stood, was empty. "This vase is very valuable and has been in the family for generations. Oma gave it to me, when I got married," Mother had said to me many times. "One day it's yours." What would I have left, when I got married? All this losing of possessions worried me.

The bomb, the fire, the vase buried in the garden, they were all left to fester undiscussed and unexplained in my young heart and mind. I knew that my parents had reasons for what they had done and they talked to each other about it, but not with me. I felt left out and had no one to ask.

My parents whispered a lot and fell silent when I came close. Visitors stopped by from out of town, not to socialize or eat, but for discussion and consultation. I was sent to my room to play with my toys. The talk between adults went on behind closed doors, sometimes got loud and went on for hours.

There was no more laughter, no more positive speeches by Father about how we would overcome evil in the world. My mother stopped playing the piano. Our life had changed drastically. In this new anxious period, which I hoped would quickly pass I was no longer the center of attention. Everyone around me was preoccupied with something I did not understand.

Most days I was kept inside and not even allowed to go out on the front balcony. Not so long before my father and I had stood on it. We had waved and saluted our proud soldiers who had marched by singing their fervent songs. Those were the days when I had jumped up and down at my father's side and squealed with excitement.

We still lived above the classrooms, but I heard no more laughter and lectures by Father going on below. "The children have to stay home with their parents," Mother said.

Father left our home early in the morning, sometimes before I got up. He didn't even say good-bye to me, his Wunschkind. We ate dinner in silence. I pushed the food on my plate from side to side which always succeeded in getting my mother to pay attention to me.

"For God's sake, Liesel! You get me very upset, when you don't eat. You are a spoiled little girl with all this good food I make for you."

I sighed. I had heard this speech many times and knew what came next. "At least think about our poor German soldiers on the Russian front. They are cold and hungry, at least eat for them."

That always did the trick. If I could help our soldiers I would put a little more food in my mouth. Sometimes it stayed there for a long time while I pondered if I should swallow or spit it out in the toilet after dinner. Whatever I left on my plate when I was allowed to get up from the table would be warmed up for my next meal until it was gone.

One day different soldiers rolled into town. I knew how our German army looked from their gray uniforms and the shape of their helmets. These men were also soldiers since they wore a uniform, but theirs was brown. They didn't go past the school singing and on foot, but whisked by in trucks. I wanted to take a closer look and say hello when they stopped in the town square.

However, before this could happen, Mother issued a warning. She looked very unhappy and told me in her strictest voice: "Never ever go near them. Das sind unsere Feinde. (They are our enemies). Promise me, never ever. You must stay away."

"Why, Mutti?"

"Because I say so, and because they take little children like you away, never to come home to their families!" This was definitely a deterrent and frightening prospect.

When Father came home in the evening, he confirmed my mother's assessment. He sounded more hopeful though, when he put me on his lap. "These foreigners are not here to stay long, we're in transition. They're full of themselves and believe they can destroy us, which will never happen."

"No, Papa. Never!"

"We're Germans and stronger than anyone. Everything will be right again, Liebling, don't worry about a thing, you are always safe here at home."

I rubbed my face against Papa's rough cheeks and put my arms around his neck. It didn't take long for him to dispel my doubts, and I was convinced that this "transition" would be over soon.

After these much hated foreign troops came to town I learned another new word. I don't believe I was supposed to hear it since Father and Mother spoke in hushed voices to each other. But I was nearby and had developed a very good ear that picked up things it was not supposed to hear. The word was Kzet or Konzentrationslager (concentration camp).

"They've found the concentration camps."

"They" were everyone who was not us. To me a camp was a happy place. We had sometimes gone camping in a tent by a stream or river. But since the talk about this camp was in undertones I sensed it held some kind of problem.

"What is a Kzet?" I asked Father.

"Hush, Liesel, don't say that word, it's bad."

I put my head down.

"It's a place where our soldiers suffer beyond belief. Some have been captured by the enemy and put in camps. Don't you think that we must defeat the enemy and bring our poor soldiers home?"

"I hate the enemy," I said.

My father smiled and gave me a pat on the back. "This is our Heimat (home), yours, mine and all Germans; no one can take it away." Father took a piece of paper out of his pocket and handed it to me. "Here, hold on to this. Your Papa wrote it; keep it in your heart." I took my father's note, written in blue ink on lined school paper, glanced at it and later put it in a drawer in my room.

*

Money began to get tight. Never extravagant, my father and mother didn't waste a Pfennig and frowned on people who spent too much on unnecessary things and lived above their means. My father told me our family had accumulated some wealth which was kept in a bank savings account. "If you ever need it, Liesel, it's there for you!"

Papa came home one day and said it was all gone. All our Reichmarks had evaporated into nothingness just by sitting in a bank. "I'll never put money into savings again," he said. "It's best to spend, eat, drink and be merry." This was a complete turn around from what he had preached before.

Mother, trying to comfort him, succeeded in alarming me. "We still have property in Bottrop. I don't know how long we're going to be able to remain in this apartment."

I knew the property in question. Several times we had made a trip to my grandparents' home in Bottrop, a large gloomy house with a musty smell. After my initial gladness when I saw Oma and Opa I always wanted to get away and come home. Mutti was convinced that one day we would have to leave the town of Schaale and make our permanent move back to Bottrop. I hoped that day would not arrive soon.

Chapter 8

Schokolade

DURING THESE CONFUSING times I tried to be very good. Most of my days, I spent alone in my room. I role-played with my dolls, became Mutti who instructed Liesel to stay out of her mother's way. Now, more than ever before Mother was preoccupied with order in the home and keeping everything spotless. This was her world, and she was in control. She cooked, baked and often adjusted her recipes to include substitutes for ingredients that were no longer available.

A few special things denied us I only knew by hearsay. I had never tasted chocolate, a banana or an orange, but my parents raved about these delicacies. My mother said, "I can't wait to see the look on your face when you taste your first banana or piece of chocolate." I had no idea what they even looked like and chocolate could have been a fruit for all I knew.

One day Mother had to go somewhere for an afternoon and couldn't take me. Father was also out of the house, but he arranged for one of his older pupils to pick me up and take care of me for a couple of hours. The girl's name was Anneliese. She and I took a walk to the center of town.

There we encountered a group of soldiers who stood around their army trucks talking in a foreign language. They leaned on their rifles and smiled when they saw us. I was intrigued.

"Das sind Amerikanische Soldaten," Anneliese said. She held my hand tightly and led me away. When I looked back over my shoulder the soldiers waved and invited us to come back. One man had something in his hand.

"Scho-ko-lade," he said in German. I knew that word and my eyes lit up. He held out a Hershey bar. "Suess, sweet candy, sehr gut, very good." Here was my chance to taste something I had never tasted before. I knew how much my mother craved a piece of chocolate. I figured I could bring it home and share it with her.

My young caretaker and I moved closer to the soldiers. Although they didn't look frightening my mother's warning was still fresh in my mind. I hesitated, but the temptation was too great. I grabbed the chocolate bar and put it into my pocket. Anneliese took one too. I curtsied and said a quick, "Thank you."

When we turned the corner we felt safe. We had a closer look at our chocolate present and took it out of its silver foil wrapping. I smelled mine, and Anneliese copied me. We both broke off a small square and put it into our mouths. The taste was so delicious that we looked at each other and laughed. I put my tongue around it and let it dissolve slowly in my mouth. The sweetness lingered.

On the way home Anneliese wanted me to give the rest of my bar to her. If there was no evidence and we didn't tell about the gift from a foreign soldier we avoided getting into trouble. But I didn't want to let it go. I wanted to explain to my mother that the foreigners were not as bad as she believed. They had chocolate and were willing to share it with us.

"Mutti, look, I brought you home some chocolate!"

Anneliese was right. Mother was very upset. "I can't leave you for an hour and you disobey me. Your father will be furious when he hears this."

Meekly I handed to her my silver-wrapped piece of delight and watched her throw it into the trash. I didn't want supper or a bedtime story. I just wanted to disappear.

From my bed I heard Father come home. I waited. What would he have to say about how badly I had let down our family and what would my punishment be? But he didn't come into my room. I lay very still. Sleep did not come easily to a child with a guilty conscience.

Suddenly, there was a loud scary knock at our front door. No one ever came this long after dark. I got out of bed, put on my lamb's wool slippers and came into the hall. Mutti was fully dressed in her best blue outfit with a jacket. She shuddered when we heard a second bang, but bravely she went downstairs and opened up. I followed her. Where was Papa?

Two soldiers in brown jackets with bright brass buttons, just like the men I had met earlier that day, stood in front of us. My heart beat very fast and I bit my lip. Mother was right; I had been disobedient and allowed myself to be trapped by a chocolate bar and brought disaster to my family. The soldiers had come to take us away. I expected the worst.

The man in uniform who addressed my mother was polite, knew her name and spoke in German. "Good evening, Frau Steffens. Sorry to bother you so late at night. We would like to talk to your husband. Is he at home by chance?"

I stepped forward in my nightshirt and stood next to my mother. "Papa is...." Before I could get more words out and tell that Papa was probably in the kitchen, Mutti pushed me back with her foot.

"Herr Steffens is not here. He has been away for quite some time. We have no idea where he is."

I was stunned; I had ever heard Mother lie. Since it was obvious she didn't want me to tell the truth, I didn't say another word. The soldiers asked more questions, but she held her ground.

"I have told you all I know. Herr Steffens is not here, and I don't know when he will be back." She began to close the door. "Now please excuse me. I must put my daughter back to bed, you woke her up." After she had double latched the door she leaned against it. Her face was white as a sheet. She was angry at me.

"What are you doing up at this hour? Go back to bed."

"Mutti, I am very sorry about the chocolate."

Mother didn't hear me. I followed her, biting my lips.

Papa stood in the kitchen and seemed to be searching for something. He was ready for a hike with his black trench coat and knitted wool cap over his ears..

"Willi, you must leave tonight," Mother said. "They didn't believe me. They'll be back tomorrow." She opened the pantry and got out a whole side of Speck (salted pork belly} and a loaf of Graubrot (wheat bread). "Here, Willi, mach schnell (be quick)."

Papa wrapped the Speck and Brot in brown paper and stuffed it into his rucksack. Mutti rushed to the bedroom and returned with a blanket, which went in the knapsack on top of the bread. Papa tightened the bottom of his black trousers with bicycle clips.

My parents embraced for a brief moment. I stood at the table and held on to a chair. "Papa, where are you going?"

They looked at me surprised and embarrassed. Mutti wanted to banish me back to my room, but my father came over to me. He knelt down and put his arms around my shivering body.

"You are strong, Musche Pusche. Papa has to go away. I know that you'll take care of Mutti for me while I'm gone."

I searched my mind to make sense of this departure. What had happened today to make my father leave us? All I could think of was that wretched bar of chocolate. My eyes filled with tears, but I wanted my Papa to know that I was strong and would not cry like a baby. He stood up, waved good-bye and went out into the night.

When morning came I asked, "Where has Papa gone, and when will he be back?"

"He's taking a trip on his bicycle. I don't want you to tell anyone," Mutti said.

I watched my mother pace up and down for the rest of the day. Again and again she shook her head. Then she seemed to have come to a resolution and by evening she started to work with frantic speed. Not as usual, when things were cleaned and tidied, instead she created chaos from cupboards and drawers. Pots and pans, china and clothes piled up all over the place. We had nowhere to sit. I offered to help, but she shook her head. She worked and worked late into the night and forgot about supper. She missed my bedtime which had never happened before, and when I finally said I wanted to sleep Mother also failed to brush out my braids. My hair remained uncombed for the next several days until she looked at me, noticed and said "Get the comb."

My hair was knotted through and through.

"Ouch!" I cried as my mother tried to pull the fine-tooth comb through my thin strands of hair. She held me clamped between her legs and continued to pull out every bit of entangled hair.

"We must be strong for Papa, Liesel. We must be strong," she said. When she finished with my hair, she took me into her arms. "This great injustice will pass, don't cry, Liebling."

I was not crying.

Chapter 9

Ancient Symbol

A DIFFERENT SET of American soldiers came back some time later. They didn't smile, walked right in without invitation and handed Mother a document.

"You've lost the right to stay here; the search for your husband is ongoing. Meanwhile, you must leave everything in the apartment and go away. By tomorrow it will become our headquarters."

Mother seemed somewhat relieved, but she worried about the furniture, especially Papa's bookcase. "Pigs, they'll ruin everything," she said right in front of the soldiers.

That night one of the neighbors picked up the bookcase and put it into storage for us.

"Where are we going, Mutti?"

"Where else, but to our property in Bottrop! Your grandparents will be delighted. Oma is sick, and we have to take care of her."

This made sense to me, although I was not thrilled about Bottrop and the prospect of living in the musty-smelling house.

"Pack your things," Mother said, pointing to a large pile still in the middle of my room, "but only take what you can carry." That was not much.

There was no doubt that I wanted to take my favorite doll, Maritzebelle, which had been with me for as long as I could remember. Mutti made her for me out of wax. She had blond hair and different outfits to match mine. Together, she and I said a teary good-bye to the other dolls and toys as we packed them into boxes and tied them with string. I promised to come back for them.

The last thing Mutti packed into her suitcase that night was the Swastika flag which had flown out in the schoolyard until the foreigners came. I knew it was of great significance to my family, especially Father.

"This is the ancient symbol of our party, it means good luck," he had told me. Since we needed good luck, I was glad Mutti took it.

"There's no point in wasting good material," she said. I'll make you a dress and Papa will be proud." I understood Mutti wanted to cheer us up, but I wondered why we would want to cut to pieces our good luck flag.

Early the next morning I waved to our friends as the train pulled away. Maybe, when we reached Bottrop we would see Papa.

Chapter 10

Kohlenpot

IN BOTTROP AFTER several train changes my mother sighed. "We are back in the Kohlenpot (Pot of Coal) and have to make the best of it."

We took a bus to the center of town and then the Strassenbahn (tram) down Gladbecker Strasse to Bottrop-Eigen. Mutti clenched her hands; we were both anxious as we stared out of the tram window at the bombed neighborhood until we got off at our stop. Exhausted, we dragged our belongings the last block to our house. Now we saw it up close, a big hole in the middle of the building between the grocery store and the second floor apartments. Mutti was horrified.

"Oh, my goodness, Liesel, that's all we needed. We got hit by a bomb." We climbed over a pile of rubble to get inside. "Goodness gracious, what are we going to find? Is Oma and Opa all right?"

"Papa is probably waiting for us," I said. The lights in the stairwell didn't work. We put down our suitcases and in the darkness felt our way up the steps. I was behind Mutti and tried not to breathe. When we reached the apartment door we banged on it and called out "Please open! It's Else and Liesel!"

The door opened just a crack and Opa peeped through. He held a candle and motioned us to come inside and follow him to the bedroom. Was that Oma propped up on the pillow or a ghost? Mutti rushed to her mother's side and tried to hug her, but stopped when Oma pointed to the bandages on her chest. Oma attempted to speak, but no words came out.

"Oh, Mother," Mutti wept and she brought Oma's shaky, bony hands to her face. I stood back and watched as my very sick grandmother lay on her bed in the candle light. I was scared.

"Rest, Mother," Mutti said after she composed herself. "I will take care of you. Liesel and I are here to stay until you recover."

Opa and I followed Mutti to the kitchen, where she put a kettle on the stove. Mutti was in charge and I had confidence that she would make Oma better.

The three of us sat around the table and sipped peppermint tea. Opa gave us the news which was not good. "Mimi (Opa's name for his wife) has terminal cancer. It's hopeless. Her breasts are gone and she can't speak. Her throat is full of cancer too."

Mother buried her face in her hands. "Where's Willi? Did he come here?" She finally asked. Opa was upset and didn't want to answer, but he did. "Yes, Willi was here."

"Where is he?" Mutti's face brightened.

"I don't know. He arrived a few weeks ago."

"Did he make it all the way on his rickety old bicycle? That's a miracle," Mutti said.

"He was exhausted and we wanted to help him, but he

had no time to rest," Opa continued. "Within the hour they were at the door."

"Oh my God," Mutti said.

I pictured my beloved father and the last time I had seen him when he disappeared into the night. Mutti slumped in her chair.

While Opa talked my misery increased. "Willi escaped to the attic with his bicycle. They looked around, but saw how ill Mimi was. I made a promise to let them know if he showed up here. Willi hid the rest of the day. I sent him on his way as soon as it got dark."

I had been to the attic which was reached from a small second floor bathroom by a pull down trapdoor with steps. The attic was huge and stretched along the whole building. It was dark and contained nothing but discarded furniture, junk and lots of grime and dust.

"Else, what was it that Willi did?" Opa asked.

Mother was tired and irritated and I could barely keep my eyes open. Her answer was short. "He didn't do anything wrong anytime anywhere."

I was glad to hear that, but grandfather shook his head as if he was skeptical. "I'm not saying Willi was wrong, but there are rumors in Bottrop that all kinds of crimes have been committed by the Nazis."

"Not Willi." Mother got up and took my hand. "Yes, he was a Nationalsozialist. We all were. He was nothing but an idealist who only wanted the best for Deutschland." She gave Opa a disapproving look, and I did the same.

We went to sleep in my grandparent's guest room which

was prepared for us with fresh sheets. I shared the big double bed and held myself close to my mother for the whole night.

*

For the next days and weeks I wondered why the soldiers were after my father and why he could no longer be with us. He had told me himself that he was not a fighter in the German army and had done other important work. What other important work? Opa said they were looking for Nazis who had committed crimes. Was Papa a Nazi? Mutti said he was and that it was a good thing for us. It was all very confusing.

I asked Mutti to explain but she told me not to ask questions. All she would say was, "your father is a good man. He never did anything wrong."

In my mind it could only be a misunderstanding. We waited day after day for news, but not a single message came from my Papa.

When I asked "when will we see Papa?" No answer Mother gave convinced me. It was always something like "don't worry, soon."

"Why are the soldiers looking for him?" I asked her again one day.

"He's such a good German man, an example to us all. He believes in the right things, that's why the evil soldiers are afraid of him and want to put him in prison."

This was her fullest answer yet, but I still didn't understand.

*

Since Bottrop was in the center of the Kohlenpot, the coal mining region of Germany, it was in the industrial heart of

67

the Third Reich. Like the larger cities nearby, Essen and Duesseldorf, it was also digging out after destruction by Allied bombings. The economy was in ruins; the people were demoralized. Our country was divided into four military zones -American, British, French and Russian. We were in the American zone. To me they were nothing but evil foreign soldiers who hunted my father. Why had I taken that chocolate?

Although Oma was near death she was well organized like her daughter, my mother. Before she got so ill that she had to be drugged by morphine to dull her excruciating pain she had planned her own funeral right down to the stockings Mother would wear and my navy blue outfit. Everything hung clean, pressed and ready in the wardrobe.

I sometimes said things like: "Is Oma dead yet?" This earned me my mother's reprimand and grandfather's stern looks. Death was not something I was allowed to talk about. There were a lot of topics I was not allowed to mention or ask about, anything to do with my father's predicament for one, so I learned to keep my doubts and questions to myself.

I regretted very much I didn't get a chance to develop a relationship with my Oma. She was kept away from me as if she were contagious. Opa I didn't like at all nor did he like me. He was grumpy and told me I was "noisy" and "a quick silvery little pain in the neck" and things like that. Opa also argued with Mutti about my Papa which wasn't right.

Mother nursed grandmother day and night with great devotion, but all I could do was sit in the corner with my doll and try to stay out of people's way. I longed for my father's attention and missed him and our walks together.

Sometimes my mother glanced at me and sighed. "Look

what has become of us." We were indeed miserable.

*

One afternoon, a big, jovial man in a suit arrived and made himself at home in the living room. After spreading out a lot of paperwork he called us to the table.

"Hello, Liesel," he said, stretching out his fleshy hand to me.

"I'm your family's lawyer, Herr Doktor Schmidt. It's indeed a pleasure to meet you. Your Opa wants to give you a valuable present. I am here to make sure it is done legally and right."

I looked at my mother. "What kind of present?"

The lawyer lifted a bunch of papers and showed them to me.

*

Before the war Opa had invested in real estate. Now our house was a focal point since Nazi property was being confiscated all over Germany. I overheard discussions between Grandfather and Mother about it and how afraid they were it might happen to us. All kinds of bad things had already happened with Papa away. Mutti said, "We have to hold on to what real estate we can."

"Your Opa has just signed this document," the lawyer said. "It makes you and your brother Fritz equal owners of this house. Congratulations. You are now a property owner, Liesel."

This was one of the few times I saw Opa smile at me. Mother looked very pleased, too.

" All this belongs to you and your brother now, Liesel,"

she said. "It produces reliable income from the rental stores and apartments."

The bomb damage was patched up, but I thought how big and gloomy the house was. I had felt much better and more secure in the country at our apartment in Schaale. Income didn't mean anything to me. But I had no choice. I looked at my grandfather and smiled back. "Thank you, Opa," I said politely.

Chapter 11

Traitors of the Vaterland

ONE DAY IN 1948 my father finally came home. We didn't expect him when he walked in at suppertime. I jumped up from my chair and got to him before Mutti. I stretched out my arms and expected him to lift me up, but he didn't.

"Papa, where have you been? I missed you so much."

He didn't reply and embraced Mutti instead of me. They both had tears in their eyes. I put my arms around them and sobbed. We stayed like that for some time.

"Willi, look at you," Mutti finally said. "You are skin and bones. Sit and eat."

Papa went to Oma's rooms first. Opa had not left his wife's side for days. He knew that her terrible suffering was almost at an end.

My father looked and felt very different from the time I had last seen him, but I didn't care. All I wanted was for us to be together like we were before--proud, happy and with a hopeful look towards a great future in our beloved home and country.

In the kitchen, where it was warm, the three of us gathered around the table. Father wanted me to stay and I felt grown up to be part of our reunion. I couldn't take my eyes off his haggard face. He told us how he was captured and I wondered what being captured meant.

71

"I left Schaale and was lucky to make it back to Bottrop, where I expected to hide. Opa must have told you how quickly they were on my tail. They probably watched the house. It was too dangerous to stay anywhere near. I took off right away back to the two of you in Schaale."

Mutti stroked my father's hands. "Willi, talk about it another time. Just eat."

"Papa, what happened after?" I asked. "Did the soldiers find you?"

He was indignant. "I almost outwitted those stupid Amerikaner. They don't know the woods. I slept during the day and ate of the land. Near Essen, a fatal mistake when I passed through a cornfield. Someone spotted my bicycle trail and turned me in. That is how they caught me, Liesel. I was turned in. 'Put your hands up' I heard. I had no choice, but surrender."

"Terrible, Papa! Then what? Who turned you in? Those bad soldiers! What did they do to you?"

"Traitors of the Vaterland turned me into the American enemy. I was arrested like a criminal."

"Why, Papa? Arrested?"

"Liesel, enough," Mutti said with finality. "Papa did nothing wrong. He was unlucky. You just heard some bad person turned him in."

The night my father came back I was sent to bed with my thoughts and unanswered questions. I wondered about "traitors of the fatherland" and who they might be. I felt very sad and angry that such injustices were committed against my Papa who was such a wonderful person and, as Mutti told me again and again, never did anything wrong.

Chapter 12

Oma and Opa

THE NEXT MORNING Mutti found Oma dead in her bed, Opa by her side. Mutti said she had postponed her death until my father came home.

Mother was an only child and grew up in this region. Most of her extended family lived nearby, either in Bottrop or Gladbeck which turned out to be a blessing. Tante Clara and Onkel Willi were rich Bottropers. Opa's younger brother had two sons, Friedel and Helmut, and he owned a business in Gladbeck just a tram ride away. Gladbeck was Bottrop's twin with its gray coal mining gloominess. Every member of our family showed up for Oma's funeral.

In the double grave family plot that had been bought some time before in the Eigen Friedhof (cemetery), Oma was buried deep in the earth with lots of flower wreaths on top. Some poor people showed up and stood behind us. They, too, cried that Oma was dead. "No more suffering for such a kind lady. She's at peace," I heard one of them say.

Opa was devastated. No one could console him. He pined for his Wilhelmina so much that he stopped eating. Every morning he left the house and walked to the cemetery where he stayed all day till it got dark. So strong was his bond to his wife that we soon buried him next to her.

This time of loss had a deep affect on all of us, especially Papa who seemed to have lost more than anyone. He had become a different person who sat in his armchair motionless. He did not read, listen to the radio or do anything.

I tried hard to cheer him up. "Papa, please play the violin." "Papa, can we walk in the forest?" He always shook his head no. Spending time with me, his Wunschkind, no longer mattered to him. I became listless, too, and stopped asking.

Although he was back with us at night, the soldiers picked him up in the mornings and took him to a camp from which he returned each time more broken than the day before. I wasn't sure where or what this camp was, but it must have been unpleasant. When I asked Mutti, she called it a de-nazification camp.

They gave Papa lunch, but his sandwich with Wurst was uneaten in his pocket when he came home. He would cut it into three equal parts. Mother and I each got a piece and this sharing became our nightly ceremony. Only once in a while he still made a small speech. "All lies, enemy propaganda! What they tell us could not have happened. They are very smart at deceiving us."

Mother was also subdued. She admonished me to leave my father alone. "He has to recover from something terrible," she said. "We can't help him. He has to do it alone."

Chapter 13

Knoblauch and Hamstertours

THE WAS AN anecdote often told when I was growing up about my first encounter with my brother Fritz. I stood in my crib, not even two years old, when he walked in (out of the blue) as a surprise for Mother. I stretched out my arms, and he picked me up.

"Onkel, Mutti comes back soon," is what I was told I said. Everyone thought it was cute that I had called my brother "uncle," and it became something I could never live down. Later I often referred to him as my "old brother."

Fritz was stunning; very tall, blond and blue-eyed, always trim and fit and blessed with a happy-go-lucky disposition unlike the rest of us Steffens. Father found him hard to take as his thinking was so dissimilar, but Mother made up for Father's coldness towards her first born with her warm and tender devotion. I always felt we were pairs, Mutti and Fritz (they even resembled each other physically), and Papa and I. I took after my father in looks as well as in his passionate character.

Since my brother was a man from a different generation I grew up as an only child. He had happy memories of his upbringing to cherish and his formative years were not clouded by the experiences of loss and war that marked mine.

Although my parents tried their best to keep disorder away from me, even strongly denying it was there, I felt its impact. What they didn't say affected me most. There was always something hidden and dark in the background. Things were not what they seemed to be.

As a child I always longed for my elusive brother. There were some yellowed black and white photographs of him in the family album. One showed Fritz in front of his tent on a camping trip holding oars of his kayak. In the other photo he was in a suit with my parents on a beach. And there were several of him and me, brother and sister from two different generations side by side.

"Where's Fritz?" I asked Mother after the lawyer's visit that made us joint owners of the Bottrop property.

Right away I realized this was a sore point. Mother couldn't come up with an answer because she didn't know where he was. "Somewhere at sea," she said. I avoided the subject from then on.

A couple of weeks later she brought up the whereabouts of my brother herself. "There is someone who has information about Fritz. You and I will go on the train to Duisburg and find out."

I was excited about it and wanted to tell Father, but she intercepted me and pulled me into a corner. "Do not tell anyone where we are going, especially not your father. He will be very upset."

We left very early the next morning before it was light. The train ride was a nice interruption of my daily routine. It took several hours to reach our destination, a shabby apartment complex in Duisburg near the railroad tracks.

The moment we came through the door of the tenement building Mother curled her nose and shook her head with disgust.

"Verdampter Knoblauchgestank (damned garlic smell)," she said. I sniffed the air and imitated her. Garlic smell was very bad and made my mother upset. To use it in food was taboo in our house. For Mother it meant lower class cooking and the odor always came from people with no breeding. We persevered up the stairs, and held our breath, to a waiting room on the second floor where we seated ourselves and waited. I jumped up when the inside door burst open and a crying lady ran out. Now it was our turn.

"Kommen Sie rein," a voice called us into a darkened room, where the middle-aged woman was seated at a round table. She had dark hair, dark piercing eyes and several long gold teeth which were on display when she smiled at us. I was glad she smiled and I smiled back. She motioned us to sit down opposite her.

Mutti took an envelope and a photo out of her purse and put them on the table. The picture was of my smiling brother Fritz in his navy uniform. The woman grabbed the envelope and put it on her lap. She turned Fritz's photo face down in front of her and covered it with her hands. Her eyes were now closed. I stared at the colorful rings with large stones on every one of her fingers as we waited in silence. The silence lasted a long time.

Then the woman uttered sounds I didn't understand and she shook her head. Mutti sat at the edge of the chair with anticipation.

"I have very bad news. Your son is dead, lost at sea. You will never see him again, sorry."

Mutti sat very still and let the strange woman's words sink in. This was terrible. She had recently lost both of her parents and now Fritz.

After she composed herself she picked up Fritz's photo. "Come Liesel, we must go home," she took my hand. "Thank you," she said to the woman of gloom.

As soon as we were out of the building she picked up speed on route to the Bahnhof and pulled me along. As we waited for our train I leaned against my grief stricken Mother. "Mutti, you still have me, Liesel. I am your Wunschkind."

Mother didn't speak until we were almost home. Then she said "don't tell your father. He cannot take any more bad news." She prepared supper for us as if nothing had happened, and in the next days and weeks she spring cleaned every corner of the house.

*

"Can I stay home?" I asked the next time Mutti announced we were to take another train journey.

"No." Her answer was firm. "We're taking a Hamstertour." I had heard the word before from Frau Lauder who had suggested Mother take such a tour. At first Mother didn't want to go and "hamster," but everyone did it. These were day trips town people took by train into the countryside where they bartered valuable belongings for fresh food.

We took a number of these trips and got rid off quite a few heirlooms this way, things that one day might have belonged to me. But Mother seemed remarkably unattached to silverware, Oma's Persian lamb fur coat, oil paintings and other brick-a-bra which she and I dragged on the train to find a new home with some grinning farmer in exchange for food.

I was more interested in the cows, pigs, chickens and geese while Mutti made her trade. Farmers were fortunate since they had wonderful things to eat. People in the cities had a bunch of useless items which couldn't be consumed. I grew to enjoy these trips and especially the smells which came from the kitchen afterwards. And that Father praised Mutti for baking and cooking some of her creations with real ingredients like eggs.

Since I was now old enough, she passed her housekeeping, cooking and handicraft knowledge on to me and allowed me to help. I wore my apron and had my own little bowl and spoon and vigorously stirred the dough to make special "Liesel cake" for my Papa which he seemed to enjoy more than anything else.

*

But there were childhood disappointments too. One I never forgot took place at Christmas time. We discussed and planned several weeks in advance what we would eat for our festive holiday dinner. Mother looked around, but didn't discover too many things left she could spare until she spotted my dollhouse. It was a real little house with a roof above two floors, blue and white curtains on the windows, carved wooden furniture and a stove. The moment I saw Mother look at it I knew what she was planning to do. I threw myself into play with my treasure, but it was too late.

"Liesel, you are too old still to play with such a childish toy. It will get us a nice, fat goose to eat for our Christmas dinner."

I didn't agree, but a verdict had been reached, and my pride and joy was wrapped, packed into a box and tied with string. We all had to make sacrifices. When we returned on the train the same box contained a dead bird for our holiday dinner.

What a sad sight. The goose lay on the kitchen table with all its white feathers still on its body and its eyes glazed and open. It might have gotten up, jumped off the table, and waddled away outside into the garden had it not been for its long, twisted and broken neck.

I touched the creature gently. It felt very cold.

Mother had already put on her apron and she moved into action. She put the goose on her lap and a pot on the table in front of her as a receptacle for the feathers. I watched. She used a lot of pulling strength with very little result. The feathers didn't budge. Even Father who never got involved in cooking or cleaning matters had a go at it. After all, our most important meal of the year was at stake.

It wasn't long before Mother announced that we had been conned. The goose was old and had been dead for too long. The feathers were set.

"Let's bury her in the garden," I said. "We shouldn't eat this goose." I thought my suggestion was a good one, but we were Steffens and didn't give up easily. So a lot more work and effort went into preparing the bird for the oven. The attempt was made to singe off the feathers with an open flame which was only partially successful and smelled awful. After roasting didn't produce an eatable result Mother submerged our feast in boiling water "to soften it up." We finally sat down to eat much later than usual. It was Mother's worst cooking disaster ever.

To their credit my parents had a knack for turning things around. Instead of complaining we laughed louder than ever both before and during dinner.

On this evening I heard for the first time Father tell with

glee his story of an American soldier who had gotten deathly sick thanks to Mutti. This tale later became a party piece that always produced belly-bursting laughs.

When Mutti and I were forced to leave Schaale in a hurry we were only able to take bare necessities, so we left several food staples behind. One of them was a bottle of Kneipp's Nerven und Kraftwein (nerve strengthening tonic). We drank the tonic to strengthen our nerves. However, Mother had secretly stored a different liquid in the bottle, one she didn't want anyone to know about--a cosmetic item to brown her legs suitable only for topical applications since it contained poisonous dye.

"These Americans are unbelievably stupid," my father said. "Lo and behold! One of them must have had bad nerves. He drank the whole bottle of Kraftwein. Was sick as a dog! His superior called a neighbor and questioned him on what kind of poison the Steffens kept in bottles so that the soldier could be helped. The neighbor had no idea."

Somehow this story had gotten back to us and Mutti had owned up to Papa about her secret attempt with leg vanity, much to his great delight. So this Christmas we spent not with thoughts of the birth of Christ, but with Schadenfreude about the misfortune of one of our enemies who surely deserved no better.

Chapter 14

Mushrooms

ALTHOUGH THERE WAS much sadness in connection with my father after he returned from captivity and our life was under a big and constant cloud, overall I can't remember that I suffered great hardships growing up in postwar Germany. By 1949 Father's state of mind had improved for the better and he paid attention to me again. Our life seemed almost to have gotten back to normal. There was always a roof above our head, and I always had my own cozy domain within the sanctuary of my room where I could play, read and write.

Every fall coal was delivered to fill our cellar for heat in winter, free, because we lived in a mining town and Father traded violin lessons to the son of the mine foreman. I remember that as soon as it was spring we enjoyed walks and fresh air in the woods and meadows around Bottrop. During summer I swam and became the youngest member of the swim club in training for regional championships. Papa's rope lesson had worked.

Autumn was always special, not just because September was Mutti's and my birthday, but it was also the time for Father's greatest passion. During fall we celebrated the wonders and mysteries of mushrooms.

Almost every day Father set off at the crack of dawn and took me whenever I was not in school. We sniffed the air, crawled low amongst the brush on springy, loamy soil and always found them. Many different species of mushrooms grew locally and popped up out of the ground before our eyes during and after a rain. I didn't know what the stronger attraction was for Father, finding the reward in the moist earth after a long search or what we did with the delicious fungi after we brought them home.

Mother must have had a hundred different ways to prepare them. She used them as a meat replacement, dried in stews and soups, as a flavoring and even ground up in her coffee mill for tea.

Father, who knew their Latin names, believed that some of these little dwarfs with hats -- that was what they looked like to me--had gotten a bad rap. He was going to set the record straight. Fliegenpiltze (toadstools) were said to be deadly.

They looked pretty with their firm stems and bright red tops with raised white dots. We always discovered them in areas where pine forests gave way to a group of birch trees. Father had warned me not to mistake one of them for a Kaiserling which was edible and delicious. I knew the difference.

It surprised me one day when Father cut out a toadstool cluster with his pocketknife and took it home in his knapsack. "Else, that's my dinner for tonight...braised toadstools," he said as soon as we put our day's harvest on the kitchen table.

"What? Willi you ask me to cook what?" Mother shook her head. "You are a fanatic."

Not something I had heard Mother say before. But as always Father's mind was made up and Mother had no choice but to give in.

"In the name of science," Papa said. We waited and watched. Even Frau Lauder was informed of this experiment, and she in turn told the whole neighborhood.

Father passed the evening with a botany book and was still alive and well in the morning when he announced with a triumphed look on his face: "You see this again, all lies. Nothing happened. Liesel let this be a lesson to you, always examine everything for yourself and do not believe old wives' tales." I promised not to forget.

*

Things from nature, mushrooms, herbs, leaves and plants saw us through starvation during times when we no longer had things to trade. My parents were always resourceful. The enemy had invaded our country, bombed our cities and tried to subdue us by their thoughts and culture, even gave us handouts with something called the Marshall Plan. But our family had its own beliefs. We were proud people and survived without help from anyone.

Children attended schools, but my father no longer taught. He was eager to, but he was not allowed.

"Papa is waiting for clearance," Mother told me and to Father she said "there is no better teacher to be found anywhere, Willi, you are the best." But Papa took it hard. Teaching was the only profession he knew and cared about.

I started school when I was six, sent off on the first day in the traditional way with a large paper cone filled with baked goods. Since they came from my mother's kitchen she made sure they were nutritious as well as delicious. While some of the other boys and girls kicked up a fuss when their parents left them in the care of a teacher I had no problem. I wanted to be with other children and immersed myself in their company. We learned to read and write, and our school days passed without the slightest mention of our country's most recent history.

Chapter 15

Langeoog

A FEW MONTHS into my first year at school a physician arrived with a couple of nurses to examine us. They checked our hair for lice and made us strip down to our underwear to examine the rest of us. I had never been to a doctor. After he looked me over from all directions and the nurse had lifted my arms, I was put in a separate line together with just one other schoolmate, a boy with a flabby belly.

There was something wrong with me. I was far too thin; my ribs stuck out, and I wasn't straight. They called my parents and explained to them my physical abnormalities.

Mutti did not like to hear about my thinness and imperfections. She got defensive. "The child is a picky eater no matter what we put in front of her."

The doctor had a remedy. Six weeks at a summer camp by the sea, where I would learn to eat and put on weight. As to my crookedness which my parents must have known about but never mentioned to me, the doctor mandated I get physical therapy. Still in keeping with previous Nazi doctrine no deformed weaklings were tolerated in German schools.

Several times a week I had to report to a place that took care of children with severe handicaps. I was the least afflicted. A leather harness was put around my head. With my hands, I was supposed to push down on handle-bars and lift myself as I hung from my head. I was literally being stretched out. As a follow up, a bonesetter took hold of my head and twisted it to one side, which made my neck crack. After it was over, I told Mother, "I won't go back." Fortunately, she agreed. The cause of this unevenness in my stature was a couple of centimeters shortness in my right leg, which I compensated by holding my head to the left. Father said that swimming was the best way to cure it, and that's what in time did the trick.

When Mother started to embroider my name into every piece of my clothes in preparation for the eating camp at the beginning of summer, I announced that I would rather not go.

"It will be good for you, Musche Pusche," Papa said. "You'll love the sea."

I felt I had brought it on myself every time I had not eaten enough of my mother's food. But I was an adventuress child and after Father explained about the wonders of the endless waters right up to the horizon, I got excited. I was even entrusted with the large family suitcase for my first trip away from home. My parents told me how grown up I was to travel by myself.

To leave Papa behind was something I had never liked and it was especially difficult now that he was a little better and I seemed to bring him joy again. But he said, "Don't worry about me, Liebling. You'll see how wonderful it is to spend a summer by the sea. Mutti and I always did before the war."

When the day of my departure came, Papa stayed at home. He didn't feel well.

"Are you sad Papa that I have to leave?"

He took me to the door. "Go on, Liebling, I'll be all

right."

Mother and I went to Oberhausen, where the Kindertransport (children's train) would pick me up. Always punctual, we got there early. We watched the other children trickle in. Most of them clutched their belongings in cardboard boxes tied with string. When the train arrived it was already packed with youngsters from as far away as Bavaria. Their German sounded like a foreign language. Mother said that was because we spoke Hoch Deutsch (High German) in our house, a higher class of German.

Mutti climbed inside the crowded train with me determined to find me a seat. When the conductor sounded his whistle she said "sit in the gangway on your suitcase." She gave me my box of sandwiches. "Do not eat this before you reach Muenster." She looked at my face and must have spotted a smudge of dirt. I hated when she spat on her handkerchief and wiped my face with spit. She did it now. The train was ready to depart. Mother turned around and was gone. I couldn't even get to the window to wave good-bye.

I sat on my suitcase, forlorn, unwrapped my lunch and ate every bit of it right away. The train got even more congested as it sped towards the North Sea and picked up more children along the way.

The Isle of Langeoog was a long, thin stretch of land, part of the Ostfriesische Inseln, a collection of small islands along the German north coast reached by a two-hour ferryboat ride. When we had to leave the train in Esens, I got distressed because I couldn't move my heavy suitcase.

"Just leave it and come along," an impatient chaperons said. We were put in lines, two by two, counted and marched on to the ferry.

The sight of the sea excited me. I even forgot that I had just left behind my family's suitcase with all my things in it. Father was always right, and he had been right about this. I loved the ocean. I showed my joy by jumping up and down on the boat railings. What a difference to Bottrop where everything was dingy and gray. I could breathe; the air was salty and fresh and the sky a vibrant blue.

My enthusiasm caused some concern to the adults. "The little girl over there is about to jump in," I heard and I was pulled away from the edge and made to sit down.

"I know how to swim," I said. "I am not afraid of water."

"Great! You will have your chance when we get to Langeoog."

My love of water was great; the wonderful freedom I felt when my weightless body was immersed in it. I couldn't wait. The island came into view, and there was nothing but a deserted stretch of white sand dunes battered by foam crested waves. The ferry turned to the small harbor and soon we were anchored.

Langeoog was the only hamlet on the island that bore its name. They marched us off the boat, again in lines of two. Women and men in uniforms and badges greeted us and wasted no time organizing us into groups. Each column had two adults in front and two behind so no one would get lost.

I put up my hand. "My suitcase is still on the train." It was not just that I felt responsible for our family's only piece of luggage, but I had second thoughts about this camp where there were so many children and I didn't get special attention.

When we arrived at one of the long caserns, the first

thing I spotted was my suitcase under one of the beds. The beds were lined up in four precise rows, equal distance apart with a stool in the middle.

Our eating began right away. Most of the children were very hungry after a whole day's travel; we marched over to the huge dining hall housed in another one of the barracks. It was shared by all the children at the camp. I came from such a quiet home that I couldn't eat because of the noise, even if I had been starving.

After a fitful first night, I woke up to the booming voice of the Hortnerin, the robust camp teacher-guardian. "Guten Morgen! Auftehen! Raus aus den Federn!" Good morning! Get up! Out from under your feathers!"

I had a featherbed at home, but here we just had blankets. We were instructed to call her Tante Helga (Aunt Helga). She was in charge of everything that pertained to our well being like Mutti was at home. Aunt Helga oversaw our eating, cleanliness as well as our daily weigh-ins. After all the purpose of the camp was to eat and put on weight.

I made only marginal progress. I found the Wurst too greasy, the black pumpernickel bread too hard to chew, and I often gave food to other children who ate faster and more. When Tante Helga was preoccupied I got up from the table and poured the glass of thick, heavy milk into a potted plant which soon started to drop its leaves.

A different woman, Aunt Petra, was in charge of our recreation. She marched us to the beach when the weather permitted. We marched a lot and sung the appropriate songs called Wanderlieder (hiking songs) to keep us in step. Eins und zwei und drei und vier....

Aunt Petra had to watch me the most since I would swim out deep and had to be called back by whistle and reprimanded. Except for the times I was at the beach and in the water I felt homesick.

After dinner and before bed we gathered in a circle for the daily mail. Every single night, except on weekends, I heard my name. "Liesel Steffens, you got another postcard." The postcards were from my father. I felt embarrassed that I got so much more mail than any other child, but my joy was great when I read Papa's words: "My dearest Musche Pusche," he wrote in his large handwriting. "We miss you very much and wish you were home."

The card's front always had a lovely picture sometimes a flower or a castle, and I stored them in my suitcase. I felt good that I was still special to my Papa. I even received a parcel with Mutti's baked treats.

"Everything must be shared, otherwise the other children's hearts will bleed," Aunt Helga said. She portioned out the goodies over several days and included a large share for herself.

Shortly after I returned home I celebrated my seventh birthday. I had survived on my own. I had not gained much weight, but I was taller and now I had a new self reliance and a sense of independence.

Chapter 16

Herr Sommer's Kino

I DON'T KNOW where the gloomy fortuneteller in Duisburg got her information. What she told us, thank God, was completely wrong. Mother spent more than a year in silent anguish and then a letter arrived that changed everything. It was from Fritz with a stamp of Great Britain's king. He was alive and well, although captive in "His Majesty's prisoner-of-war camp."

How he and just one other of his marine buddies survived and had gotten there when the rest of his comrades were dead in their torpedoed submarine at the bottom of the sea was a mystery that took a lifetime to solve.

The way he survived did not matter in the least to Mother. All she cared about was that her beloved son was alive and would one day come home. However, Father mentioned the word "deserter," which earned him such a horrible look from his wife that I never heard him utter the word again.

We were able to correspond back and forth with Fritz in England. One day he wrote that he had been transferred to a farm in Wales where the farmer had a beautiful young daughter. The daughter kept him warm and had knitted him a sweater and scarf.

At the same time as Fritz turned up "saved" we were hit with another, very bad tribulation. Father was put on trial for being an active Nazi and for his work for the Third Reich in Poland at the end of the war. There were also accusations of things he had done in Bottrop as a Blockwart (person in charge of a district.) He had been under investigation for a while, and now enough evidence had been found to make a Prozess. Mother said, "The Americans pinning something on him that's totally untrue."

"Your father did nothing out of the ordinary. All good Germans acted the same. We were idealists and only wanted the best for our country. They can't put us all in jail."

I knew nothing about Hitler's "Final Solution." I did not connect any wrongdoing to my father or anyone else I knew. But one thing I was sure Mother was wrong about. My father had not been like everyone else. He studied and examined matters for himself, which was the right thing to do. If other people did what they were told and did not think about it, they were wrong. My father would never be a Mitlaufer, a person who runs with the rest of the crowd. He would act and speak only from total conviction.

The world had turned upside down. Right was now wrong, and it was my father of all the people in Bottrop who had been singled out for prosecution. I thought it was very unjust that they picked on him. Of course, I understood very well who brought the charges. Not anyone from our town, but the foreign invaders who did not know right from wrong.

My father and our family remained highly respected among our neighbors and friends. Everyone smiled and greeted me and offered something for free when I walked around--a day-old cookie from the Koch's bakery or a slice of sausage

93

without garlic from the butcher who knew about Mutti's garlic aversion. And then there was our immediate neighbor, Friedrich Sommer, the movie theater owner.

Herr Sommer was the only one Mother cautioned me about. He was overweight with a skinny wife and a good-looking teenage son who was seven years older than I was.

"When der Sommer speaks to you just walk away," Mutti said. "He is a pervert, which means he is not a good person and does terrible things to little girls." I noticed she omitted Herr when she spoke about this neighbor.

I don't know if it was this warning, that he was not liked by anyone in the community or the Sommer's Kino that fascinated me more. Although Herr Sommer said several times "come and see a movie for free," I only took a peek into the dark auditorium and ran away. Sometimes he waved at me from the entrance of the theater with a smile on his fat and flushed red face.

However, without anyone's knowledge, especially not Mother's, I found a way to sneak in and experience almost every film. I can't say I really saw the movies, because once I got in through the exit door I had to flatten myself up under the screen. Sometimes, when I saw Herr Sommer leave on the Strassenbahn and knew he would be gone for a while, I dared to crawl down to a seat in the first row, where I curled up and kept my head low.

Not many people attended these shows. I don't know what it was about Herr Sommer, but people didn't care for him. For me the films opened a whole new world of wonder. Even when I couldn't understand the actors' words I still cried and laughed with them.

*

The only other person we knew who was on trial was Uncle Erich. Mother said that he was already in jail and things were very bad for him. I felt very sorry for Uncle Erich. Father was luckier since he only had to report to a de-nazification camp during the day and was allowed home at night.

Liesel & brother Fritz

Chapter 17

Fritz

ONE DAY FRITZ came home, again unannounced to surprise Mother. She shed tears of joy and they hugged for a long time. I curtsied when Fritz finally shook my hand, and he gave Father a stiff formal embrace. Reunited, the four of us sat down to dinner, and Fritz told us some very exciting stories.

"I love England and the British," he said. "They are fair-minded and have a great sense of humor." Father frowned, but unlike before when he and Fritz had argued he listened and didn't tell my brother he was wrong. I was glad.

The time before he got to England, his submarine and survival of the winter in the Arctic region of Norway as a fugitive he was not yet ready to talk about. We found out about that later.

What he did tell us was that he and his friend Karl had been stowaways on a ship bound for the United States and had hidden themselves deep in the bowels of the vessel for many days without food and water. They had lost all sense of time and direction. When the ship docked they emerged and surrendered to the captain who called the military police and handed them over to the British.

"Could you not have found a German ship in the region, Fritz?" Father asked. My brother undid the shirt buttons around his neck.

"At least it wasn't Russia," Mother said and Father agreed. Horror stories reached us out of the Soviet Union, where hundreds of thousands of our soldiers had died a miserable death in Siberian prison camps; only a few lucky ones had survived and were returning home.

Fritz continued to talk about the English prisoner-of-war camp. "I escaped six times and each time got more daring. Can you believe what the Commandant said to me after I was caught again?"

We shook our heads and Mutti looked afraid, but Fritz smiled. "He said, 'Steffens, not you again. I'm transferring you to a farm in Gloustershire where you can work to your heart's content and take your mind off escape which will save all of us a lot of time and trouble.'" Mutti and I laughed and even Papa joined in.

*

Details of my father's trial which was about to start were kept away from me. I had no understanding what the prosecution was about. Papa and Fritz didn't mention it at all and Mutti only told me: "Your Father's work during the war was good and important work." I didn't know he was in Poland and had worked for "Uncle Erich." All I had witnessed many times myself was how kind, generous and unpretentious my father was.

My wonderful humanitarian father had instilled in me lessons and values. "Don't worry how a person looks. Just see what he believes and if his heart is pure." Papa embodied all that was good and humane. He was my hero and the center of my universe.

Fritz had a different view; he and Father argued often after the first night of his return. My brother listened to the BBC on the family radio and tuned in a crackling English voice whenever he could. Father called it backstabbing and got mad that he allowed "enemy propaganda" into his own home. Fritz sometimes blamed Father for his Nazi views and called him a fanatic before storming out of the room. I didn't know what "Nazi views" were and felt sorry for Papa who didn't feel well.

I never did anything wrong like that and Papa was never in the least cross with me. Everything I said and did seemed to delight him again, although more in a subdued way without the enthusiasm of my earlier years. Fritz didn't bother to explain what he heard from the BBC. I wasn't interested since it was clear to me that it was bad news we didn't need.

Father's daily reporting to the de-nazification camp stopped, but even though I was a child I could see that it had left a mark. His once athletic body had changed too. I could no longer put my arms around his body because he had much more bulk around his mid section. He kept his hands in his pockets when he walked. His hair was gray now and falling out and his posture was no longer straight and upright. The confidence and hope for the future was gone from him.

Chapter 18

Final Departure

MOTHER SUGGESTED A short vacation by the sea which the three of us took in August of 1950. Fritz stayed behind in Bottrop looking for work. My parents decided that we would not sail to one of the islands, but remain on the mainland. The small, secluded town of Norddeich was named after the strong, grassy levees (Deichs) which went along the coast all the way to Holland and the town was Papa's choice. He told me about dykes. "They protect the fertile lowlands which have once belonged to the sea from rough tides ready to reclaim them. Instead of sand dunes this area has marshes and they have a special beauty all of their own."

The purpose for our holiday was to give Father renewed strength for the ordeal of the trial ahead. We lodged in a guesthouse surrounded by pastures just below the dyke where we had rented a large efficiency room with a stove and three beds. We were the only visitors. Most families who took vacations by the sea went to enjoy the more scenic islands off the shore. Father did not want the hustle and bustle of a lot of tourists. The inhabitants of Norddeich were Friesen, a melancholic people of few words.

On the first morning, August 8, Mother was making breakfast. Papa suggested an early morning walk first and of course I wanted to go with him. "Let's work up our appetite.

What you think Musche-Pusche?"

I was happy to see him in such good spirits. Mutti got the camera, and the proprietor of the inn took a picture of the three of us and one of just Papa and me. Papa put his arm around my shoulder and had an adoring look on his face just like in the picture we took in Klingenberg. I felt warm and secure that I was his pride and joy, his Wunschkind again.

I wore a light cotton sun dress over my bathing suit and a small matching scarf over my pigtails. We climbed the embankment and I ran down on the other side, almost tumbling. Then I waited for Papa who moved slower. Together we strolled in the sunshine along the water's edge. I skipped by his side and chit-chatted about things I had not had a chance to tell before. "Papa, I wrote a play in school. All the children have a part. Will you read it?"

"Of course, I will. You're very smart, Liebling. You watch and see, times will change soon and our beloved Deutschland will be like it was before, the greatest country in the world. We have to hold our Vaterland dear over everything and everyone. You understand, don't you?"

"Yes, Papa, I understand."

"It'll happen because of Germans like you. Remember, you are our Wunschkind, our hope and dream for the future?"

"That's right, Papa."

"Now more than ever this is true. Your Papa tried hard and can't do much more, it's all up to you now."

We continued to walk. I was silent and pondered my father's words. He was always able to sway my emotions. A few moments before, I had been carefree. Now I looked up at him and deep sadness engulfed my heart. He was a disappointed man who had so completely believed in a cause that it was impossible for him to comprehend any new direction. I felt my father's rejected passion and vowed somehow to make things right again for him.

He wore his shirt open at the neck on this lovely mid-summer day and he had rolled his pants up to the knees. Mutti would be sure to scold us if we returned soaked or dirty. Of late he had taken to listen more to her, when before he hadn't cared. Before, when everything had been normal and he had been strong and in control. How I wished we could go back to those times. Father had just told me that there was hope and that the hope came from me. I wasn't sure if I was up to the challenge.

"I don't know which is more beautiful, the sea or the forest. I guess they are equally special. Do you still have the poem I wrote for you about our Heimat?"

"Yes, Papa. It's at home in my drawer. I love it by the sea just as I love to walk with you in the woods."

"Always remember, Liesel."

I skipped ahead a little, splashing the water with my bare feet. I waved my arms and mimicked the seagulls overhead. They sailed on the breeze in the blue sky. Then suddenly they swooped down to catch their breakfast of silvery fish.

When I turned around to wait for my father I saw that he was quite a way back and on his knees. He must have found something interesting on the ground to show me. He always had an eye for things other people overlooked. I ran back to see what it was. When I reached him he didn't look well. He tried to use his hands to get back up.

"Papa?" I felt a pang of misgiving. "Let's go back."

He tried to speak, but all that came out was my name. "Liesel...."

His temples bulged and turned a transparent blue. His eyes stared into space as if he was surprised by something he saw in the distance.

"Papa, Papa, get up."

He gasped for air. Just a couple of wheezes, then he let out a deep sigh and fell backwards with his head near the water. I looked around panic-stricken, but the beach was deserted. I shouted in horror. "Help, help my Papa!"

There was no one to hear my cries, just the screeching seagulls overhead and the roar of the incoming tide. I sank down beside him. The waves lapped closer every time they rolled back in from the deep. Soon they would sweep us away. Have to move Papa away from the water, I said to myself. I can't let him drown.

I picked up his head and kissed his cheek. Then I tried to turn his rigid body. It wouldn't budge. What to do? I yelled at the top of my lungs. The breakers now splashed over us. I could never abandon my Papa. I held his head up high.

When I looked up I saw a man on the dyke. "Help, help my Papa." But he went away. Soon after three men appeared and ran towards us. One fished me out of the water, screaming "Papa, Papa!"

The two other men went into the sea up to their waists and dragged Father by his arms. Now he lay stretched out on the beach. More men hurried down the dyke with a ladder. "Poor little girl, you were almost taken by the sea," they said, shaking their heads.

I sobbed. "Please help my Papa, make him better."

103

They placed my father's body on the ladder. He was very heavy and it took several men to carry him. His arms hung down and I held my Papa's cold wet right hand as we took him back to the guesthouse. A small crowd had gathered. Mutti ran towards us. I had never seen her run before.

We were surrounded by strangers, Friesen, people of few words and questions. Mother and I only had each other for comfort, but she didn't take any notice of me so completely stunned and submerged she was in her own sorrow. The center of her life was gone, the only man she had ever loved.

I was put into dry clothes and offered a hot drink to stop my trembling; it didn't help. No tears came; I just shook like a leaf in a thunderstorm. Was I responsible for my father's death? Only I had been with him. Father had relied on my strength. I had failed him.

The unusual death of the stranger with his young daughter who had clung to her father's body made news through the villages along the seashore. People came from all over to look. I overheard commiserations about our tragic misfortune.

A woman said "he was already dead for a while. The little girl clung to him and almost drowned herself. If we could only have gotten there sooner and brought him to a hospital. They might have been able to revive his heart."

I overheard another say "a beautiful death. Ein schoener Tot. So swift and without pain."

*

Mother informed Fritz and made arrangements to return to Bottrop. A special metal coffin had to be made so we could bring Father's body with us on the train. The people around us

104

were kind and tried to cheer me, even brought over children my age, but I was inconsolable. Mutti and I exchanged no sympathies with each other. I felt hat I had suffered the greatest loss and was alone in my grief.

That first night I had an overpowering desire to see my father. The only place to store a body had been in the guest house's tool shed. I got up out of bed in the darkness. Only a full moon gave a little light. I put on shoes and in my nightshirt made my way to the shed.

My father lay covered with a sheet high on a workbench by the window surrounded by rusty equipment. I walked over to him needing to see his revered face once again. I brought a wooden block over to elevate myself and folded back the cloth that covered his head.

I looked at my father's cold and impersonal face and realized that what I saw was no longer my father. He was gone from me forever, leaving nothing but an empty shell.

*

On the train ride back with my father's casket, Mother and I were silent. From the window I watched the countryside, black and white cows grazing peacefully by a stream, dotted windmills and straw-covered farmhouses--the land of marshes and purple heath that my father had loved and his body now passed in a coffin sealed shut with heavy screws.

Back in the Ruhrgebiet, where the air was always heavy and one gray town followed another, Fritz and several relations picked us up at the station. I watched Father's casket unloaded like a piece of cargo.

Some family members thought I was too young to be part of the funeral procession since it involved a walk several kilometers long behind the hearse, but they were wrong. I positioned myself right behind the horse-drawn hearse in front of Mother and Fritz. She was dressed in black head to toe, a black lace veil covered her tear-stained face. She leaned on her son during the funeral march. Fritz and all the men wore black armbands. I wore my best navy blue velvet dress and I pinned a black armband on my sleeve, too.

We proceeded along Gladbecker Strasse to the Friedhof in Bottrop-Eigen, where my grandparents were also buried. Church bells rang and the procession stretched a long distance. More and more people joined in along the way. Men removed their hats as we passed, and I saw people stare through windows and dab their faces with handkerchiefs.

Whatever the meaning of Father's arrest and trial this tribute was proof, if I ever needed it, that he was an important and well-respected member of the community. Through my sorrow I felt pride.

I was his daughter and a Steffens.

Chapter 19

Living or Dying

IN TIME MUTTI and I settled into some kind of normal routine. Her world now revolved around me, on rent collection from the tenants and her worry about Fritz who had moved into his own apartment in our building. Mutti complained that he brought home Flusen (loose women) and had not found a job yet. I spent my days more and more according to my own plans which I didn't share with her or anyone.

Often after school I walked to the cemetery and visited my father's grave just as Opa had done after Oma died. I brought special gifts of stones or wild flowers for decoration on the marble monument which had the inscription "Eheleute Steffens." It meant that the grave was for both of my parents and Mutti would join Papa's side when her time came.

I didn't believe my father was really under the earth but that he had transcended into the sky above. The peacefulness of the cemetery became one of my favorite places, where he and I could have intimate conversations and no one disturbed us.

Mother's obsession with my cleanliness became more and more bothersome. No matter how hard I tried I always collected grime somewhere which was not hard to do in a mining town like Bottrop. Dirt just seemed to stick to me, my shoes and clothes. It was a constant battle to keep clean.

The moment I came home Mother said "take your shoes off and wash your hands before you do anything else." She rushed over to wipe the doorknob and checked where I might have left finger-marks. Coarse, homemade soap and disinfectant was always on the kitchen and bathroom sinks. She investigated to make sure I washed my hands on top as well as on the inside and checked behind my ears every night. Even behind my ears I got dirty.

My mother made a variety of aprons for inside and outdoors which I was supposed to wear over my outfits at all times for filth protection.

I complained to my brother once, "Fritz I look silly."

He laughed. "The same aprons plagued my childhood and they are even sillier on a boy, don't you think?" He told me he had found a way to discard them the moment he was out of Mother's sight and suggested I do the same. Picturing Fritz with one of Mutti's aprons gave me the giggles.

Every week or two when the Kino showed a new film I still crept in through the backdoor. One day Fritz confided to me his own illicit activities in the Sommer's movie house during visits to our grandparents as a boy. Always the practical joker that he was he committed pranks. He placed stink bombs or smelly cheese under the seats and one time a whole swarm of insects which flew into the stream of light from the projector and appeared huge on the screen. "Herr Sommer had no idea who the culprit was. He's just a stupid, fat, ridiculous man," Fritz said.

I kept quiet about my movie secrets. I did, however, feel sorry for Herr Sommer whom I had never seen do any harm to anyone. His wife was always out of sight, and we didn't know if she was sick or had died. Friedrich Sommer junior attended a boarding school some place out of town. I couldn't figure out what it was about this family that made me always feel uneasy and strange. It was different from the way I felt about the backbiting Frau Lauder whom I didn't like at all.

Even Frau Lauder whose large nose with a wart on one side was always in everyone's business had very little direct information about the Sommers, so she made up unbelievable stories about them. She heard cries from their house. Herr Sommer beat his wife. Frau Sommer had delivered a stillborn child and gone mad.

Out of curiosity I hung around the Sommer's three-storey property quite a bit. I investigated from all directions and strained my ears but I heard nothing. I never went inside their apartment which was above the Kino.

*

The big void left by my father was hard to overcome. I was in the close company of my heartbroken Mother who still wore only black. Even for her to smile would have been inappropriate during her year of mourning.

Mother had not always been this matronly sullen figure. We had pictures of times when she was a stunning beauty, a champion athlete and kayaker who beat even Father and Fritz in her single kayak. As a radiant bride and young mother she had explored different scenic parts of Germany like the Spreewald, where people still wore their traditional costumes, and the Sauerland with its secluded lakes and streams. She had slept in tents and paddled into areas so remote they could be reached in no other way. All this was long before I arrived.

Now she rarely left the house. Even inside she didn't feel like doing anything other than cleaning and housework.

109

She no longer played her piano, but talked of giving it away along with my father's huge collection of leather-bound sheet music. It would be a waste if no family member used it and Fritz wasn't musical. Nor was I.

However, she got the idea to put the piano back in use-- piano lessons for me from my aunt Ilse who was a professional pianist.

Ilse was the young wife of Uncle Friedel, who had just become a doctor and already made a name for himself in Gladbeck looking after women as a gynecologist.

Ilse came from Southern Germany, and the family considered her talented as well as exotic. The way Mother said "exotic" in connection with my aunt made me wonder if it was a compliment or if it meant she was considered undesirably foreign.

Ilse Menken tried her best with me. Twice a week I took the tram and showed up, sheet music under my arm, for the hourly lesson on the Steinway in her elegant parlor. I quickly learned to play a couple of short sonatas but soon Ilse complained that my heart wasn't in it, and she was right. She said it was hopeless, and I wouldn't become a renowned musician which was fine with me. Since she really wasn't interested in wasting her time teaching a child of no musical talent (which she implied but not stated openly) the lessons were discontinued. Mother was disappointed, but I was relieved. I could spend more time on sports, outdoor activities and swimming again.

*

For Opa to sign ownership of the house over to Fritz and myself had been a deviant formality. At that time we were in danger of losing the property to confiscation by the Allied forces. The family understood that Mother had inherited it from her parents and was the true owner entitled to collect all the revenue.

Fritz lived rent free in our building. "He tries hard to get on his feet after the disaster of war," Mother said. I knew that the sea was my brother's great love but somehow he couldn't return to it professionally which might have been because of the way he had deserted the navy during the war. The only work he could find was as a sales representative for shoe polish.

I imagined my handsome, charming brother as captain of a great ship not selling tins of smelly polish. But that's what he did with little complaint. After a while he traded in the shoe polish (of which we retained a lifetime supply in all colors) and became a liquor salesman.

He didn't confide to Mother or me about his plans or his life goals. I was sure it wouldn't be selling things. I was hopeful that something great connected to the oceans of the world awaited my brother just around the corner. His blue eyes and face always lit up when he spoke about the ships he had sailed in the navy.

My brother was also fond of animals but like me he had never been allowed a dog or cat. Mother considered them dirty and an affront to her crusade to keep us all germ-free and clean. Now that Fritz lived in his own apartment he thought to get a dog. Mother tried to talk him out of it. That's when Fritz told us how he had once loved a dog called Bonzo. The story held me spellbound.

"Bonzo was not really my dog, but belonged to my friend Smutje who had no family to leave him with when we sailed out of Hamburg. So he smuggled Bonzo on board. The dog was as good a sailor as any of us and never lost his balance, not even in a storm. He kept us warm in our berths when we made our way through the icy waters of Norway almost at the top of the world. He ate the same food we did, and the three of us were the best of friends."

As Fritz continued he no longer smiled. "One day out of the blue I heard a commotion on deck and laughter from a bunch of sailors. Since there was not much to be merry about I rushed over to see what was going on. They had thrown Bonzo overboard. He thrashed around in the ice and the pigs pushed him under with a stick. 'You damned ass-holes!' I screamed. Smutje was right behind me and everyone disappeared below deck. We managed to get the poor creature out but he was half frozen. We wrapped him in a blanket and tried to give him some warm soup."

Fritz couldn't go on. He was more moved than I had ever seen him before. I waited for a happy ending but all he said was, "Bonzo didn't make it. He's buried at sea." I reached my hand over to my brother who out of all the tortures of war had chosen to talk about the fate of a defenseless dog.

*

The next day Fritz got himself a lanky, happy puppy. Mother didn't protest as long as he housebroke the animal and kept him at his own place. I was elated for Fritz and by Ajax. Every free moment I spent with the dog. I walked him and threw sticks and a ball for him in our garden.

As soon as Fritz returned from work in the late afternoon he got himself ready to go out with the ladies. Papa hadn't cared how he looked but Fritz wanted to impress his dates. He knew that wasn't hard to do, his only worry being his

112

receding hairline. For a couple of hours each night he wore a hairnet to coax his thinning, blond strands of hair forward across his bald spot.

What kind of woman would care about hair if they got to go out with my brother? I thought. Not me. I would be ready in a flash if he came calling to take me out. To spend more time with Fritz was something I craved. Father had always enjoyed my company, but to Fritz I was just a bothersome little sister.

*

This distance and difference in age became crucial after my encounter with the Jewish stranger and my outburst against Mother. Fritz was the only one left I could have confided in and received answers from. The day this life-changing event took place I was overwhelmed with conflicting feelings. I waited and listened for Fritz to return home before I came out of my room. I didn't want to encounter Mother.

I sneaked over to my brother's apartment. At his door I heard hushed voices, one belonged to Mother. I was too late. She had gotten to Fritz first and told him. I tried to eavesdrop for a moment, but it did not feel right and I got frightened about what I might hear. I retreated back to my room. Fritz would be on Mother's side. I had nowhere to turn. She would make sure that Fritz hated me too for what I had done.

What had I done? I had brought a stranger into our house, someone who had lived next door. Somehow he had turned out to be an unwelcome guest. Not just unwelcome, but feared and despised.

Instead of standing by my family I had taken the side of the stranger whose name I did not even know. This all happened in a split second without time to think it over. In an

113

instant, spontaneous, emotional outburst I accused my mother of being a murderer, somebody who had committed a terrible crime.

I couldn't figure out where my outburst had come from. I frightened even myself. All I know is that I had believed the stranger's story without hesitation, and my instinct and memory told me his story was true when I saw my mother's reaction. I knew at that moment that everything I had believed about my family's goodness and innocence was a falsehood. I had been betrayed and lost my father for the second time on that day. He had not been the man I thought he was, and I realized I had not ever known him at all. I could not forgive him for that.

It was knowledge I carried with me from that day on, that we are forever strangers to each other. No one ever knows another person, nor for that matter knows oneself.

I lost so very much on that day in 1951. I no longer believed in myself and was no longer proud of who I was. The love and devotion of my mother, my only remaining parent, could no longer reach me. These were unbearable damages for a child my age, and I felt the impact instantly.

The atmosphere at home now became one of suspicion and condemnation. Neither one of us was able to understand or explain what had happened or why. Father had been the lucky one; he died early. I became obsessed with death and dying, and saw it as an escape from my pain.

The day the stranger came no one ate in our home, but the next day Mother expected me back at the table. My chair remained empty. I didn't touch food for several days.

My schoolwork suffered. I no longer saw any purpose in learning. I wondered about my teachers. What had they done during the war? Where had they been when a little boy was being thrown from the balcony? Yet I asked none of these questions, afraid of the answers. Besides, I had already made up my mind. I turned away from everyone.

My diary became my confidante and I wrote in it almost every day seated at my father's large oak desk. I covered the pages when Mother came in. The lock and key were the most important parts of this small book with blank pages I had received as a Christmas gift. After each writing session I locked it and I slept with the key under my pillow. One entry read: "It's over! When someone finds this I will no longer be on this earth of misery."

I saw no way out and a couple of calamities hastened my resolve to make my permanent exit from the world.

Chapter 20

Liar's Exit

THE FIRST WAS Ajax's untimely death which was my fault. Fritz allowed him to roam the neighborhood during the day. The dog had gotten very attached to me and waited for my return from school near our house.

On this day he was across the street and when he spotted me he made a mad dash to greet me. At the same time a motorcycle zoomed around the corner. I knew the outcome even before it happened. "Stay," I shouted. "Ajax, please, please stay." I ran to reach him, but-- bang! The motorcycle couldn't stop and the dog was dead with a broken neck.

When I carried him to the back garden I got blood all over me. A neighbor tended to the injured cyclist. Fritz cried when he got home and had to bury his pet. We hadn't talked in private since the day of the stranger. It was obvious that he blamed me for the grief I caused Mother. Now he gave me accusing looks for killing his dog.

The second hurt came from one of my teachers whose name I still remember, Frau Zurmuhle, my German instructor. I enjoyed writing and had produced a true-life essay about a beggar in the street whom I had seen everyone pass by. Frau Zurmuhle chose my work to read out loud to the class.

"Nicely written," she said, "but what do you think? Is

this story true? There are no beggars in Bottrop, and if they were we would all help them, would we not?"

She called me a liar in front of the class for writing something that wasn't true. But I knew what I had seen, and my observations were correct. The beggar in the street had been an embarrassment and citizens had looked away, hurrying past him.

I got bright red in the face with embarrassment. It was the last time I handed in any work to her. In fact, I decided this would be the last time I would ever write anything for anyone to read. I was only going to confide in my hidden diary. How sad that I saw and felt so different from everyone around me. I couldn't win, no one understood me. What a strange and pathetic outcast I had become.

On the day I decided to end it all I picked out rat poison from Mother's storage below the sink. I hadn't seen it work on rodents, but the sign on the canister showed a deadly warning. So I poured some into a paper bag, went to my room and locked the door. The poisonous wheat grains looked no different from wheat I had picked in fields and chewed on before but these had a sweetish smell. I put a handful into my mouth and grinded them between my teeth. I swallowed hard and started to gag, but I took deep breaths to prevent this. I forced myself to lie motionless on my bed.

The next thing I remember was that I felt very sick and someone lifted me. I didn't come to until I was in hospital. I kept my eyes shut, but I could hear the commotion around me and my mother's anxious voice when she addressed a stranger. I moved my head and Mother leaned over me. "Why did you do it, Liebling? Why? You are so very young and have your whole life before you."

I opened my eyes and looked at her for just a moment before I turned my face to the wall. My mother knew very well why I had done it.

Medical attention restored me and I was sent home after this botched attempt at taking my life. When I looked at myself for the first time in the bathroom mirror I saw my ashen face and sunken eyes. They didn't belong to a child.

Three months later I attended the funeral of my cousin Gudrun who had been more successful. Gudrun was a few years older and had just begun training as a nurse which probably gave her access to more lethal potions. I looked at her young body in the coffin and admired what she had done. She was dead and had gone to a better place. All we living could do was weep for her.

What Gudrun's reasons were I had no idea. We only saw each other on occasion at family gatherings where we shared food but not thoughts. Nor do I know why several other young people in Bottrop committed suicide. One hung himself in his attic. Another girl threw herself in front of the tram. There was a self-inflicted, premature death epidemic which our parents and elders tried to hide. Each one of these suicides was reported to have been an accident.

Chapter 21

Konfirmant

MOTHER REDISCOVERED RELIGION. She talked to the pastor of the Evangelical Church in Bottrop-Eigen as well as my teachers. Together they came up with a plan to help me recover and get back to normal. Since I was beyond human help (they must have reasoned) only an all-powerful God could do the trick.

At my age it was the custom for a young person to become an active member of the church by being "confirmed."

This involved the study of catechism on a weekly basis with the Herr Pastor and to pass a verbal exam in front of the congregation. I found it ironic and ridiculous that Mother had become so pious and such a church seeker and I pointed this out to her. "Can't you stick to anything you believed in? Why are we now running to church when I haven't even been baptized yet?"

I also told this to the pastor who conducted an investigation. At first Mother denied it but when she couldn't produce my baptism certificate she admitted the transgression without going into details about the Nazi naming ceremony. I had been dedicated to a different God as was the custom and the demand of the National Socialist regime, but now we had seen the light. Mother had no problem in convincing the man of the cloth who seemed to understand her plea very well.

What light we now saw I wasn't sure.

To rectify my lack of church standing and to keep it away from a gossipy community the minister agreed to come to our home secretly on a Sunday afternoon instead of performing the ceremony in church. With water in one of Mother's china bowls and candles lit he baptized me in our living room at the age of thirteen. My name hadn't been changed, but everything else had. It made no difference in the way I felt.

Confirmation was next, and on a Sunday in April I passed my test by reciting several psalms in a clear, loud voice in front of the congregation. A week later I stood with my fellow Konfirmanten and faced the altar.

The pastor directed us as a choir to speak together words from the Evangelical Lutheran church service. I just opened my mouth and voiced what I was supposed to, but what I said on the inside was nothing but: "Blaa, baa baa, blaa bla. Baa baa blaa bla."

Mother outdid herself with my dress which was very pretty and maybe even a work of art in antique, black lace. As always the confirmation was memorialized by a group photo with the pastor outside the church. Mother couldn't wait to pick up our copy to see just how lovely I looked in my outfit. Was she disappointed!

There in the back row with the group of straight bodied, solemn looking youngsters stood her daughter with a silly grin and crooked head. A sudden recurrence of an earlier affliction had been reenacted.

Konfirmation

Chapter 22

Slaughter of the Innocent

AFTER THIS FAILED effort at my redemption via the church Mother made another attempt "to bring us close again like we should be as mother and daughter." During my summer vacation she took me back to the North Sea. I didn't object.

An efficiency room had again been rented, this time in a private home on the island of Norderney. Mother had found our lodgings through an advertisement in the newspaper. "Scenic and quiet," it stated. "Close walk to the beach. Advance payment required." It sounded like a good deal and Mother sent in her bank draft.

Again we went by train. The last time we had gone north we were a family. It was the same countryside we had seen when we had returned in the other direction with my father's coffin. Now I was glad he was in a box under the earth and away from me. I didn't want to think about him in any other way. Certainly not looking down and guiding me from above. At the same time I felt guilty.

Mother couldn't have picked a worse place in all of Germany for a vacation to heal her child. Everything looked peaceful enough when we arrived late on Friday. Our housing wasn't as close to the beach as we had expected, but we could make the half-hour walk. The building had window boxes with red geraniums and was part of a compound, fenced in all around, with a big iron gate and a small pedestrian entrance on the side. We unpacked and settled in.

The weekend was fine, but when Monday came, the floodgates of hell broke open. We were woken by the loud rattle of the metal gate and a line of trucks with shouting drivers who sounded their horns and demanded entry. When I saw that the trucks were full of squealing animals--cattle, sheep and pigs--I got dressed in a hurry and ran outside.

Never in my life could I have imagined such horror. Mother had gotten us to holiday on the property of a slaughterhouse.

Big men with coarse, pimpled faces and stained, white overalls lowered the back flaps of the trucks. They pushed and beat the animals off the vehicles. The desperate creatures tumbled and fell on top of each other, broke their limbs and let out the most terrifying screams. I joined in at the top of my lungs.

"What are you doing? Get away, get away!" I shouted and stood in front of the perpetrators. I stamped my feet and demanded an end to the mayhem. The butchers who, not surprisingly, had never encountered a young girl attempting to interfere with their work were amused. They saw my anguish and it made them laugh loud belly laughs. I winced and they slapped their fat hands together and applauded me. After they had enough fun they said, "silly, little girl get lost."

One nasty man with a big grin put his hands on his hips. Then he pulled out a long blade and stabbed the air.

"Soon the blood squirts everywhere," he shouted. "Ha, ha, ha."

"Don't," I begged. "Don't do it."

All the animals were forced inside the big stone building and the door slammed shut. For the next few hours the bleating, mooing and squealing continued until there was silence and then the stench of blood and death.

I ran around the outside of the building, jumped up on windows to see inside. I saw the animals and saw some of them killed. I cried and banged on windows and doors. They stabbed a calf in the neck with a knife, and the calf looked at me with huge brown eyes before he was slaughtered.

Mother was furious with our landlords, a smiling couple who needed the money. "I brought my daughter here because of her frail nerves. Now she throws up all day. I demand a refund." Nothing else was available on the island in August. We were trapped.

I wanted to go home but Mother said, "we can't give in. It's best to be strong and stick it out." She reasoned that it wasn't quite so bad since the slaughter took place just on Mondays. By Wednesday all the blood was hosed off and the corpses were gone, including the skins which had been left outside on racks to dry. "It's not right if we return early. What will the Bottropers say? We have to have a good time."

"We have to have a good time in a slaughterhouse?"

"No one must know about this. We can't let anyone know, can we, Liesel?" Mother said.

"Of course we can't." The word "Mother" or the endearing term "Mutti" had not come from my lips again.

*

On the first Sunday in September Mother invited her female relatives and her spinster girl friend, a retired teacher and mother's advisor on my misbehavior, for her birthday

124

Kaffeklatsch, the German institution of catching up on gossip over coffee and cake.

"Liesel and I had a lovely time in Norderney," Mother lied.

I sat with a piece of apple cake and Schlagsahne (whipped cream) and didn't contradict her. I smiled at the women around the table and they remarked how well I was growing up and becoming a young lady.

Aunt Clara said, "Not long before a wonderful young man will come along. He'll marry our Liesel and take her away from us." They all agreed. "Yes, that will be a shame."

What popped out of me next was not something I had planned to say or thought about but it seemed appropriate at this gathering.

I said, "I'm going to marry a Neger (Negro)."

A collective gasp, followed by silence. The air in the room was stifling. Everyone looked down at their plates-- Mother's finest Meisner--then attacked pieces of birthday Stollen with pastry forks. Mother's face was hot and red. She wiped her forehead with her starched and ironed handkerchief. All the attention now shifted from me to her and the commiseration was heartfelt. "Poor Else. What a cross to bear."

"What's wrong with marrying a black man?" I said and left the table. Back in my room, I submerged myself in one of my very favorite library books, *Uncle Tom's Cabin.*

*

Every week I took out books from the local library. I had already read Dickens' *Oliver Twist* and Tolstoy's *War and Peace.* I also had great interest in the fate of American Indians, and I read books about them whenever I could find one. I read late into the night and I slept very little.

Yet at school I was a failure. Time and time again Mother was called to the Gymnasium (grammar school) where I was now schooled in the center of Bottrop. I had passed the entrance exam with ease, but during the year my work was marginal at best, and I wasn't easy to get along with. Fortunately I never had to repeat a class. My teachers were only too glad to pass me on and I made always a last minute academic effort to reach the next grade.

My friendships were few and never with popular youngsters. I sought out the company of children who had something wrong with them--bad body odor, extreme fatness, and as in the case of sixteen-year-old Peter whom I met in the street outside school, a missing right arm. I fiercely defended them from bullies who called them stinky Scheine (pigs) and misfits.

Chapter 23

On Wings of Budding Sisterhood

IN THE SPRING following our slaughterhouse vacation Mother took a trip of her own.

"Where're you going?" I asked.

"I'll be home late this evening. Your dinner's prepared. You can eat with your brother."

I decided I wasn't hungry and Fritz went out somewhere by himself.

She did return late. I had waited up to find out where she had gone. "We'll talk tomorrow. I'm tired and have to go to bed." I stayed awake that night and wondered what this mystery trip was all about. I found out soon enough.

The next day she called me into the living room. "Sit down. I have come to a decision regarding your future. Things have gone downhill here at home and you are a constant embarrassment.

"How so?" I said.

"I don't know what to do with you and we can't keep on living like this. At the beginning of next month you will start boarding at the Theodore Fliedner Schule in Duesseldorf-Kaiserswerth."

"Wonderful." Sarcasm marked a lot of conversations

with my mother. I got up and headed for the door.

"I had to beg them to take you. Your grades aren't even good enough. This tremendous financial sacrifice is for your benefit."

I didn't care about her sacrifice. I didn't know what I cared about, but I didn't relish the idea of banishment to the prison of some faraway school. I wanted to stay home to confront Mother and keep hurting her.

I knew I had only myself to blame. I was persistent in my belligerence, was rude and disrespectful. No one liked me, not even Fritz. I soon concluded that to leave was the best for everyone, including me.

*

By the time I departed I was thrilled at least on the outside. Bottrop, its secrets, gossip and bad memories would soon be gone I told myself. I would miss a few things, films at the Kino next door, my room and my familiarity with the neighborhood. But the big city of Duesseldorf awaited me. My mind was made up. I would spread my wings and never return.

Mother accompanied me and my belongings to my new school and watched and listened to me hum the latest Schlager (pop song), even laugh hysterically on the train. Our separation was imminent. I noticed tears just behind her eyes. She spoke only two sentences on the trip shaking her head: "What would your father say? You were our Wunschkind."

What my father thought didn't matter anymore in the slightest. I was determined to make a fresh start with new people who didn't know anything about me or what my father had done. He was dead and gone, banished from my mind, the good times as well.

All the students arrived around the same time we did, most of them by car. They looked like city girls with fashionable parents to match. I told Mother to leave as soon as possible.

Until now I had not paid much attention to my clothes which had always been unique and homespun. Since I would be living away Mother's hands and sewing machine had been busier than usual. She made a bunch of complete outfits that would last some time while I grew into them. In other words they were much too big. I had a whole suitcase full of oversized garments.

My clever Mother had even made my cotton underpants and sanitary pads which buttoned into them. The only store bought concession was four white cotton bras in two sizes to allow for growing breasts. As far as colors, there were great limitations on what she considered to be in good taste and not vulgar. Nothing bright, nothing largely patterned just small paisley flowers in pale blue and a lot of beige tweed, brown and navy.

The lined, tailored suit I wore for my entrance into the school was beige and brown with a white removable Peter Pan collar. A skirt covered my legs well below the knee and a buttoned jacket hid my hips.

The school which charged extravagant monthly fees was modern and luxurious. Just two girls shared a room. I watched Mother leave. She looked very old and dejected and didn't turn around as she walked slowly down the street towards the train station. I also felt miserable deep down in my heart but didn't allow these feelings to linger.

Upstairs in my designated room on the second floor my roommate was already unpacking. She looked amused and

129

inquisitive. This was a big moment. We were assigned to be together for the year and would have to get along.

"Hello, nice maternity outfit," she said. "When's the baby due?"

How embarrassed I felt. My face got hot. "I hate you Mother, you made me a laughing stock," I wanted to say, but she was gone. There was nothing better to do than laugh myself. My roommate had found her match.

"In five months. You can be the midwife."

She laughed. "Come on, quite honestly. Where does one find such a terrific outfit? By the way my name is Ingrid. Ingrid Neul."

"Only I know where you can get one. If you're really good I'll have you an outfit made just like mine. I'm Liesel Steffens."

"Where does the Liesel Steffens come from looking so divine? Have you ever been to a city like Duesseldorf?"

"Of course."

"Okay then let me see what your haute couture looks like on me."

She pulled her pink sweater up over her ample breasts and stood in front of me in her skin-tight blue jeans and lacy bra. In Bottrop we didn't wear blue jeans.

Ingrid was a great beauty, very different from me, the pale, delicate girl with straight, thin blond strands of hair pulled back in a tight French twist. Everything about her was voluptuous and curved while I was plain and flat like a board.

Her thick, curly hair, cut fashionably short, framed a

strong face with beautiful, tanned skin and sparkling large brown eyes. Sophia Loren was the film star of the day. Ingrid looked like her, but I thought she was even more gorgeous than the Italian actress. Only our height was the same.

"Why have you been sent here? This isn't a maternity ward as far as I know."

"It's not?" Wait till I tell my mother."

"Come on Steffi, take it off and turn it over."

"Okay, Neuli."

We had found nicknames for each other. I hesitated only for a second before I took my jacket off and handed it to her. Ingrid managed to button it only around her waist; the rest was too tight. We laughed till our sides hurt.

After the initial kidding around Ingrid never made reference again to my lack of sophistication. In fact she was always very careful not to say anything that might hurt my feelings. I appreciated this very much and adored her for it.

She offered to let me share her things."Everything I own is also yours. Wear whatever you like. Just do me a favor and hide all your funny stuff in your suitcase under the bed."

I liked the new me when I looked at myself in the mirror. Ingrid's designer jeans were loose but she handed me a nice, buckled belt to hold them up. Her lacy, silk panties gave me a wonderful new sensation against my skin. Even my hair was not so bad hanging now shiny and loose to below my shoulders.

When the bell sounded it was time to come downstairs for supper and a welcoming speech by our governess. Ingrid and I made our entrance into the dining hall together. I had

131

been transformed into a city girl.

*

Neuli, which I always called her now, had a secret. She probably had many but this one she shared with me after just a couple of days. I was surprised at myself that I hadn't noticed before.

"Pick a hand, Steffi."

She always played games and gave me surprises. I chose the right. She stretched it out upside down with a clenched fist. I thought she held something in it. "Come on Neuli, show me." I turned her hand over.

"Wow." I was startled. Ingrid's fingers were missing. Her manicured thumb was next to a stump of an index finger. The rest were gone.

There was a brief moment of sadness on her part that upset me. "Oh, my God? What happened to you?"

Ingrid shrug her shoulders and laughed. "Don't be a baby Steffi. It's nothing. Just don't tell anyone."

"I swear I won't." I reached for her mutilated hand and brought it to my face. A strange sensation. She moved the thumb and stump then she slipped it into her pocket. That's why I hadn't noticed before. Ingrid's right hand was always hidden nonchalantly in a pocket.

"How did it happen?" I asked. Oh, how I wanted to find out all about her.

"Just an accident. I cut them off in an electric food slicer. No big deal. Come on, Steffi. Don't look so shocked. Let's go down to the Rhine and take a swim."

By the time the Rhine River which started out as a pure mountain spring in the Alps reached Duesseldorf it was murky with lots of debris and litter and it stunk. But Ingrid liked the water just as much as I did and it didn't keep us from enjoying ourselves. We swam in the polluted waters often.

Since there was a strong under-current and swimming was forbidden as per large signs posted along the shore we took our lives into our hands every time we left our clothes by the riverbank and floated downstream in our bathing suits. We climbed out reeking of river at a special spot where we could get hold of a reef. We laughed and embraced that we had overcome danger and made it once again. These were very intimate moments.

The buildings where we girls boarded were a ten-minute walk away from the historic schoolhouse. There was no supervision after we left our living quarters and before we had to arrive for our classes. The two of us sometimes took this window of opportunity and disappeared on adventures.

On our very first Saturday together Ingrid told me that she would be picked up and return home for the night. "Don't worry, Steffi. I'll be thinking of you and I'll bring you a nice present."

I didn't care about gifts although hers were always thoughtful and special like the twenty-four carat gold bracelet she gave me. I came to dread weekends because I missed my friend and didn't want to be left behind. There were also feelings of jealousy. She meant the world to me and I wasn't prepared to share her with anyone. Maybe there was another girl friend near her home?

Ingrid's mystery remained her secret for a while. She was always understated, unpretentious and never boasted about

133

her family's opulence. They were prominent Duesseldorf industrialists who owned a luxurious mansion with a swimming pool-- the greatest sign of affluence--and a department store on Shadow Strasse, the main shopping district just off the Koenigsallee. Ingrid's older sister was married to a high ranking German diplomat.

The car that picked her up was a black Mercedes. It was our governess who informed me one weekend about the Neuls. I was flabbergasted.

What a difference. My mother traveled on the train, we lived in an apartment above a grocery store and my brother was a salesman.

"Tell me about your home, Steffi. I want to know everything about you. What is Bottrop like?"

No way. I couldn't tell my precious friend. How could we still be close if she knew what I had discovered about my family? My father had been a Nazi, I was at war with my mother, didn't speak to my brother and Bottrop was a miserable dump. Somehow I had to invent a new family and history for myself, one that was more likable and noble. It was vital to do so if I was going to make it and have any friends. While I tried to figure it out my focus was on Ingrid.

"Why have you been sent here?" I asked her one day. "I'm sure it's better for you to live at home."

She got serious. "There were difficulties. My father felt a more strict routine would help straighten me out. He doesn't know yet what we are up to here."

I didn't see anything that needed to be straightened with my amazing friend and she never explained her difficulties. Anytime the past came up in our discussions we changed the subject and started to laugh at events or people at the school. We laughed a lot.

Ingrid had everything imaginable in the way of clothes and material possessions. She was worldly, humorous and free spirited. Yet, there also seemed to be an underlining sadness not unlike my own. Something had happened to her and she wasn't telling anyone, not even me. That made me feel better about my own secrets. Why tell?

We got into oodles of mischief together. I often led her astray and couldn't believe how much we got away with without getting caught.

Our parents paid a lot of money to have us under strict supervision which they had been unable to provide themselves. We were both strong and willful characters and our governesses and teachers didn't do that much better.

At night we often escaped through our window on the second floor. Sometimes we walked four kilometers to the Duesseldorf airport and watched planes and passengers from destinations like London, Paris, Rome and New York. I longed to fly away with them.

I said to Ingrid: "One day you and I will be on a plane and take off to faraway countries. I can't wait for that day."

"I can't wait either, Steffi. Where shall we go first? Paris or London?"

"How about Africa? We can roam about in the bush and no one will find us."

"I don't know about Africa. We'll be bitten by snakes. Let's go to London."

"All right. I don't care where we go as long as it is far

135

away from here."

Our travel plans would have to wait and only one of us was destined to realize dreams of international travel and adventure.

Meanwhile we tried to make our boarding school life as exciting as possible for ourselves. We found ways to go over walls and fences into people's gardens. I climbed trees and threw apples and pears to Ingrid below. Boxes full of stolen fruit were under our beds.

*

Our room was off limits to the other boarders. Ingrid had an aura of authority and had made sure of these boundaries right on the first day. I had never shared a room but with Ingrid I lost my self-consciousness and didn't mind dressing and undressing in front of her. In the communal bathroom where in the German tradition we took cold morning showers to develop character I preferred to be covered with one of Ingrid's robes.

We were kindred spirits and sisters, protective of each other and our relationship. For the first time since I had lost my father I felt close to another human being. But it was a different intimacy and it felt good. I began to see my glorious Ingrid through the prism of love. Everything she did and said was perfect and adorable.

One chilly morning when it was still dark she spoke to me. "Steffi, are you awake?" Ingrid's bed was by the window and mine near the door.

"What time is it?"

"Don't know but it's cold. Can you come over here and warm me until we get up?"

I was sleepy but got out from under my covers and snuggled under her featherbed next to her warm body.

"You don't feel cold to me, Neuli."

"I don't? You do, Steffi. Let me warm you."

She gently turned me around and wrapped her arms and legs around me from behind. I wore a cotton nightshirt, Ingrid a satin pajama. She brought her left hand to my nipple and massaged it, her mangled right hand to my belly. I felt soaring, intense sensations all over. My heart raced.

"How do you feel, Steffi?"

I was speechless. We were close like two peas in a pod and it felt wonderful beyond words, beyond heaven. I never wanted this moment to end. I wanted to melt into her and never leave.

She kissed my neck and put strands of my hair in her mouth. She made wet circles on my back until it became unbearable and I turned around.

"You're wicked, Steffi. You're seducing me." She blew in my ear and brought my hand between her legs. She moved it back and forth, back and forth. It slid around on the wet, slippery satin.

"Faster, Steffi, do it faster."

She panted harder and harder and then let out a loud moan. After a moment she brought my hand to her face, kissed it tenderly and lay still.

"Oh, Steffi. You're outrageously wicked, and I love you for it."

I loved her, the sensations I had just experienced and

my new identity, "outrageously wicked." I wanted more of this incredible closeness.

After that if I woke up first and there was time I didn't wait to be invited into Ingrid's bed and it was always just like the first time.

*

Since our forte lay in our private, extra-curricular activities it was no wonder that neither one of us did well in school. We had no plans or ambitions for our future and we lived for the moment.

Ingrid's artistic talents despite her handicap amazed me. I couldn't take my eyes off her when she sat at her easel and created vibrant pieces in the style of Gauguin, her favorite painter. She held a pencil or brush between her thumb and stump.

I strung together words that rhymed...laut with Haut and I wrote short stories. We exchanged gifts of her artwork for my silly poems and essays.

*

History lessons in this institution for German girls and their higher education like in my previous school did not touch our recent history and focused instead on the Middle Ages, a time when persecution had been rampant. Not a word about the camps of our recent past where fellow human being's lives were hell on earth and our Jewish neighbors were persecuted to their deaths in the millions.

Our country had eased into some outward changes like replacing parts of the national anthem. "Germany over everything" was now "Unity, right and freedom."

Unity with whom? Right to what? And freedom? How could young persons like Ingrid and me be free to live our lives unencumbered by our dark heritage? The full and unfathomable horror of mass murder was still officially concealed from us. Each one of us was alone and had to unearth the truth for ourselves, one by one and over time.

I had books on the subject but didn't want anyone to know what I was reading and turned the sleeves inside out. What I uncovered confirmed the horror I already had concealed in my heart. My father's preaching about inferior races and how they needed to be overcome had not been empty words. He had acted on them with great success. My father had done what he said he would do. He was always a man of his word. And after his deeds he came home and was my Papa who lifted me into his arms and kissed me as if nothing had happened.

I came to think that in my ordinary, loving German home I was taught a most deadly culture, so despicable and wrapped up in deceit that to free my conscience I had to free myself from everything German about me.

My father was dead, but the world around me was full of others like him, the fathers and mothers of other young Germans who seemed to have shed as irrelevant the absurd doctrines of their Nazi revolution that shook the whole of civilization. These dogmas were no longer worthy of discussion so they concentrated on their own survival and future prosperity. The victims lay forever silent in their graves, they hoped, and their own children would be silent and not ask questions. The consensus was: Let's not think about it and it will go away.

Surely I was not the only one whose future had been dedicated to an ideology of world domination and destruction.

For myself and young people like me the burden was so heavy and we were so confused in our void that we did not seek, even shunned, connection with each other.

What could and should we believe in now? Which road should we travel that would lead us to freedom from our overwhelming guilt? How many tears would it take to fill a bottomless pit of evil? We got no answers. Each one of us had to begin the search for our individual path and new destiny alone.

My future was uncertain. All I knew was that I didn't want to be around my mother with her hypocritical behavior and thinking nor anyone else in authority. They were all guilty in my eyes, undistinguishable, and had left us with a heritage we were completely unequipped to deal and live with.

*

When it was time for school vacation and Ingrid extended an invitation to come home with her I was elated. I had no hesitation to call Mother. "Hey, I'm not coming back to Bottrop."

There was great disappointment in her voice. "I was looking forward to seeing you."

"I look forward to spending my holidays with my girl friend and her family in Metternich."

"When then are you coming home?"

"I don't know. Maybe never."

*

Metternich was a beautiful, tree-lined suburb of Duesseldorf. Ingrid's elaborate home and grounds intimidated me at first but she was always by my side and helped me feel

140

comfortable. At mealtime the table was set with exquisite bone china. Which fork or spoon should I use first? I watched Ingrid.

Her mother was warm and sweet and her two brothers, one older and one younger, were polite and upright young men, but Ingrid's father made me tremble when he looked at me. I couldn't wait to be out of his sight. He controlled the family and reminded me of my father in a frightening way.

At the end of the school year our delinquent undertakings caught up with us and a letter was sent to our respective homes:

"Your daughter has passed the Mittlere Reife (half maturity). However, we regret to inform you that during the next school year there is no longer a space available for her at our institution. May we take this opportunity to suggest that it is in the best interest of both young women, Ingrid Neul and Liesel Steffens, to be separated. Their behavior together may become criminal in the future. On their own they will have a better chance of success."

The shock of this letter was only that we were to be separated. To see ourselves as criminals made us roar with laughter. The Mittere Reife was a middle of the road educational passage which led to vocational training and a few special colleges, but it meant we were not eligible for the Abitur, the prerequisite for university.

Our good-bye was emotional. We promised to stay in touch. Pricked our fingers and mingled our blood in forever sisterhood.

We were fifteen.

Many years later we saw each other again briefly but by then our closeness had evaporated.

141

Chapter 24

Middle Maturity

I WAS A reluctant and rebellious young person when I returned home to my mother. I was there in body only. Laughter, warmth and love had been left behind in Duesseldorf. The heaviness of Bottrop dragged down my soul, making it bitter and silent. The silence could be heard and felt by all.

Mother quickly found a space at a "finishing school" where young women not bound for universities were prepared for marriage instead.

We learned how to become good hostesses, an asset to our future husbands. There were classes on starching and ironing a man's shirt to perfection, how to make a budget, to arrange flowers and set a table and how not to drown our first-borns in their bath water.

Having returned from Duesseldorf with Ingrid's dressing know-how and tastes as well as a bunch of her clothes I was now the most sophisticated person around Gladbecker Strasse. I knew people talked behind my back. "Where does she think she comes from?"

"Not from around here," I said to myself.

*

Once a month I spent a week doubled up in agony with

painful menstruations. Mother made an appointment with gynecologist Uncle Friedel in Gladbeck. He was Mother's cousin, the son of grandfather's brother.

The well-known physician with lots of patients and no time to spare agreed to take a quick look (for his usual large fee) at his mousy, unimportant great niece. We had not seen each other since I took piano lessons from his wife Ilse. Mother had already clued Uncle Friedel in on my female problem and he would prescribe a remedy.

I sat in his waiting room when he swept in all dressed in white. He looked at me twice and showed great surprise.

"Is that you, our little Liesel? Mei, mei, how you have grown. Come in and let your dear uncle have a closer look at you."

Caught off guard by his unfamiliar attention I smiled nervously. I had done something right in the way I looked and presented myself to my uncle that was obvious.

"How have you been, my dear little one?"

"I have been well Uncle Friedel. Thank you for asking. I just returned from a year in Duesseldorf."

"That's what it is! You have explored the big city and have turned into a beautiful young woman. Who would have thought that you had it in you born so late to Else and for such a crazy reason?"

I paid close attention to every one of my uncle's words.

"Do you know it's because of your Uncle Friedel that you are here in the world? It was me who had the connections with the brilliant Herr Professor. Your mother Else came to me and wanted to use her body to bear another child that she and

143

your father could present to the idiot they called our Fuehrer. The demented lunatic led us into a fine mess. I told your fanatical father so at the time."

I shook my head no. But of course I knew. During my childhood I had heard too many times about the purpose for my birth and I didn't want to be reminded.

Uncle Friedel talked about it as if it was all a big joke to him. I hid my embarrassment. He was oblivious to my emotions, brimming with delight at the way I looked and his part in my creation.

His comments about Father shamed me. He made it clear that he was not a fool. He hadn't fallen for the same outrageous nonsense my gullible father had. I felt that I should somehow speak up for my parents. But how could I? They had willingly chosen to participate in Hitler's plan.

"Now, let me see what's going on with you down there," he said and pointed to my "private parts."

"Take off your panties and let your uncle have a closer look." I hesitated, and then he watched me as I slipped out of my underwear.

"Hurry up. We don't have all day. I've lots of patients. Take everything off and put on the gown over there. You do want your uncle to help you, don't you?" I was not so sure anymore.

"I'm all right. My pain already cleared up. I'll come back if I've any more problems."

"Not so fast," Uncle Friedel said and blocked the door. "What will your mother say if you don't let me help you?"

I had no choice. After I put on the robe he guided me to

the gynecological chair.

"Lie down. That's right; just relax. Every woman in Gladbeck has been spread out in this chair before you. Your uncle is the expert. Your legs go right here in these stirrups." He separated my legs and tied them down.

What he did was horrible and I tried to get up.

"You are a woman now and your uncle needs to have a look." He pushed me to lie down.

His soft, spongy hands felt my nipples, the right first and then the left. They hardened and stood up as did every hair on my body. When he leaned over me I closed my eyes. This medical exam was humiliating. I willed myself to think of something else more pleasant like a walk through the meadows on the first day of spring. I was far away, his voice in the distance. "That's right. Very nice. Very nice. Uncle Friedel's little niece is a lovely woman now."

When he poked with something hard between my legs I let out a scream and opened my eyes. He had perspiration on his forehead, and he wiped it off with the sleeve of his overall.

"All right, you're done. Get dressed. You're in perfect health and everything is still intact down there. For your pain take these pills." He handed me a foil wrapper. "You'll be cured in no time at all."

He left the room and I was glad, but on the way out he called me into his office.

"I have to see more of you now you have grown up and your father is gone. After all we are family and I have to keep an eye on you. How about coming to one of your Aunt Ilse's house concerts next Friday? Our parties are always the talk of the town."

145

"I'm not sure, Uncle Friedel."

"Ilse told me how bad you were at your piano lessons. You really have no talent, but looking as beautiful as you do now it doesn't matter in the least. I'll see you on Friday around seven. Say hello to your mother for me."

I wondered if I should mention to Mother there was something funny about Uncle Friedel. What was the point? She wouldn't understand. We had stopped meaningful talks long ago and ever since I had disregarded her views and opinions. As far as I could see, she was wrong about everything.

What could I have told her anyway? Uncle Friedel was untouchable with his high standing in the community. He was the only one in our family who had become a Herr Doktor.

Mother paid and thanked him for his help with my pain and the pills we got for free. "Have her start on them right away, Else," Uncle Friedel said.

Dr. Menken's stupendous comments about my parents struck a cord. He had disdain for them as crazy followers of a lost cause. He had been smart and fearless enough to speak up to my father and had distinguished correctly between right and wrong. At least there was one member of my family with whom I had something in common.

*

It turned out that the high potency birth control pills my uncle put me on had just been invented. I had no idea I was an experiment for his medical practice. They gave me violent morning sickness and made me dizzy. I threw them out and I didn't mention my monthly aches again.

*

I wasn't sure yet what to make of all the attention I was beginning to get from men. They whistled, waved to me from cars and stopped on the street to watch me go by. And now my uncle had invited me to a musical evening at his home which was quite exciting although daunting as well. What if I made a fool of myself in his social circle?

Mother who had not been asked to attend sulked to show her disappointment. After all, she was the lover of classical music, knew far more about it than I did, and the piano was her instrument. She was also too proud to request an invitation for herself. When I left for the evening she was halfhearted. "Have a nice time," she said with a sad smile.

*

My first time as a welcomed guest at a Menken's house concert was a marvelous experience. I tried to behave as ladylike, witty and grown-up as I knew how. Ilse's performance was stirring and it made me one of her followers and a classical music lover that night. I slept over at their home and in the morning I got another surprise.

Uncle Friedel came into my room and said, "Ready for breakfast? Come." He took my hand and led me to the master bedroom where a smiling Ilse greeted me. Breakfast was served in the Menkens' marriage bed.

"We're free and easy here in our house," Uncle Friedel said. "Get in." I climbed into bed next to my aunt. My uncle got under the covers on the other side of me.

"I bet you anything your mother wouldn't approve. Else's so prim and proper. There's nothing wrong with our physical natures and our sexuality." He squeezed my leg under the covers. "Always do what you enjoy best, dear little Liesel,

147

and listen to your uncle and aunt. Life's too short for bourgeois rules and regulations."

The maid brought in a large silver tray with boiled eggs in china egg cups, buttered toast, English orange marmalade and delicious, strong coffee. The three of us spent the next hour and a half in bed together eating and conversing.

*

How different this branch of my family was from the rest of us. I made a promise to myself that I would change and fit in with them as a way of transcending my conventional background. My aunt and uncle were freethinkers and very un-German. I felt lucky that they were spending time with someone like me and teaching me to become like them. Since I was about to spread my wings, nothing was off limits or improper, although my uncle's actions in his office still bothered me.

*

One day Fritz announced to Mother his intentions to marry. She said right away, "This isn't something my son really wants to do." Frau Lauder was put on the case and as expected came up with concrete serious objections. At a private session with my brother, Mother issued her warnings and divulged to Fritz the secrets Frau Lauder had uncovered about his betrothed. I watched Fritz storm out of the room. He disappeared for a few days after which he reappeared with Anna on his arm. "We just got married. Mother, Liesel, please meet my wife."

Anna had a look of triumph on her face and gave my handsome brother a big juicy kiss in front of us. Mother excused herself and took to her bed for several days. I was more welcoming to my new sister-in-law and curious about the allegations against her that barred her from becoming a member of us Steffens.

I never found out from Anna herself, but Mother pulled herself together and stated her case.

"Fritz got himself captivated by a lecherous seductress."

I wondered what that would be like and what it would take for me to become captivating and seductive myself. Anna was not physically attractive, missed a few teeth and looked older than Fritz, but nevertheless he had married her.

The fights between Mother and Anna soon started. Mother didn't mince her words. She freely insulted her son's wife to her face and behind her back. She called her an imposter who had no right to her wonderful son. The newlyweds lived in Fritz's apartment next door to us.

Anna was no pushover. In fact she cursed and screamed the loudest. The whole neighborhood heard her, but everyone was on Mother's side of course. I tried my best to listen to the complaints and not take sides. Fritz did the same. Since he hated to be caught between his mother and new wife he stayed away from both of them. That made Anna even crazier since she now believed Fritz was unfaithful and slept with his previous lady friends. Probably true knowing my brother.

"I'm going to sell the house. Liesel and I'll move away," Mother announced one day. "I've had enough."

Fritz evoked the legal document Opa had signed that transferred ownership of the property to him and me.

Mother said, "Fritz you know very well that was just a formality to keep the house from falling into a stranger's hands."

Fritz knew, but now said this wasn't the case and his grandfather who he was named after, had wanted no one but him to inherit it. The quibbling went on for many months. Fritz seemed very bonded to our property which had been in the family for so many years. I wasn't attached to it at all and pointed out again and again that Mother was the rightful owner and could do as she pleased with it.

*

It was Fritz' disillusionment with Anna which eventually provided another twisted real estate solution only the three of us knew about. If something was ever going to happen to my brother he didn't want Anna to receive a Pfennig not even her rightful share. In Dr. Schmidt's office--the lawyer didn't make house calls anymore--he signed his half back over to Mother who felt vindicated. I confirmed again to myself that we Steffens weren't as honest as we appeared to be.

Mother negotiated a cash settlement with Fritz and made a rental agreement which was legally binding on a prospective new owner. I still had my half share and was happy to consent to put 332 Gladbecker Strasse up for sale.

Chapter 25

Wittringer Forest

HIKING THROUGH WITTRINGER FOREST had been something I had often done with my father. These woods were close to Bottrop and Gladbeck and I always found them enchanting. There was a lake and a small castle that made the coal mines of the region seem far away.

After Father's death I had continued these walks on my own lost in brooding thoughts and feelings of abandonment. I did not see a happy life ahead for myself and wondered if I had any future at all. On one of these solitary walks I encountered a man walking his dog. The dachshund saw me and pulled the man in my direction.

"Good afternoon," he said, tipping his hat. I smiled at the adorable dog and bent down to pet him.

"Seppel must find you attractive. He is usually more protective of me and doesn't behave like this towards a total stranger."

"You need protection?" I glanced at the man and tickled the dog who had rolled over on his back.

"What do you think? Of course I do. The woods are full of dangers. Aren't you afraid?"

"Should I be?"

"Not of me and Seppel, but anyone else...I'll say yes."

His sausage of a dog waggled his tail.

"The dog's a killer. I feel safe walking with him. Wouldn't you know he likes you so you must be okay."

I grinned.

"Hello, my name's Wolfgang, Wolfgang Ligges. I don't bite either, especially not young women. As a matter of fact I always try to stay on the right side of the law. Law and order is going to be my profession."

"Hello, I'm Liesel Steffens. I'm not a lawbreaker myself."

"I wouldn't think so." He gave me an approving look and smiled. I was pleased how this chance meeting had developed.

We continued our stroll around the lake together. I kept my eyes on our path and didn't have a full look at my male companion, but he was attractive, a little taller than I was and looked studious with his eyes hidden behind thick glasses. The sun began to set and it was getting cool.

"How far do you live and how are you going to get home, Freulein Steffens?"

"I'll walk," I said.

"May Seppel and I drive you home?" I accepted without hesitation and he led me to his red Volkswagen. On the way to our house I learned that he was twenty-four, eight years older than I was, and a law student at Muenster University. He was from Gladbeck and returned on weekends to visit his widowed mother. He worked on his dissertation; his law doctorate no less.

I asked him what the word "dissertation" meant and he explained that it was the comprehensive written essay that would render him a doctor of law.

We said our polite good-byes and used the formal Sie (you) as was the etiquette in our country. Only after a lapse of time and a mutual agreement could the protocol be changed and the Sie, Herr and Freulein converted to the less rigid and familiar Du. When the time was ripe there was again a prescribed formula. The woman had to offer it to the man and in the case of two people of the same sex the older person made the request. An exception to the rule was an evening of alcohol. Two drinkers, each with a heavy pitcher in their hand, interlaced their arms and drunk themselves to brotherhood and an instant Du.

Mr. Ligges said he wanted to see me again, so we made a date for another rendezvous for the next weekend. Same time and place in the Wittringer Forrest. The week couldn't pass fast enough.

From then on our relationship developed steadily. He was witty and self-deprecating which I liked and his looks were ruddy rather than handsome. He had thick, brown hair and strong features. I teased him that he had an extra amount of gray brain mass behind his very high forehead, and he seemed to enjoy the compliment. I still laughed at things he had said long after we parted and planned appropriate replies for next time.

He was a born lawyer. Interrogations came natural to him and his memory was excellent. That made it somewhat stressful for me to keep in mind what I told him about myself and my family. I couldn't let him come across any inconsistencies about my father's past. A few times I saw him come to a halt and frown.

Mr. Ligges had other talents besides being an intellectual as I found out one weekend when he surprised me with a large oil painting.

"Here Freulein Steffens, I'm better at painting houses, but I hope you don't mind accepting this still-life. This is for you."

He painted it for me. How touching. I was ecstatic. "Thank you so much. I will hang it up in my room and always treasure it."

I put my arms around his neck and kissed him on the cheek. From that moment on the formality was gone and we were Wolfgang and Liesel.

I lacked much confidence in myself because I felt so uneducated and untalented compared to him, but he was patient and seemed to enjoy teaching me. He was masterful in the way he articulated his many, varied interests. For my part I tried to act charming and laughed at all the right moments to make him feel important.

My musical ear was not nearly as sharp as his. He had great fondness for jazz and could distinguish between different musicians just by the way their instruments sounded on his car radio.

"Do you hear that trumpet? Only Dizzy can play like that." Other times it was Miles Davis or Duke Ellington. He knew all the famous jazz musicians and the pieces they played. One afternoon he invited me to his mother's house and played his own trumpet for me. I couldn't hear any difference; to me he sounded just as wonderful as any of the greats. Or maybe I was just falling in love with him.

154

I got a library book to read up on jazz and I hoped to hide my ignorance going forward with our relationship. In the back of my mind I was always afraid that because I was so ungifted and unaccomplished our relationship could be wrecked and at any time he would stop seeing me.

It took a while to find a buyer for our property and a new place to live. Mother and a realtor made trips to an area called Westerwald, a region of woods, hills and small villages, three hours south on the Autobahn near Wiesbaden and Frankfurt.

Finally the day was close when 332 Gladbecker Strasse would no longer belong to us. Mother was ambivalent, but mostly sad. It had been her parents' home and had helped see us through financial worries after Father's death. To sell and move away also meant that Oma and Opa's and Father's graves were left behind in the Bottrop cemetery.

Frau Lauder, our tenant, stressed herself out that she now had to deal with a new landlord. Mother promised to put in a good word. After all, Frau Lauder had been very loyal, kept Mother well informed and was never late with her rent. I was still underage. A court appointed trustee signed off on my behalf which was agreeable to me as I had no interest in the money due to me from the sale.

I would not have had the slightest reservations about moving away had it not been for Wolfgang and our blossoming relationship. Another fact was that I still would have to complete my education and become something with the finishing school now over and done.

Mother, unable to find a house which met her standards, bought three parcels of farmland in the small town of

Wallmerod in the Westerwald and paid cash to build our new home.

"I'm doing this for you," she pointed out. "Once we leave Bottrop our mother- daughter relationship will improve."

I didn't hold out much hope. Our problems would follow wherever we went.

Wolfgang was unaware our move was imminent. I always kept my interactions on his ambitions and activities, not mine. As for Mother, she didn't know there was a Wolfgang.

"Why did you decide to become a lawyer?" I asked one day.

"I want to be an advocate for justice," he said. "Also it's not a bad way to make money. I can't stand the sight of blood. Wouldn't make me a good medical doctor."

I laughed. "I faint at the sight of blood myself."

"We will make a fine pair," he said. "I may go into politics some day."

"That's great. We need to change this country and make up for what our parents did."

I saw right away this wasn't a conversation he wanted to get into with me or anyone. I shouldn't have brought it up. He disapproved and got silent, and then he took off his glasses and looked at me.

"It's best we put the past behind us and not dwell on it. We can't change what happened. We have to move forward and prosper. That's what we Germans are good at, besides our many other fine qualities."

He cheered up and poked fun at our country's ability to

156

adjust to change. "We turn in the opposite direction and there you have it. Forward we march and onward we go."

I wasn't sure what to make of it. I didn't know what his convictions might have been at the end of the war when he was a boy of only twelve. How far had he believed in our indoctrinations of blood and honor for our Fatherland? And how devastated had he been that our nation was defeated?

I took this opportunity to tell him a lie, a lie that would become part of me for many years to come. I told him about our neighbor, the Jewish man who returned and spoke to me in the street. "It was my father who caught the little Jewish boy in his arms and saved his life. My family was never part of the Nazi insanity. They didn't believe in it."

I told him (and myself) what I wished had happened, what I wished my father had done, not what in fact did happen. Wolfgang didn't seem interested one way or another to hear more about it or about my father's heroism.

"The past needs to stay the past," he said. "Right or wrong we have to forget about it. I can tell you many stories about my father who was a foreman in the coal mines. He always carried a gun. Accidents happened; miners disappeared into the pits and weren't seen or heard again. I'm not saying my father was right, but what he did had nothing to do with me and I can't judge him."

We drove home in his car, both now silent and absorbed in our private thoughts. I wondered what this future advocate for justice would leave unjust and unresolved, how much injustice he was willing to accept. I felt alone and misunderstood. When Wolfgang wanted to give me his usual good night kiss I turned away and got out of the car. His tires screeched as he sped away.

157

Chapter 26

The Lawyer

WHAT A BAD idea. Wolfgang didn't take lightly to being refused or slighted. He was late for our next date and when he did show up he was in an angry frame of mind. I noticed right away that things between us had changed and that made me very nervous.

I blamed myself. Instead of our usual walk he pulled up in front of a Gasthof in town and ordered a large beer for himself. I didn't't drink so I ordered apple juice.

He came straight to the point: "Sorry this relationship isn't going anywhere. We should wind it up."

"What did I do wrong?"

"Nothing. I'm just frustrated. You must be sleeping around with men all week and feel you can tease me on the weekend. I don't need it. There're plenty of beautiful women at the university."

I got red in the face and couldn't find the right words to express my devastation.

"How in the world can you believe I would do something like that?" If he called me stupid and ignorant I would understand, but this accusation was preposterous. I had never so much as kissed a man before Wolfgang.

There were sensations in my body which I knew had to be ignored until I was married. I had stayed away from my uncle and aunt after I met Wolfgang. I had doubts about the way they lived and expressed themselves. No decent man would want a woman who wasn't virtuous. I was also terrified of pregnancy. In our society a baby out of wedlock made the unfortunate young woman an outcast. I was already ostracized enough. I said unpredictable things that outraged people. Already I had upset Wolfgang with my mention of the Nazi past.

Even my brother's wife had been a lesson on what not to do. Fritz's marriage was on the rocks and the sexual attraction hadn't lasted. I wanted to keep Wolfgang in my life and earn his respect. I longed to be loved in a different way, for the sensitive and thoughtful person I was.

Now he was accusing me of something very hurtful. I was speechless and stared into my juice.

"You're old enough to drink a beer. Don't you think I want to be with someone who can share a beer with me?"

He had asked me right in the beginning how old I was. I had lied and made myself eighteen when I was barely sixteen.

"I'll try a beer. Can you please order me one?"

If it were just a question of beer our problem would have been solved right away. I didn't't like the taste of alcohol and had stayed away from it, but now a big cool pitcher of golden beer with foam running down the sides was placed in front of me. I took a few sips. The taste was bitter, but what it did to me was very pleasant. It made it easier to talk about myself and Wolfgang smiled again.

"I'm sorry you think that I have messed around with

159

men," I said. "You're the only one I go out with."

"What do you mean? Are you telling me you have never slept with a man?"

"Of course not. Never. You should know me better than that." He ordered another beer for himself, which he drank quickly.

He paid and we drove off in his car. I felt fewer inhibitions around him because of the beer and this loosening up of my body and mind felt liberating. I leaned my head against his shoulder, and he put his right arm around me. He moved it only to shift gears. We drove to the woods. He came to a stop at the entrance of a deserted path that was off limits to cars. He removed his glasses and hung them over the rear view mirror. We faced each other, and he pulled me very close. He brought my face towards his and gave me a kiss, not just with his lips, but his teeth and tongue parted my lips and pushed deep inside my mouth. He tasted of beer, but I didn't care. I gave myself to his superior experience, my rising desire and the intimacy of the moment. His hands moved to my breasts and felt through my blouse.

"You're beautiful," he whispered in my ear.

I had intense feelings of pleasure like I had during my closeness with Ingrid. I pressed myself against him and didn't want him to stop. We panted and rocked from side to side. It was wonderful. Suddenly he did stop.

"Are you taking the pill?

"The pill? Of course not. What would I need it for?" I felt he was testing me once more, looking for confirmation that I did this with other men.

"You can't do it without a safety net, you know," he

160

said.

I giggled. I was unsure how he wanted me to act and what I should say. Did he want a woman who was sexually experienced? Was it more attractive to him if I remained shy and modest?

I was so mixed up that I did a bit of both. I pulled him to me and kissed him hard. Then I felt we got too close and I stopped. I pushed him away and straightened myself.

"What kind of safety net?" I wanted to keep our conversation going until I figured out what was going on and how this might end.

"Condoms. We have to use condoms to be safe."

I had never heard the word before.

"What are they and how do we get them?"

"That you can leave to me. I've a huge supply. They're rubbers for protection. We get them wholesale by the case at the university."

He kissed me again and undid buttons on my blouse. I got less and less concerned with trying to figure out what was happening and the consequences. I pushed myself against him and allowed his hand to explore under my skirt. As he stroked his fingers up and down my thighs I started to tremble. An uncontrollable and embarrassing shudder came over my whole body.

"Why do you shake like this?" he removed his hand. His mood had changed again. "Isn't this something you want too?"

I didn't know what I wanted. I didn't answer. He put his glasses back on and started the engine.

161

"I'm sorry," I said as we drove back home.

"Do I repulse you so much that I make you tremble?"

"No, you don't. You mean the world to me. It's just that I couldn't't help myself. It's all so new and fast."

"Not fast, my dear. We've gone out for several months. How long do you think you can be such a coquette, make a fool of me and keep teasing?"

"Oh God, I'm so sorry. I don't want to hurt you any more. Two weeks and I'm gone."

"What?"

"We've sold our house and are moving to the Westerwald."

"When were you planning to drop this bombshell on me? Moving without telling me? Deceitful, lying woman. I hadn't the slightest clue."

We had come to an abrupt halt outside our building after bumping the curb. He kept revving the engine and didn't bother to come around to my side to open the door.

I got out fast. "Can I at least write to you?" I said miserably.

"Nothing more to say. Good bye, Liesel Steffens." He sped off.

162

Chapter 27

Blemished Love

I HAD WOLFGANG'S address in Muenster and sometimes had sent him humorous little notes during the week, but now I sat down and composed a long letter. I told him that he was the first and only man in my life and that I loved him. The word "love" was easier to write than to say.

"Can you please give me another chance? I want to do whatever you want and make you happy."

I half believed he would not show up for our weekly meeting on Saturday, but the other half held out hope. I arrived early at our usual place and waited for a long time. I was just about to give up and walk home, heartbroken, when I saw his Volkswagen pull up. I jumped in. We went for a long drive and made small talk as if nothing had happened. I didn't care or ask where he was taking me. We left Gladbeck and finally came to a stop in a wooded area outside Gelsenkirchen.

I tensed when he took my shoulders and turned me towards him. He removed his glasses and put them over the rear view mirror, a sure sign that we would be close again and I had been forgiven. I could not wait to return his kisses.

"Did you get my letter, Wolfie?"

"Yes, I did. I am glad you wrote and explained. This changes everything."

"Are you no longer mad at me?"

"No, Liebling, I am not. You have something the girls at the university have long lost and therefore you are special."

I drank in with joy every one of his words and felt special, "chosen" for his love above a bunch of gorgeous and accomplished students. I would not disappoint him.

I returned his kisses passionately, my eagerness belied my nervousness. He pulled me over to the driver's side. The gearshift hurt my stomach, but there was nothing I would not endure for his love.

"Let's move to the backseat," he said in a husky, urgent voice. "We have more space."

I took off my shoes and without opening the doors we climbed over the front seat. He went first and I plopped on top of him. The world was gone, the windows steamy. We were locked in his Volkswagen, a small space for two grown, stretched-out bodies.

I wore a tight dress, which rode up on my hips. He pulled me very close. My legs hung awkward and bent. He fumbled with my zipper. It took too long and he pulled it over my head instead, which ripped the neckline. I didn't care. Nothing mattered. He undid my bra and took a close look.

"Your bust is beautiful. Small and white like milk."

"Am I not too small for you?" I said. I remembered Ingrid's full form.

"You're perfect. That's how I like it. Small and tight." He took my hand and guided them to the zipper on his pants.

"Go ahead, open it." I felt something hard that had not been there before.

164

"I can't."

"Yes, you can." He did not let go of my hand and helped me undo his trousers. I stopped thinking. At that moment only he and his passion for me mattered. I had something he wanted, and I was not going to disappoint him.

I ended up underneath him, our bodies entangled. I had no objection to anything he did to me. Just a vague feeling of obligation and oblivion, no splendor. My needs were immaterial. I was committed to only him.

A sharp, stabbing pain, then he moaned and shook and finally lay still. He was heavy on top of me, panting, I was suffocating. Tears came to my eyes. He lifted himself to his elbows and knees. Then he wiped my tears with his hand.

"Now I know you were right. You were a virgin. Next time it's not going to hurt you anymore, my love."

He had already planned the next time. I had become a man's lover, could never go back and I didn't know if this was good or bad.

He pulled up his pants and composed himself. I covered my nakedness. There was blood on my dress and underwear. I was wounded. He spotted it at the same time.

"For God sake, don't move. Here, use this and don't get blood on the seat." He handed me a box of paper towels.

On the drive home I asked him, "Have you ever done this with other women?"

"No. You're the only virgin I've ever made love to."

"Do you think I'll get pregnant now?"

"Don't be silly. I used a condom." I had no idea if this

was true or not.

"Will you come to see me in the Westerwald?"

"Absolutely. Now you're mine and we are lovers I'm going to see you whenever I can."

That was what I wanted to hear. The pain and unpleasantness had been worth it. I belonged.

I crept into our apartment so Mother wouldn't hear me and washed my clothes while she slept.

The soreness in my body caused by Wolfgang lasted for many weeks. It was a reminder of him every second of the day. I visualized again and again what we had done on the back seat of his car. It made me feel better about myself and affected everything I did and how I behaved. I walked more erect and put my chest out in front. I got hold of makeup and started to paint my lips a crimson red, shaped my cheekbones with highlighter and made my blue eyes wider and more haunting with dark shades of powder eye shadow.

This was how I entered the convent school in Limburg: worldly and experienced in making love to a man.

Chapter 28

Convent and Impunity

WOLFGANG KEPT HIS promise! Not every weekend, but whenever he could. He met Mother, and her heart rejoiced. She approved of the man and the lawyer he was soon to become. A big worry off her mind! Her rebellious daughter had been lucky enough to make a good catch, unlike her unfortunate son Fritz who had not listened to her and was stuck in a miserable marriage. Her daughter was being tamed into submission by a man and would become like her after all, dedicated to her respectable German spouse and her future children. Everything had turned out right.

Wolfgang was welcomed and trusted to stay in our home overnight, and Mother fussed over him with the foods he preferred. He did have strange eating habits and never touched vegetables, chicken or fish. Our palate changed to accommodate him. When Mother knew he was on his way, the delicious smell of a fresh Apfelkuchen (apple cake) emanated from her kitchen.

I dressed to please him. He liked stiletto heels and tight skirts, so that's what I wore, even though the footwear was painful and unsuitable for the hilly terrain. I had learned to sew and take in any loose fabrics at the seams of my clothes. One week he mentioned he liked redheads, so while he was gone I dyed my blond hair flaming chestnut. A change too drastic

167

even for me and I changed it back. The chemicals made my hair fall out.

Wolfgang and I explored the forests around Wallmerod together and still made love in his car behind Mother's back. When we walked arm in arm through villages and towns I had to be careful. Wolfgang liked having other men lust after me with approving looks, but I couldn't enjoy the attention and appear flirtatious. That would get him mad. I walked a tightrope, always conscious of his desires.

A twenty kilometer, one hour bus ride from our new residence in Wallmerod, was Limburg an der Lahn. The historic town, with its timbered houses and narrow cobblestone alleys, had a famous seven stories high cathedral with seven steeples that could be seen from far and wide.

During the week I attended Limburg's special convent school, Marienschule (Mother Mary's School), which had been founded in 1895 by a devout order of nuns who called themselves Arme Dienstmaegde Jesus Christi, (poor handmaidens of Jesus Christ). The school was respected as an excellent humanistic grammar school for women as well as a college for kindergarten teachers.

*

I had been intrigued by a brochure that arrived and detailed the school's turbulent history during the previous fifty years.

The Third Reich had taken it over in 1939 and replaced Mary, the Mother of Jesus, with Hans-Schwemm. It became Hans Schwemm's school. Whoever this Hans was I had no idea, probably some local Nazi hero. An announcement had been made to the town. "The new school's headmaster is happy the will of the people has been heard and acted upon. The right to totalization by the National Socialist Party cannot allow any other educational and pedagogic methods to take hold of German youth."

During this time the nuns had been forced to stop teaching and had taken care of the sick in the local hospital instead. In December of 1945 "the will of the people" demanded their return and the school was reopened. Young women from all over Germany proceeded to flock to it.

There was something about this story and the nuns' dissent from the "Thousand Year Reich," which made me interested in going to the Marienschule and becoming a kindergarten teacher. Since I had not succeeded at the Theodore Fliedner Institute in Duesseldorf, I decided to try this convent school to see if I could pick up some useful education.

One of the first and foremost teachings of the nuns was, "protect your maidenhood under all circumstances. It's a special gift which you must preserve and give to our husbands on your wedding nights."

I was very aware that I no longer had this gift to give. I was damaged goods. But well and good, I had my Wolfgang already and our wedding night would therefore not be such a painful ordeal.

During my two years at the school, there were other teachings I did take to heart. I learned not so much from the nun's words but from their cheerful example. It was clear that they had found the road to happiness. They were content.

Where their strong Catholic convictions were concerned they practiced remarkable tolerance and never tried to proselytize. During classes with religious overtones, it was always "Freulein Steffens, as a Protestant you are excused." I was excused a lot. Just as well. Any efforts to convince me to believe and follow the command of a single man, even though he was the Pope, would not only have been wasted on me, but I would have been an unwelcome disruption to the rest of the class. The nuns were wise.

"Always examine things for yourself, Liesel," Wilhelm Steffens had taught me. He could not have foreseen how well his daughter absorbed this lesson above all others and applied it even to him and all he stood for.

Although Catholicism was not for me, I never made fun of the nuns and respected their earnestness and purity of heart. I was aware that I felt a secret longing for something I could trust and believe in myself.

During classes I was aloof and did my own thing. I sat by the heating radiator in winter and breathed in fresh air from the open window during warm weather. I was suspended in time and space and I felt like a prisoner might feel serving his sentence before being released to freedom. Sometimes Sister Rafaela, one of the teaching nuns, called on me: "Freulein Steffens, are you still with us? Do you have an answer to this or that?"

I usually came up with something spontaneous that made my classmates laugh. They watched me write love poems to Wolfgang, knit him a sweater--my hands moved under the desk with no problem--or read something that was unrelated to school. They expected to see me get in trouble, but the easygoing nuns laughed as well.

At the end of the second college year I wrote a 120-page essay entitled: "Threatening Youth, Threatened Youth" which earned me the highest marks in my class for delving into what I thought was wrong with German youth. That, plus a passing grade in an oral exam in front of a governmental commission, and I had a profession. I was a kindergarten teacher.

Chapter 29

Father's Vocation

I WAS DELIGHTED when Wolfgang told me that he had transferred to the University of Heidelberg for final work on his doctorate. We would be closer and able to get together more often. But I also felt a nagging worry about attractive women he was sure to encounter in his new environment. Had I been more studious and reached my Abitur I would have chosen to study law as well. I could keep my eyes on Wolfgang and make him happy every night.

Now, at the age of eighteen, my vocation was to take care of children as my father had done. The moment I graduated employment offers flooded in. I picked a Jugendheim (reform school) in Wiesbaden where I had room and board.

My job was to care for and live with thirty young female lawbreakers. Too young for prison, they had been banished to this institute for rehabilitation. I took on the challenge with interest and it was a responsible position for someone just out of college.

When I told Wolfgang I would live in the Wiesbaden school he was annoyed, especially since I hadn't consulted him.

"All those hours taking care of delinquent kids for next

to no money. What were you thinking? Surely not of us. When will you get time to see me?"

I assured him he was always the most important person in my life and if he felt neglected I would give up my job. We compromised with the understanding that within a year we would have our joint future mapped out and I would change my work to fit in with his. Meanwhile, he could visit me in Wiesbaden and we would spend weekends in Wallmerod.

On my first Saturday off I took the bus home and waited with Mother seated at the dining table for Wolfgang. The cake for him was already in front of us, but couldn't be cut yet.

"What time will Herr Doctor Ligges arrive?" Mother asked.

"He should be here soon and don't call him Herr 'Doctor.' He hasn't finished his dissertation yet."

I could see Mother was alarmed at the way I spoke about the man she thought of as her future son-in-law. She always addressed him with formality.

"Did you by chance say something out of line? Remember how lucky you are to have the Herr Doktor in your life."

The phone rang. It was Wolfgang. "No," he said. "Can't make it this weekend." I felt let down, but bit my tongue. Mother showed her disappointment by the way she cut big slices from Wolfgang's cake.

"You must have done or said something foolhardy."

"Probably. Who cares?"

"I care. Too much foolish talk and your ship will sink."

173

"I bet you hope I'm not sinking this ship with the Herr Doctor at the helm and off we sail to my salvation."

"There's no talking to you."

I left Mother with her cake and the other elaborate "Ligges" food she always prepared for him. I threw myself into work with my charges, girls who ranged in ages from six to fourteen. Their parents and society had failed them. I was determined to make a difference in their lives and to a small degree I did.

My essay at the Marienschule started with the Chinese proverb: "Even the waters of the Yellow River are sometimes clear. Is there a living being that is never good?"

I saw goodness in "my" girls. I knew what they needed to thrive. It was hope and love! Something I did not have for myself. Yet somehow I was able to guide them to find self-reliance. We bonded, grew and learned together.

The school board recognized our artistic endeavors when we exhibited paintings and performed plays and musicals. My monthly reports on each and every one of the youngsters were always positive. The headmaster remarked that maybe I was a little too naive and overlooked wrongdoing that was unreformable. I argued my case. If we believed in someone strong enough, they would turn out to be the person we thought them to be.

Wolfgang was busy with his research and came to see me less often. I understood and didn't make demands. We wrote to each other and talked on the phone professing our love.

"Ich liebe Dich."

"Ich liebe Dich auch."

I knew that after the year was over I would have to keep my word.

The school had male and female staff members and I enjoyed their company. Wiesbaden with its casino, many beautiful gardens, fountains and elegant shopping arcades was an exciting city to explore.

Men wanted to invite me out, but my commitment to Wolfgang made me decline. He had no reason to be concerned about competition, but he was. One day he confessed that he had hired a detective to follow me around for a week. He laughed about it. "Cost me a fortune," he said. "For nothing. The poor guy got bored following you around with the children."

If Wolfgang was so suspicious and mistrusting I began to think that maybe I shouldn't trust him. He didn't care about my work. Maybe there was a budding lawyer in his life. The thought took hold and didn't let go.

Chapter 30

Tango and Waltz

UNCLE FRIEDEL AND Ilse's house concerts came to my mind and I decided on the spur of the moment to call and visit them on my next long weekend.

Dr. Friedrich Menken was no longer in Gladbeck. Hearsay in the family had it that he was forced to exit in a hurry due to a fatality. A woman had bled to death in his medical office during an illegal abortion. Her husband stood outside afterwards and shouted words like "murderer." Uncle Friedel had packed up his practice and family and relocated to Wuppertal.

When he picked me up at the railway station he looked rosy and happy.

"Much better town this is. Not half as stuck in the mud and backward as Gladbeck. That town didn't deserve me." I was tempted to ask him about his sudden departure, but thought better of it.

"Let me look at you again, little Liesel. I missed you. Is there a young man in your life who now plays the lovely instrument, that luscious body of yours?"

"Don't be absurd, Uncle Friedel," I said and laughed. He had the strangest expressions, flattering but silly. I had to humor him and not mention Wolfgang.

176

"How lucky can you get? I have a special surprise for you this weekend. Guess who's coming to Ilse's concert tonight?"

"No idea, Uncle Friedel."

"Go on, have a guess. He is very tall, very famous and very black."

"Who is it?"

"No other, but the great baritone Kenneth Spencer."

"What?" I couldn't hide my excitement. This was a dream. Kenneth Spencer was my favorite artist. He appeared on radio, television and concert halls all over Europe. I listened to his entertaining whenever I could and read stories about him in magazines. Now I remembered he lived in Wuppertal.

"I must have known. I brought my midnight blue chiffon dress," I said.

"Smart child."

My uncle was in the best of spirits the rest of the afternoon. To have a great concert artist join his wife for a private performance wasn't a common event. Everyone who was anyone in Wuppertal had been invited.

That night, when Kenneth Spencer entered the room, I was instantly smitten. He was a huge, powerful man and the first black person I had ever seen face to face. My eyes remained fixed on him.

It didn't take long for him to notice me and stretch out his hand. He was elegant and confident. He was a star.

"Hello, my name is Kenneth." His voice had command.
"I know."

"You must be Friedel's niece I hear so much about. Are you not a teacher in Wiesbaden?"

"Yes, I am. Do you come to perform in Wiesbaden?"

At that moment Aunt Ilse signaled she was ready to start the concert. That's when I noticed Kenneth hadn't come alone. A much shorter black man stood behind him.

Kenneth introduced him, "my manager, agent and impresario, Hugh Scotland. Why don't you sit together during the performance."

That was what we did. My eyes and ears remained glued on Kenneth. The lit white candles in the heavy silver candelabra on the grand piano Ilse played flickered with the timbre of his voice. When it was over everyone in the room was intoxicated by the music and exclaimed "Bravo!"

The evening was far from over. In fact, it had just begun. Ilse shifted from pianist to charming hostess. There was plenty of wonderful food and the finest champagne and brandy. This was the right kind of Germany again. Culture, good food, drink, and illustrious company. The hardships of the postwar years were behind us, forgotten like a windstorm that had come and gone. The sky was clear again and the future brighter than ever. My father had died a bitter and disappointed man, his vision of a pure Germany fortunately not realized. Uncle Friedel thought of that time as a sick joke.

"People had no taste during the Nazi years," he had said in the car. "They left behind nothing but ugly architecture, hideous Wagner music and a bunch of other kitsch. Good riddance."

I was silent and thought of what else had been left behind. Millions of bodies. And no one seemed to care.

178

After his performance Kenneth joined us.

"We've just finished a television taping in Cologne. Hugh came from London to choreograph it." His manager, who spoke no German, nodded agreement. The gramophone played the latest songs and dance music, the chandelier was turned off. Kenneth lifted his hands with the grace of a ballet dancer.

"Would you care to dance, Freulein Steffens?" I popped straight into his arms. He towered over me and swirled my eager body around the parquet floor. I felt feather light and rhythmic, not the clumsy clod I usually was. We tangoed and waltzed and I didn't step on his foot once. It was heaven.

Out of the corner of my eye I saw Ilse approach. She tapped Kenneth on the shoulder. "You two seem to enjoy yourselves. My turn."

As soon as Kenneth turned to my aunt the manager from London stood in front of me and took over the rest of the dance. His dance ability was just as good, but since he was shorter, his arms didn't feel secure; I stiffened, lost my step, stumbled and asked to sit down.

I watched with envy how Kenneth and Ilse moved their hips to the music. There was a certain intimacy between them and I sensed this was not new to them. They were both artists, which created a bond I could not hope for.

Hugh Scotland interrupted my thoughts. "Kenneth is married," he said. So was my aunt I reminded myself.

Uncle Friedel came to look for me. He swayed from side to side with his brandy glass. "Oops. Are you having a good time my little niece?"

"A great time, Uncle Friedel, thank you." I felt slightly irritated that there was always 'little' in the way my uncle addressed me, although I was five foot eight and now had a responsible job.

"You're the most beautiful woman in the room. What a gorgeous dress. I saw everyone staring at you."

"Enough, Uncle Friedel."

"You're your dear uncle's favorite. He is exceedingly proud of you, let's dance."

I smelled the alcohol and cigar on his breath. His hands were clammy. Compared to my two previous dance partners, Uncle Friedel was heavy-footed. We lumbered from side to side. I held him up and prevented a crash into the pedestal with the antique Italian vase. Thank God the dance was over soon. He collapsed into an armchair and waved the maid for another drink. I sat down and had more champagne, altogether quite an unusual large amount for one evening. But this night was special and unforgettable, and I felt safe in the bosom of my family.

Chapter 31

The Sofa

IT WAS QUITE late before everyone left. Kenneth took my phone number and promised to come to Wiesbaden and sing for the children. Hugh Scotland gave me his business card and invited me to London. Ilse was tired and went to bed. Uncle Friedel and I remained in the room, chatting about the evening and finishing another bottle of champagne.

I was full of thoughts about my first discovery of "colored people" and was eager to have a discussion about them with my uncle.

Three images of this exotic and foreign race had stuck in my mind. The first came from a Wilhelm Busch cartoon in Father's library. A character with an oversized nose but no real name just called "schwarzer Mann" (black man) was being ridiculed. He had a huge ring through his large, flat nose. A smart monkey who did have a name (it was Fipps) had his way with this hapless creature twisting his nose ring around tree branches, ripping it off and leaving a gapping, bleeding hole. Busch was the most famous cartoonist of the time. "Is that not hilarious?" My family said. I didn't think it was funny and felt sorry for the poor man.

My second childhood impression came from my father's words and his experience when he had attended the 1936 Berlin Olympic Games. He condemned Jesse Owens, the

181

super-human black man who ran side by side with our so-called superior athletes and won every race. It wasn't fair, he said. "They have animal strength, but no intelligence."

During the reading of *Uncle Tom's Cabin* I sobbed many tears in my room. The poor black race had endured so much injustice--forced from their African homeland only to live in cruel slavery.

Much to my delight and satisfaction none of this fitted even remotely the two men I had spent time with at my uncle's tonight. They didn't need sympathy. They were equals. No, more than equal it seemed to me. More fascinating.

When I brought the subject up, Uncle Friedel said, "you really liked those two, didn't you?"

"I think they are amazing."

"Stick with your uncle and you will find out more amazing things." He grinned. "Kenneth depends on me...a huge demand on him...comes for vitamin injections...Ilse enjoys to branch out...."

"Who's branching out? You're Kenneth's doctor?"

"I'm the best medicine man in town." Uncle Friedel slurred his speech. I realized no sensible discussion could take place at this time.

"Fantastic night, Uncle Friedel. Thanks." He grinned.

"Will you excuse me? See you in the morning."

"I'm happy, Liebling. Come; give your uncle a kiss." When I bent to give him a goodnight kiss, he pulled me down onto his lap against his protruding stomach.

"Missed you," he whispered into my ear, "don't see

nearly enough of you. Your boyfriend...what's it like to make love with him? Tell your doctor."

"As a matter of fact I do have a boyfriend. He's in Heidelberg working on his law doctorate."

"Should work on you instead," Uncle Friedel giggled. "How come he neglects someone like you?"

"He's not neglecting me."

It was the early hours of the morning. My head was foggy; the stagnant air of cigar and cigarette smoke in the room got to me. I thought of Wolfgang and the two men I had met on this extraordinary evening. Not one of them was within reach, but my uncle was. My uncle thought I was desirable.

I wasn't a seasoned drinker. The euphoria of the evening combined with too much alcohol made me dizzy, and I leaned my head against my uncle. He clamored and got up and led me over to the sofa. I heard his voice, but could no longer make out what he said. I just knew it was soothing and pleasant. We laughed and tripped and fell on to the couch.

His lips were soft like the rest of him. His hands caressed my thighs, and sent a tingling sensation up my spine. I closed my eyes and pretended this was no longer my uncle, but a new lover, someone who desired me just the way I was and made no demands on my tomorrow. I leaned back against the velvet cushions and let him have his way.

Chapter 32

Waywardness

AS SOON AS I woke up alone on the sofa covered with a blanket I was nauseous. I dashed to the bathroom and was violently sick. Friedel and Ilse were up and about already. After breakfast and the couple of pills Friedel dispensed I felt better.

He wanted me to stay. "Why don't you come down to my practice and give me a hand? I have a few patients to see this weekend." He studied my face to see if I remembered the finale of the night before. I did! I knew my uncle had seduced me, and I had let him. I was guilty and surely would not tell anyone about it, which I was sure, he expected of his little niece.

Like in Gladbeck his medical practice was on the ground floor. "Here put this on." He handed me a starched nurse's uniform. I became an instant nurse, and Dr. Menken treated me as such.

"Hand me the speculum! Bring gauze." That afternoon I fumbled around with instruments and equipment at the lower end of several women's bodies.

I wanted to call him by his first name, but he stipulated it was to be either Dr. Menken or Uncle, whichever was more appropriate for the situation. In the practice he was Dr. Menken and I, Nurse Steffens.

When the patients had their eyes closed he pinched my behind and gave me knowing looks. We were a team of conspirators who examined women's genitals together.

As weird and lecherous as my uncle was, he was brilliant. He had developed an early detection technique for uterine cancer which saved lives. His book, *Photokolposkopie und Photodouglasskopie,* was used nationally and internationally as a teaching tool.

"I'm the inventor of a camera which, inserted into the uterus, can photograph the internal cells," he explained. "This means that a cancerous mutation can be detected early and the patient treated."

"Impressive," I said.

"I'm impressed with you and your quick learning ability in the medical field. Come here my beautiful assistant."

Exhausted and too much on my mind, I returned to Wiesbaden after my first sexual encounter with my uncle. Wolfgang had called and I felt guilty, remorseful.

As if he sensed something was amiss Wolfgang arrived unexpected in the middle of the week and spent the night. Something had changed, and I wasn't as eager as usual to be in his arms. In a way I was more liberated. I had put distance between myself and the people who cared about me. I wasn't sure where it would lead or if I could find my way back or if I wanted to.

*

Hugh Scotland called and we struck up a long distance relationship via mail and telephone.

"Our meeting has indelibly changed me," he said. "I

185

can't get you out of his mind for a second."

"I have thought about you too," I said. I had, but not in the way it sounded.

"You have to come to London and allow me to show you the city," he wrote. I knew a little English, but I learned more from our talks and letters. He was no Kenneth, but he was a black man, which was very much in his favor as far as I was concerned.

My uncle also called with an invitation. "You have to come to Paris and help me present slides of my work at the gynecological convention." I agreed. How exciting, my first trip out of Germany would be an adventure. "I'll buy you anything you want in the city of love," Uncle Friedel said.

My uncle took me to Paris and showed me the parts of the city that he regarded as a haven for love. I thought they were sordid. We crept around corners and in alleyways; he was offered dirty postcards which he was eager to purchase.

At the large convention hall full of doctors from around the world, I manned the projector and showed his medical slides. I had no idea which picture was up or down, but everyone smiled and said I did a great job and looked beautiful doing it. Naturally Friedel had taken just one room at the hotel and kept me close.

When I told him about my future plans with Wolfgang he pointed out that a boring lawyer would bring me nothing but disappointment and unhappiness. I now saw myself as decadent, more like my uncle from a different and more exciting side of the family. I couldn't settle for a lifetime of faithfulness like my parents had. I was more like my uncle's wife, the gorgeous and unrestrained Ilse.

186

In my heart I knew he was only partly right. I had become different and had fallen into a well of waywardness, but it didn't excite me that much nor did I believe myself to be that exciting. It was more like a curse. Once Wolfgang discovered who I really was and what I had done he would leave me. And he would be right to disappear. There could be no fairytale ending. I had no right to hold on to him. In my mind he was as good as gone.

So was Uncle Friedel. I never saw or spoke to him again.

*

When I returned to Wiesbaden I gave a month's notice at the school. I told the headmaster I wanted to travel and explore different parts of the world. I knew that to save my soul I had to give up everything--my country, my family, my lover.

My country didn't face up to its sordid past, and as long as I remained I was as polluted as everyone around me with their lies, pretense, and decadence.

Hugh Scotland had continued to woo me. He sent long love letters in which he laid out the wonders of London and the life that waited for me there with him. When I wrote back that I wanted to take him up on his offer, he was ecstatic. "Give me a couple of weeks to get your ticket and immigration papers," he wrote. "I have connections at the home office." That was fine with me. I needed at least two weeks myself.

*

I made a final visit to Mother. While there, I picked up a few mementos--my doll Maritzebill was still around, Father's poem, a few selective pictures and a couple of books. I spirited them out of the house.

187

"See you next month on my weekend off," I told Mother.

I had no money. Most of my small salary I had spent on the children. Borrowing was not done by our family, but I made an exception and spoke to Brigitte Hartman, a friendly farmer's daughter in Wallmerod. I sometimes volunteered to help her with crop harvesting and she said I did really well for a city girl.

"Take sixty marks," Brigitte said.

"I'll pay you back soon."

"No need. You've helped us a lot."

Chapter 33

Heimat

AFTER THE DOCUMENTS arrived from London my next trip was to Heidelberg. Wolfgang was bright and happy that I had come to see him. We enjoyed ourselves over dinner at a student tavern and a jazz club afterwards. He showed me the romantic side of Heidelberg. Goethe fell in love in this town; Schumann serenaded it in his music.

"Tomorrow I'll take you to see the spectacular views from the castle."

"I'll make us a picnic."

"Great, we'll spread a blanket on the grass by the Neckar and watch the river flow by. We'll drink in the atmosphere and a bottle of wine."

We walked arm in arm, like in the olden days, enjoyed the charms of the city and his words of endearment captured the mood for the last time.

"You're constantly on my mind," he said. "I love you and can't wait until we live together and get married."

"I love you too," I said. "You're my life."

My feelings for Wolfgang filled my heart with hesitation. There was still time to forget my plans and give myself back to my first love and future husband.

189

On that romantic night we made love like never before, not just with eager passion, but also with tenderness. I was snug in his arms as he fell asleep.

In the darkness a clock ticked and his breathing was deep and even. My anxiety returned. This could not last; I knew it was an illusion. There was no way I could stay. The arms which held me now would suffocate me tomorrow.

I moved myself away from him to the side of the bed. I got up and dressed without putting on the light. I made sure he was covered with the blanket. Shoes, knapsack and windbreaker in my hands, I left and closed the door behind us.

It was before dawn when I walked through Heidelberg to the Bahnhof. Chilly dampness hung over the river. I pulled the hood of my anorak over my head. I didn't want to be heard or seen on the cobblestone streets. I left Heidelberg, the city of romance, like a thief in the night.

The words my father wrote to me about Heimat when I was eight years old came back to my mind. I carried his note with me, but I dismissed the feelings he had expressed in "My Home--My World" as sentimental nonsense:

"Your home can be the world to you, but never the world your home. Sweet sounding German word Heim, blessing to have one just like mine. Personal culture, family culture, national culture all start at home. In poverty and housing needs these high values cannot develop and grow. Home is a resting place, escape from hurry, haste and noise. A sanctuary, letting the soul return to itself in spiritualization away from shallowness and desolation. Treasures and rare objects do not make a home. The center is Man and his thoughts and actions. If there is a sense of beauty and inward looking, the home too will carry a personal, spiritual note. All objects take on a breath of his soul, are part of his world, beloved and valuable, not dead material. Stormy weather, rain or snow outside, inside is the physical warmth of a fireplace, apples baking, warmth of the soul, tender connections, priceless treasures, the wealth of the nation…family."

*

All lies. I was glad I was about to abandon the "wealth of my nation." I would make the world my home. By quitting I disowned my country, my family, my lover, my future. Yet I wasn't brave enough to leave words and explanations. I didn't have words and didn't know the right sentiments for what I felt compelled to do. It was painful and confusing and on this morning in Heidelberg it wouldn't have taken much to persuade me to stay.

Wolfgang would wake without me, but he would recover, become the successful lawyer he was destined to be and get on with his life. I had no idea what tomorrow held for me.

Part Two

Promised Land

Chapter 34

Voyager

THERE WAS NO turning back now. I ran down the last few streets to the station and arrived breathless just in time to make the train for Cologne. I had planned day and night for this very moment and for at least a week I hadn't slept. Darkness was about to lift and a new morning had arrived.

I was numb as the train sped through the familiar countryside and I sat amongst my fellow Germans on the early commuter train. Any of the women around me could have been my mother or sister. They spoke my language and like me drew their first breath in Germany, but I felt no common bond, no attachment. I was alone amid familiar strangers.

In Cologne I picked up the Transcontinental Express which was already full to the brim. I climbed over boxes and luggage trying to find a seat. My fellow travelers spoke foreign languages and looked and behaved differently. Most were immigrants, whole families from Italy, Bulgaria, Spain, Greece and other Southern and Eastern European countries. Young and old, we were all headed towards the United Kingdom and a new life.

They had brought belongings from home that would help them settle in their alien surroundings, but I traveled light with just my knapsack. My heart was somber and heavy with sadness and guilt. I settled on a fold-down seat in the gangway and watched the international commotion around me.

A silver-toothed Greek offered me a fruit. I smiled, took it and thanked him. There would be no box of sandwiches from Mother on this trip. No return home from summer camp after six weeks. I was on my way into a lifelong, self-imposed exile.

Wolfgang would wake up by now and reach over in the bed for me to make love again. When he discovered I was gone he might smile at first. I had probably gone to the bakery to surprise him with fresh breakfast rolls and would be back any minute. I always did thoughtful things like that for him.

He had no idea I was already far away. Emigrating. By nightfall I would be in a new land with human beings who didn't know me. My heritage and wrongdoings would be left behind. By nightfall I would be free of guilt and shame. All the people I knew would fade away and be better off without me anyway.

We reached the Belgium seaport of Ostende where we transferred to a ferry, a huge ship with restaurants and bars. My fellow migrants reveled in duty-free drink and merriment. I stood on deck and let the cold wind blow my face and hair. I thought how significant it was that I had left land, was crossing water and would settle in the British Isles. Masses of deep, dark sea separated me from my abandoned world.

From the moment I laid eyes on the white cliffs of Dover I knew that England would become the new home I was destined to love. By the time I cleared immigration and was seated comfortably on another train bound for London I was moved to tears with gratitude. A man who barely knew me had made this possible. He was my benefactor and had supplied me with my ticket out of Germany. Therefore he had given me something immeasurably valuable--my freedom. I couldn't wait to tell him how appreciative I was.

How can I ever forget arrival at Victoria Station for the first time? I was overwhelmed with excitement. This was truly a foreign, final destination. Even the train had to reverse direction to leave the terminal. I stood still on the platform and took in my busy surroundings. People rushed to and fro. The air seemed permeated with energy.

The train passengers all disembarked. I looked around for Hugh, my host. Hadn't he received my letter that told him I arrived tonight? What would I do? I had immigrated almost penniless and knew no other person in London or England.

There were many black men who dashed around at Victoria. My memory of what Hugh Scotland looked like was obscure. We had met only once in my uncle's home during a euphoric night of music, alcohol and laughter. On that evening my eyes had been on a different, very attractive man, and I had paid very little attention to Hugh.

The crowds cleared, and then I saw him. His face beamed, and he made a beeline for me with great speed, arms stretched out in front of him. "Welcome to her Majesty's United Kingdom. I have waited too long for this moment."

I leaned over to kiss the short, chubby man with a clean-shaven face and slicked down black hair who had stuffed himself into a suit that was much too tight. He picked up my knapsack.

"You traveled light. I hope this does not mean you plan to leave again soon. You and I will have a beautiful life in the greatest city in the world."

"I am very happy to be here," I said in broken English, "Thank you very much for all you have done for me. I am here to stay."

"That is exactly what I want to hear." I noticed he checked to see if everyone around us saw that he was the one who picked up the tall blond. He ushered me to the exit with his arm around my waist. I realized that without the platform heels on his shoes he would be even shorter.

Outside the station he waved for one of the funny-looking taxicabs. We zigzagged in and out of heavy traffic. I laughed and was startled at the same time that we drove on the left. Hugh pointed out landmarks, famous buildings and places I could not wait to explore when I was settled in. My first impression of London was one of awe. My first impression of Hugh Scotland on his home turf was one I was too weary to want to think about.

The taxi pulled up outside a tenement building on Queensway in Bayswater. I followed him inside. Instinctively I curled my nose and raised my brows as Mother had in Duisburg. These were the same pungent cooking smells only more exotic. Garlic mixed with Indian curry. We moved along a dingy hallway on the first floor to the back where he unlocked the door.

"Welcome home, my darling." He was ready for a close embrace, but I tightened as I stared at the place he called "home." It was no more than a narrow room with two narrow beds, bare walls, a sink and a burner on a shelf, one chair which held some of his stuff and a short rail to hang clothes. Harsh lighting came from a couple of unshaded light bulbs way up on the high ceiling. The unpleasant surprise froze my smile. He had an explanation ready.

"This accommodation is just for the time being. I'm never home and don't need anything more. Now that you're here my life is complete. We'll move together."

"For the time being" was a phrase I would hear over and over. I already disliked it the first time. I had run out of English for the night and signaled that I was tired and needed to rest. The communal bathroom was across the hall. It smelled of urine and the toilet didn't flush.

In my mind I heard Mother's most disgusted voice. "Gitti, gitti! Such filth. Liesel don't touch anything."

I felt a pang of regret that some of her cleaning compulsions had afflicted and followed me to London. First thing tomorrow I would have to look for disinfectant and a scrubbing brush. I pulled back the tattered, pink candlewick bedspread and with all my clothes on curled up in a tight ball. A merciful sleep overwhelmed me quickly on my first night in a foreign land.

Chapter 35

Agency

ALWAYS AN EARLY riser when I woke it was still dark. I had to get my bearings. A baby's cry came from above, a door shut with a bang, cars sounded horns from the street in front and at the back. But the loudest sounds came from the other bed in the room and the snoring human being in it.

After a quick visit to the unhygienic bathroom I fled to the street.

"Morning, love. " The friendly milkman made his rounds with clinking crates of silver and gold foil topped glass bottles. "Just moved in? Here's a bottle of free milk. I'll be around every morning about this time."

"Thank's very much." I smiled. It was summer, but London's smog was like a cold blanket that dampened and engulfed every part of the street. I shivered inside and out as I explored a couple bocks of the neighborhood.

When I returned to the room it was just getting light and Hugh was still asleep. I half hoped he would stay that way, but I needed him. I pulled back the tattered window curtains.

"Hello, good morning. Where do I get bread to go with this milk?"

He wiped the sleep from his eyes. "We have food right here, sweetheart. I'll warm the chicken and rice I prepared for you to eat last night."

I looked and smelled inside the pot he retrieved from the shelf under the burner. Not good, but I didn't say anything.

A thick layer of grease dissolved as our breakfast warmed. Again I caught myself thinking like Mother. "There's garlic in this pot. I can't eat it." I watched Hugh as he enjoyed his cooking, digging into chicken legs, garlic and rice for breakfast. Oil dripped from his mouth and trickled down his neck. I wasn't hungry anymore.

We reached "Scotland, Inc., Talent Agency" by underground and got off at Piccadilly Circus in the heart of Soho. We walked a few blocks down Shaftesbury Avenue to number 66.

"No better location for show business anywhere in the world," Hugh said. "Do you realize where you are? This is Piccadilly Circus. We are in the center of everything."

He led me up a tight staircase to the third floor and unlocked one of the doors. The office matched our living quarters. A lone bulb hung from a wire in the ceiling and was the only light source for the two rooms that faced out onto Shaftesbury Avenue.

The shrill hooting noise from the avenue could be heard but not seen since the windows were coated with sticky grime. I wondered if anyone had ever made an effort to clean anything and how long it would have taken for the dirt to reach a saturation point and not get worse. The furniture consisted of two big wooden desks covered in piles of paperwork, one in each room, a couple of office chairs and a manual typewriter. From almost every inch of wall space smiled glossy, eight by ten images of hopeful men and women of every ethnic background.

"I'm their agent," a self-important Hugh said. "Without me they're nothing in this town." He looked at me and smiled. "But no one is as beautiful as you. You're the queen of my heart and will be forever. I need you and the business needs you."

"That's lovely," I said, reminding myself that I needed to overcome whatever negative feelings and prejudices I had brought with me from back home. This was my life now. I had to let go of the past and start work on the future.

The first couple of days I cleaned. From Soho Market I bought a bucket, mop and disinfectant that I transported back and forth on the underground from office to home. After two days I saw other things that needed my attention more.

Hugh made it clear that I was the biggest asset in his life and that touched me. I felt needed and therefore I couldn't just pay lip service and say I wanted to help us build a future together. I had to show integrity of commitment. That's what my father had taught me. I had walked out on Germany, but now I had a second chance to fulfill my responsibilities. A 45 year-old man had a dream to succeed in show business and I would help him to realize that dream.

It was necessary to improve my English, so I enrolled in a language school on Oxford Street. Hugh was right. We were in the center of everything. Theaters, world famous stores like Selfridges and Liberties on Regent Street, Trafalgar Square, the National Art Gallery...they were all in walking distance. Life wasn't so bad.

My profession as nursery schoolteacher came in handy for our talent agency. "You do a great job," Hugh said. I answered the phone, wrote letters, nurtured prospective clients and kept things straight, but it was an uphill battle.

There was much interracial mingling in London in the early 1960s, but Hugh informed me that there was also a lot of racial prejudice. "Black agents have much less of a chance. I'm trying hard to break through the barriers. You're vital to me. To be white is always better for business."

Not what I wanted to hear about the country that was now my home. "That's not right," I said. "We have to change it."

Chapter 36

Talent to Change

CHANGE BROUGHT CHALLENGES and adjustments. My surroundings wouldn't adapt to me. I had to fit myself in. I worked from morning to night to make that happen. Surely dirt on the windows was not as important as racial prejudice and the dark, evil hearts and deeds I had left behind in Germany.

*

Hugh and I operated on different clocks and were fundamentally different natures. A blessing in disguise.

He was a man of the night who came to life as the sun set and he functioned until the early morning hours in cabarets, clubs and discotheques, the venues of his trade. When he arrived back at our Bayswater digs he reeked of drink and smoke although he personally neither touched alcohol nor tobacco. He suffered from hay fever and other breathing problems, and made it clear that to walk through greenery in one of the beautiful London parks would be his death. The air in nightclubs was more conducive to his health.

As soon as I heard and smelled him arrive I was eager to get up and begin my day. The morning was my time. The parks were my favorite places. I ate nutritious foods while he never put anything green into his mouth. Unbeknownst to him though, I cut the grease and garlic out of his "one pot on one burner" meals.

Soho Market with its street vendors and selection of small bargain stores was a great and inexpensive place to shop for almost anything. I prided myself on needing very little money to run our home and office. A couple of pounds a week would buy enough rice, vegetables and meats as well as toiletries and writing paper. The source and amount of our income I had not figured out yet. Meanwhile, I felt the need to conserve.

Most of the photographs on the walls belonged to phantom clients whom I never saw set foot in our agency's office. The deal in Cologne with Kenneth Spencer had been a one-time shot at fame and soon evaporated. Hugh talked of the big shows he would produce, but for the time being we waited.

"What does 'time being' mean, Hugh? Tomorrow…next week…when? When are we able to move from our one room flat in Bayswater?"

"Aren't you happy? You're in the heart of London what more do you want?"

I wasn't happy. I didn't expect to be. What was happiness anyway? Regardless, just to live in a little more comfort would make life easier. But he was right; I had no reason to complain.

*

We were not totally out of "talent" and almost daily a new aspiring artist would find his or her way up the stairs to the third floor eager to audition for us right in the office. We wrote down everything they had talent at and promised that Hugh Scotland had the right connections to get them where their artistic gifts would shine like stars. For the time being their photographs would go up on the wall with the rest. Sometimes, if they had a day job, Hugh escorted them outside and got an advance on our future commissions.

The only two sources of business that were somewhat real and lucrative belonged to artists who had made a name for themselves. One was a duo, an act called the "Clarke Brothers;" the other a well-known bandleader and singer who toured in Europe, George Browne.

The Clarke brothers, Jimmy and Steve, were real brothers from Jamaica. They sang and tap danced together and flew all over the stage. Bookings kept coming in for them without much work.

One day Jimmy came in. "Hey sista, I'm here to pick up our money. Gotta pay the rent."

"What money, Jimmy?"

"Money. You know, when ya work ya gets money. Me and Stevie work sing and dance our heart out all over town. Club managers tell us your man come in and collects the dough. It's chickenfeed, but pays the rent."

"Hugh got your money? He hasn't paid you?'

"No, sista. His cut's ten pacent not tha whole deal."

I didn't doubt for one minute that Jimmy told the truth. "Can you come back tomorrow? I'll make sure to have your money."

"Alright than. Stevie or me will be by for it tomorrow. Tell me lav, how does that Scotlandman gets so lucky to find someone like ya? If ya ever want a change Jimmy Boy's available. Just say the word. Don't forget now."

I smiled at the good-natured artist, but inside I was furious. When Hugh showed up--he never arrived in the office until one or two in the afternoon--I let him have it.

"Where's our client's money?"

"What client and what money?"

"You know very well what client. We don't have too many. The Clarke Brothers. Jimmy was here looking for his rent."

Hugh laughed. "Just last night I made the rounds and picked up what's due. No other manager would do that for them." His English always got lilted when he was defending his actions. He pronounced his words like British royalty. "You just don't understand show business, my darling."

"I understand show business, dear Hugh. Very soon we may show no business."

"What do you know? Nothing. I haven't even told you about the magnitude of my work. The greatest show ever to hit London, and I'll produce it at the Windmill Theater."

"That's very nice. Meanwhile pay Jimmy his money. And by the way it's a perfect time to keep your word and move us out of our one room digs in Bayswater."

"What do you mean?"

"What I mean is we need to move. No more excuses."

"Why now?"

There had been a few times I had felt obliged to let Hugh make love to me. It wasn't something I wanted to think about when it was over.

"I…I'm expecting a child," I said.

"What? Woman, why haven't you told me? That changes everything. My son will have the best. I'm the happiest man in the world."

*

We got married at Westminster Town Hall. A time tested, magnificent setting for a far from magnificent, uneven union of two lost souls. The only witnesses were two strangers from the street and the official registrar. When I first arrived in England I had changed my name to Liza Scotland. Now it was official. I was Mrs. Scotland. Even my name signified I had changed countries and allegiances.

Hugh was oblivious to my feelings and desires, which were to do good and rid myself of my family's shameful past. He didn't know me and only bathed in the glow that I was his. I didn't belong to anyone, most of all myself.

*

Together with the certificate of matrimony came a one year lease on a large flat at 44 Exeter Mansion on Shaftesbury Avenue a few doors down from the office. The rental agreement was his wedding gift.

Mother had no idea where I was. I don't know if it was to hurt her or a secret longing to connect, but since a new life grew inside me I reached out to the old. I called her.

She cried and lamented. "How could you do such a thing? Take off in the middle of the night and not tell anyone."

"I had to get away."

"Away? Away from what? Didn't you have a loving home, a good job and a wonderful man? I knew right away you were up to no good and did something crazy again."

206

I was silent and let her tirade wash over me.

"Brigitte Hartman told me you borrowed money. How could a Steffens stoop that low? Of course, I repaid her right away. And poor Wolfgang. How could you do such a terrible thing to poor Wolfgang?"

"I guess he's been a big help to you," I said. In my mind I could see them on the sofa commiserating together about me over apple cake.

"What a wonderful man. And he's still prepared to take you back."

"Take me back? What for? I'm already happily married. No, thanks."

"You're what?"

"I'm married to a Negro just like I told you. He's as black as the Kohlenpot. I'm happily married. Soon I'll give birth to our first child. London, the greatest place in the world, is where I live."

Silence. I hyperventilated and knew my behavior was rotten, but I couldn't help myself. My words stabbed my mother's heart. There was no bigger, more hurtful transgression. Although it was a lie, at that moment it seemed like the right thing to say. My new life was no bed of roses. I suffered, so why should I give Mkother anything to be happy and proud about?

"What would your father say?"

No answer was needed. We both knew it only too well.

*

By marriage and my soon to be born child I had

cemented myself into a different race and culture. Like my father I didn't take half-hearted measures. I was no outsider who looked in on how black people lived, how they talked and what they thought and felt. I had become one of them and they were my new tribe. Their sorrows and fights for justice and equality were mine.

*

Barely of age, always of a passionate nature and with a heart on fire I stormed into London's black life in the early 1960s. This was the world of my new and chosen clan. With the bravado of a young person (and a damaged one at that), I thought of myself as a gift not to Hitler for whom I was created, but to every black person on the planet whose cause I would gung-ho defend. And how could I not have been damaged? I had cut myself off from any and all parental love and guidance so early on.

*

It took awhile to see all the nuances. To me a German was a German, but I soon discovered a person of color was many different things and could not be generalized. The man I had married came from the West Indies, the former British protectorate of Trinidad and Tobago. He was born in the capital of Port of Spain, a tropical, multi-racial island melting pot. He proudly stated that some of his ancestors were white settlers and he was as British as the Queen.

"Why do you deny your African heritage?" I often asked with an accusing undertone. "Black is beautiful."

"Don't call me black. Don't you see these refined European features and my fair skin?"

Hugh was not quite as black as the "Kohlenpot," and

208

therefore he thought of himself as better and elevated by several steps above his darker-skinned kind. He was also stubborn and had all the earmarks of a racist and bigot which felt strange coming from a black man. Through me he hoped to assimilate himself into the white race in the same way I was trying to become black.

We often had race related arguments. "The one problem that holds me back in the entertainment business is color," he said. "I have to work a lot harder. Even black artists who are any good want white representation."

I found this outrageous. "To think you're white isn't going to help you one bit," I said. "Straightening your hair won't do it either."

Hugh had come up with a unique beautifying regime for himself. He plastered his hair flat to his head with a rich and creamy black shoe polish. Voila! The kinkiness and gray were gone, and the lingering odor was neutralized by a heavy dose of "Old Spice" cologne.

At the Laundromat the black grease from his pillowcase spread to the rest of our washing. In response to my persistent nagging he did make one adjustment: he placed his shoe polish laden head on the daily late edition of the *Evening Standard* and would wake up at noon with the previous day's headlines imprinted on his face.

*

In spite of my loveless marriage I acclimatized myself to my new life well. I managed the talent agency with cheer, solved problems for others and discovered that I had strength, endurance and freedom. There was no other place in the world I would rather be. I was of no particular nationality, no religion. I hid the truth of my background from questions like: "You have an accent, where did you come from?" I would answer Holland one day and Sweden the next. To play fast and loose with the truth about such minor matters as one's place of origin was no problem, and it had a definite advantage if that place happened to be Germany.

Mother and son Hugh

Chapter 37

A Son for Africa

OUR NEW FLAT was huge, so huge it could not be heated. In winter during the persistent damp and biting cold, we took turns warming up. We stood in front of the one small gas log in the living room. It hit the immediate surroundings with force and toasted our calves while every body part above the knee shivered and goose bumped. London had all kinds of nasty atmospheric conditions besides fog and freezing smog. The weather of the day was always the main and first topic of any conversation.

"We" was an odd collection of people. In no time it got around that Hugh Scotland now occupied a spacious West End flat. The black London artists he had made promises to and owed money were out of work and starving. They resented the hell out of him. I felt responsible to at least get them nourished.

There was Rudolph Dunbar, the orchestra conductor who had "taken Egypt by storm" in the 50s conducting the Cairo Symphony--those were his words--but he hadn't conducted anything since. Around six o'clock every night Rudolph and at least four or five other men showed up like clockwork to share what was in the pots, which wasn't much.

In the small kitchen we had a real gas stove now. Even a couple of pots. One was for rice and the other for a meager amount of protein with vegetables and lots of spicy, exotic sauce. The sauce could be stretched with flour and water to accommodate any number of dinner guests. Everyone left happy, with a full stomach, full of hope--and without lifting a finger towards doing the dishes.

The aging Exeter Mansion had eight large rental properties, two on each floor. The ornate elevator was ancient and consisted of a metal cage brought up and down by wire ropes. The doors were also metal and clanked open and shut manually like an accordion. The whole system creaked and was on its last legs. We had no choice but to trust it if we didn't want to climb the concrete stairs to the fourth floor.

A flat in the "Mansion" had possibilities which I discovered when I once peeked into a neighbor's. Theirs was done up while we lived with the barest furnishings. Hugh had managed to get some basics on credit, but the time was near when the creditors lost patience and our table, sofa, chairs and beds would be repossessed if they didn't collapse first. We made it a rule not to open the door unless we knew for sure who was on the other side.

As in our office down the street the apartment windows didn't open and were permanently glued shut by dirt and coats of century-old paint. I had given up cleaning London windows as futile and now tried to hide rather than remove the dirt. I bought a roll of shiny pink fabric that was on sale at the Soho Market and a hammer and nails. In the absence of curtain rails I nailed the large panels I had hand sewn, to the window frames.

Sine we had no ladder, a couple of chairs and books stacked together did just as well. I dangled precariously and pregnant with my hammer and nails while the dinner guests watched and waited to be served their food. They were "artists," brought up in a society where women did most of the work. Gentlemanly gallantries were foreign to them.

I could do very little about the rest of the flat. The lone light bulb in the corridor made the black wainscoting appear even gloomier. Some tenant before us--not a handyman-- had tried to varnish over a bad wallpaper job. The walls were an unappealing dark brown and peeling. The floor throughout was brown, cracked linoleum that lifted around the edges. However, I had my own bedroom away from Hugh's snoring, and we had a bathroom with hot water in the tub. Things had improved as far as I was concerned.

I knew one of our clients, George Browne, worked on a regular basis although I had not met him yet. Hugh owed him a lot of money and for that reason had kept us apart. "George performs in Europe," Hugh said.

George also came from Trinidad, and Hugh's eyes lit up when he talked about his countryman. He considered him easy going, almost saintly. George didn't make a fuss about his dues, and for the time being we were living off it.

One day in the show business trade press I read that our star client George Browne was in fact in London and was starring in a musical he had written and produced. "I want to see it," I declared to Hugh who couldn't find an excuse not to take me.

"You'll love his performance," he said. "George is royalty amongst blacks and his following is all white. They love him at the Blue Angel night club where Princess Margaret and her entourage are regulars." Hugh mentioned British royalty a lot.

*

213

The theater was indeed filled with white women of all ages. We took our seats in a place of prominence in the front orchestra row. After all, we were the star's agents. For the first time I felt some pride in our show business enterprise.

It was his voice I heard first. He began to sing offstage as part of the performance. A deep baritone of such magical richness it had no equal. When he entered the stage with his guitar it was to thunderous applause, and although slight in stature he dominated the set with his charisma and talent.

The show was a calypso musical and featured a steel band. The tones that could be produced by beating metal drums were new to my ears. The drums could turn from happy, up-beat chimes of a faraway island into soulful, penetrating outcries in the night.

"Take a trip to Trinidad and you'll be oh so glad

It's the home of calypso and the land of flamingo

Rich in sunshine rich in rain

Rich in Laughter rich in pain

But above all gloriously

Rich in good humanity."

*

After the show we went backstage and Hugh introduced me to George.

"What a wonderful performance," I gushed. "I have never heard anyone sing like you before. And I have never seen steel drums used as instruments."

"Thank you. I appreciate the compliment. Steel bands are a part of Trinidad. We are a musical nation and ingenious in the way we extract sounds out of almost anything. The drums were once used for transporting oil."

"They were?"

"Yes. You must come again, Mrs. Scotland." George took my hand and kissed it in a courtly manner. I was charmed.

"Hugh told me that you love music and the two of you met at a classical concert. I perform more simple styles of our islands."

"You are too modest, George," Hugh said and put his arm around my waist. "You have immense talent from jazz to classical. I'm working on very important bookings for you right now that will make the world see your greatness."

"Thanks, Hugh. You're the best."

As we left the theater together, Hugh said, "Liza makes the best West Indian stew in London. Why don't you stop by sometime."

Making stew was my biggest asset. "I don't know about the best," I said, "but you are more than welcome to join us any evening."

George promised to take us up on the offer and a few days later he did.

*

Soon I looked forward to his visits. He showed respect and treated me as a friend and not just a maker of stew. We had interesting discussions about a multitude of subjects from reincarnation to world politics. I discovered that he unlike Hugh was comfortable with himself and his heritage. He would make a better role model for my unborn child.

215

National Health, what blessing! No matter who you were or where you originated, if you found yourself on England's shores the British welfare system came through for you no questions asked. Everyone, young and old, rich or poor fared equally well. I took advantage of all the services offered for an expectant mother, from vitamin and iron pills to doctor's examinations and free milk. The responsibility for a new life was not to be taken lightly.

The delivery was by forceps and complicated, but out of pain and darkness emerged great light. My world became sunny and blissful on March 27, 1964 with the birth of my son Hugh at Charring Cross Hospital.

As I was born a gift to the Fuehrer, so was this child my very own gift to Africa.

Chapter 38

My Son's World

HUGH JUNIOR WAS welcomed into the world not just by me--his delighted mother--but also by his proud father and family friend George Browne who came to visit the hospital ward every day.

The best thing parents can do for their child is to love each other, but the feelings I had for my son's father I knew were not love. What he felt for me was the best a man could do who did not like or respect himself.

There was a lot of underlying bitterness and sadness in our home which I hoped my baby would not feel. I loved motherhood, and my son was the most important person in my life. From my own life and from my studies of child psychology I knew about the importance of the early, formative years. I wanted the life I constructed for us to be as normal and happy as I was able to make it.

I worried a lot about the world my boy would inherit. The ideals of his German grandfather had been so inhuman and wrong. My son and I belonged to a race my father's band of thugs wanted to see exterminated. Hitler was gone, but how different was apartheid and what happened to my black brothers and sisters in Africa, America and all over the world?

I was at the right place and time to become part of long overdue change. The London of the early 1960s was the heart and soul of emerging Black Nationalism. People from all over the world gathered to demand social and political revolution.

One charismatic South African had come to the forefront. He demanded the abolition of apartheid, demanding justice, freedom and dignity for the black majority in his country. It was Nelson Mandela. He had remained dignified and noble in his fight for liberation, but he had landed in a notorious prison.

I began to educate myself about what it was like to live under apartheid. To be white meant ownership of land. Land was power--the power to enslave people with no-right to own land, to keep them uneducated, poor and living in ghettos. The land was the black man's ancestral home and this was a great injustice.

My soul and heart felt for the disenfranchised people of Africa. I identified myself as a black woman and I had hatred for all white oppressors. Injustices that had taken place in Germany I could do nothing about. Our Jewish neighbors I did not even dare bring back to my mind. But to throw off the shackles of apartheid--that was a cause I could fight with passion here and now.

Being inexperienced I didn't look for integration and common ground. My world was black and white, and I saw no reason why a single white person should have the right to remain in any part of Africa.

There was a lot of my father in me, but I was not aware of my own self-righteousness at the time. Fortunately, the militant blackness of my heart was mitigated by my interracial baby who was neither black nor white.

My interest for office work in the show business agency

waned. I saw no improvement. Hugh was still not getting work for our clients and I could make no real difference to anyone. I gravitated outside and pushed my baby carriage into the London parks, where activist speeches sang to me and sparked me into joining rallies and demonstrations.

We rallied and marched to free Nelson Mandela, we vowed to boycott any companies and goods that came out of white South Africa. We stood side by side with the civil rights movement in America and the Soledad Brothers. Our fight for racial justice was right and just and gathered momentum. I believed we would win if we fought hard and long enough. I had found my voice, and every voice mattered.

Where was Hugh Senior's voice in this fight for justice for his people? It was nowhere. He did not identify with either me or any of us who looked for revolution. He was stuck in the past and according to him Trinidad had done better under the British. His main concern was how to get his big break as an impresario and this meant aligning himself with people not of his own race.

"I am an Englishman. Damn you woman, you married an Englishman. What you are doing will harm us."

"I married a black man. We have a black child."

"You're insane. Don't drag my son into this. He's as white as you and I."

There was no point in arguing with Hugh. I found myself caught between two worlds. I had left one, but I had not received entry into the other.

Blacks who saw me married to the shorter, older, unattractive and no-money Hugh Scotland thought I was an easy target for sexual advances. Why otherwise would I have married someone so unappealing if it wasn't for sex?

Whites must have thought of me in a similar way. One day after I had traveled on the underground and walked around town I returned to our flat and found a note had been pinned to the back of my coat. It read: "White whore, go back home." I had my suspicions that the note writer was a white male in our office building.

In the circles where I moved Jews were hardly ever mentioned. I was taken aback one day when Hugh said, "Jews control the entertainment industry. They don't give blacks a chance. Your Hitler had the right idea."

I was outraged. "What? How can you make such a foolish statement? And don't call him 'my' Hitler. My family stood against everything that crazy idiot proclaimed."

"You claim you care about justice. Just think how injustice affects us."

"Where are you going with this statement?"

"Haven't you noticed how black entertainers are stereotyped? They don't get leading parts and are always relegated to play servants, clowns, prostitutes or criminals? Don't you see that is unjust?"

"That would be unjust if it was true." From then on I watched to see if he was right. He was.

I still did not know any Jews. The only Jew I had ever met was the stranger in Bottrop whom I had last seen flee from our house. My thoughts of him and other Jews were neither negative nor positive. I avoided any opinion. I did not want to think about Jews at all. They were stranger and more mysterious to me than any African, and I was terrified of them.

220

Chapter 39

Gloria

ONE COLD AND foggy evening Hugh made a shocking announcement: "We got to move."

"In heaven's name, why?" I had visions of the three of us cramped back into one room in Bayswater.

"We're three months behind in rent. The flat's too big for us anyway, and you always complain about the cold." His tone was pompous and nasal.

I grabbed baby Hugh and put him in his stroller. For the rest of the day I walked with him through the foggy streets of London with despair. It was like we were already a homeless mother and child with nowhere to go. I only returned to the flat after I knew Hugh had left for the clubs. For several days we did not speak. I was out when he was in.

Hugh came to the realization himself that to lose the roof above our heads might entail the end of our relationship. He tried to solve the problem.

*

By the end of the week he had found the solution. He was excited and waited by the door to tell me. "Darling, you've the greatest husband in the world, ME. You're so privileged. We will continue to live in the heart of London in this very flat."

221

"Where did the money come from?" I asked.

"This idea should have come to me sooner. It's so brilliant."

"What?"

"We'll sublet the two front rooms. Never use them anyway. I've found a lovely lady who'll take them over and pay us a very nice rent. We'll be landlords."

He pulled out a wad of money from his pocket to show me this was real and not just another empty promise. "Let's go out to eat and celebrate," he said.

We went to a Chinese restaurant and when I wanted to find out more about the person who was going to share my home all he said was, "her name's Gloria. Have to respect her privacy."

"No big deal," I said. "I want to be left alone too and mind my own business."

My home-saver and good fortune appeared the following afternoon. When I opened the door, in front of me was this huge Jamaican woman with the whitest teeth and an infectious smile.

"Hey, Sista. It's Gloria. Already paid ma rent. Bringing in ma belongings."

"Happy to meet you, Ms. Gloria," I said, pointing to the two front rooms.

"Likewise, darlin."

Up the stairs lumbered two men with a mattress. They cursed about the lift being too small.

"Come along fellows," Gloria said very much in charge. "Right in here." She directed her moving in without lifting a finger herself. I watched and wondered what she had that I didn't. Men labored for her.

Since standing in the hall became too exhausting for our new tenant, she sat herself down on the sofa in the living room and with the door open she directed the arrival of several more pieces of furniture and a bunch of boxes.

"Are you in show business, Gloria?" I asked.

"Yes, darlin. Gloria's doing show business." She giggled, and I laughed with her.

My baby woke from his nap. She reached out to hold him. Hughie gurgled with happy sounds when she pressed him to her overflowing bosom and blew kisses on his belly.

My new flat mate worked out really well. She was warm and self-confident.

"Gloria, you have children?"

"Gloria has two babies, a long way from here, back home in Jamaica."

"You left your babies?" I couldn't imagine parting from my child.

It turned out she missed her children, but they were well cared for by Gloria's mother and her extended family. She sent regular money back to Jamaica from her show business work. I assumed Gloria was a jazz singer.

*

Gloria was a Trojan horse! Behind her arrived several more young women, some white and with showgirl looks, as well as a constant stream of men of every persuasion. Gloria began to run her trade from our flat, and that was how my baby and I came to live in a brothel.

We flourished on the rent money for several weeks, even months. After I found out what went on in the two front rooms, I didn't want to think about it. I kept myself to the back where the kitchen was located. A few times a week Gloria would join me and fry herself a juicy, sizzling steak and we had friendly chats.

Since the walls were thick I only heard telltale noises once in a while. Occasionally I saw a man stagger out intoxicated. The girls must have done a good job; they were cheerful and prosperous and the men kept coming.

Prostitution was widespread in Soho. I had no idea if it was legal, and I never witnessed the police take action against any of the street-walking working girls.

One spring day in the middle of the afternoon, our front door was kicked in. "Hands up. Scotland Yard!"

Hugh, who had just gotten up was seated in the living room with the *Evening Standard* and I was feeding the baby.

When the officers saw we were a peaceful, wholesome looking couple, they changed their tune to the usual, polite British manner. They informed me that I had been under surveillance for a while and had done nothing wrong. It was Hugh they were after.

Hugh was indignant and shouted like crazy, but that didn't help him a bit. They handcuffed him and took him downstairs to the waiting "Black Maria," the cockney name for the police van.

He was joined in the van by several occupants of the

front rooms who had been unlucky enough to be in for the afternoon. It included a handcuffed Gloria. She took the event in her stride.

"Look after that beautiful baby boy now will ya, darlin," she said before the police van doors slammed shut.

Several male and female police officers stayed behind and combed through every corner of the flat. In the front they collected evidence, all kinds of tools of the trade, including whips and chains. Things I had never seen before or thought existed were now piled up in the corridor.

"The back part of the apartment doesn't have anything awful like this," I said. The officers didn't take my word for it. I endured a thorough search of all my belongings.

"Please believe me, my husband's innocent," I said. "We own a talent agency down the street. This is a mix-up."

A female officer took me aside. She came across my box of family photos: a smiling Fritz next to me, Mutti and a little girl in pigtails.

"You and your baby should return to your family. This isn't the right place for you."

"Oh, no," I said. "This is my home. When will my husband return? He did nothing wrong."

"The arraignment is tomorrow morning. Bring your solicitor."

*

After they had left with Hugh's briefcase and all of his paperwork I was alone with my broken door and pounding heart. The charge was "running a house of prostitution and living on immoral earnings." I needed help.

225

That night Rudolph and the other regular eaters were nowhere to be seen. Word got around fast and they were not about to come anywhere near a place just done over by Scotland Yard.

George Browne was giving a concert at Cambridge University. I could not reach him until early the next morning.

When I got hold of him his voice was calm and sensible as always. "I'll get my solicitor and come straight to Westminster Court."

"Thank you, George. I know I can count on you."

"How could Hugh let this happen?"

I didn't tell George that it was because of me and my need to have a decent roof over my head.

"Why don't you and Hughie return to your family till this blows over? I'll be happy to pay your way." This was the second time I was given unthinkable advice.

"Oh no. There's no way I'll run away from Hugh now he's in trouble." I expressed with the greatest ease and conviction my self-deceit and any untruth that seemed appropriate at that moment. I knew very well that I didn't stay because I was a devoted spouse. I would never return to Germany for any reason.

"You're a wonderful wife. I hope one day he appreciates you," George said.

*

Hugh spent the night in jail. He was released on bond the next day after George put up his house as bail. At the hearing a couple of weeks later Baby Hugh and I were presented to the judge as evidence of a stable and devoted family unit. A generous Gloria took the blame and testified it was all her fault and that Hugh had no idea what business she was in. George was a credible character witness.

Hugh was lucky and got off with a fine and no prison time. He didn't leave the flat for a while and whimpered, "The whole world is against me. No justice for a man like me."

The eaters came back and commiserated with "poor Hugh."

I compared the two men from the same background, Hugh and George both from Trinidad. In Hugh I saw the victim he had turned himself to be, and although I could appreciate his intelligence I had lost faith that he would succeed in anything. George on the other hand had made a success of his life and things would continue to go his way.

I was joined in marriage and parenthood to "poor Hugh" and like him I would fall short.

Chapter 40

Charge D' Affaires

ONE DAY WHEN Hugh showed interest in my African liberation activities, I told him about a rally that started at Hyde Park and marched to the Houses of Parliament.

"Would you like to join me and your son in our grassroots efforts?"

"Oh no! For crying out loud have you forgotten my hay fever? Can you imagine what the park will do to me?"

"It's only a corner of Hyde Park, covered in cement."

"Pollen will seek me out from every corner of the park. I will be destroyed."

"You destroy yourself."

"Anyway, I have something much bigger in mind."

"Another big idea?"

"I'm a black man."

"No kidding."

"I'm serious."

"You are?"

"Go and buy yourself a new cocktail dress," Hugh said. "We have an invitation to the Congolese Embassy in

Knightsbridge."

"When?"

"Tonight, and I'm about to look into helping my African brethren from a more important position than aimless walking in the park."

"It's never aimless."

"Don't skimp, I want you to look stunning." Again a substantial roll of money appeared from his pocket. He peeled off several large pound bills and gave them to me.

*

I checked out the sales on Oxford Street and parted with most of my cash for a red chiffon, off the shoulder, designer creation at Selfridges. I thought of Mother and my liberation from her tastes. Red looked good on me.

Hugh in his too tight tuxedo-- I had already replaced the buttons twice and moved them closer to the edge -- and with his slick hair and signature fragrance of "Old Spice" had a new lease on life when we pulled up with our baby at the official residence of the Congolese Ambassador. A chauffeur driven Rolls-Royce had picked us up at our "mansion" on Shaftesbury Avenue.

I was surprised that my husband seemed already to be among the inner circle of the debonair Charge d' Affaires Thomas Kanza, a tall, handsome African man in his thirties who had been educated in the United States. This acquaintance was very recent, and I couldn't decide who or what it might have been that got Hugh a foot in the high society door of the embassy. I didn't ask.

His Excellency was very kind and accommodating. He

229

pointed the way to his private quarters should I need to rest and nurse my baby. A young woman in a colorful African caftan was appointed to look after Hughie so I could enjoy the reception without worry. And what a grand and elegant affair it was.

I was in heaven when the great South African singer Miriam Makeba arrived. She rendered a wonderful impromptu performance in her unique style with an accompaniment of Zulu drums. We were in London, but she transported us to her homeland through music and allowed us to partake of its beauty, artistry and struggles.

Afterwards I got a chance to talk with her about her beloved country and our joint desire for its liberation from white imperialism. She was surprised how passionate and well informed I was. So was Hugh who took in every word of what he had previously dismissed as foolish talk designed to bring us down and alienate us from the British. All of sudden he was a changed man.

We were the last to leave and it was the first of many such posh and swanky soirees. After a couple of evenings we were on a first name basis with Thomas. He was an eloquent charmer. Luminaries from all over London enjoyed themselves at his well attended parties. Great food and drink and even better conversation. Thomas, the consummate diplomat, was hailed as a future leader of the Congo.

"Do you know how rich the Congo is in precious metals, minerals and diamonds?" Hugh asked me one night on the way home. "It's no wonder Belgium tries to hang on to the richest country in Africa and bleed it dry."

Until now I had not imagined Africa's troubles from this materialistic point of view. I had been naïve enough to believe white settlers wanted the land just to homestead their families.

There's much more at stake," Hugh said. The black population isn't just enslaved. Great riches are plundered and exported to Europe."

My face clouded.

*

The Congo's troubles were similar yet different from South Africa's. The Congo had black leadership now, although that leadership may as well have been white. It was neither freethinking nor interested in lifting the population out of bondage and poverty. It catered solely to its own whims and pandered to the interests of its European lords and masters.

I didn't know what went on in Hugh's heart. I wanted to believe he saw the light about racism and he now agreed his own and our family's destiny was tied to Africa.

"My son hasn't been baptized yet, "he said one day. "Let's honor Thomas and make him godfather." I agreed and envisioned my boy one day on a liberated and prosperous African continent.

Thomas had an entourage of beautiful women, but he was not married and had no children as far as we knew. He held our son during his baptism in the beautiful St. Martin's in the Field Anglican church on Trafalgar Square. It was an emotional moment.

*

I was still feeling my way in diplomatic circles, and diplomacy was not something I found easy to practice. There were occasions at the consulate when I came across diplomats from African nations who enjoyed the good life in England and here was I, a white woman, telling them what to do.

The Ethiopian Ambassador was one of them. We met at a cocktail party where he sipped champagne. Horrific pictures of starvation in his country after a year long drought had just reached us. I expected more involvement, more urgency from him to rally relief for his people. When he continued to make small talk with me I cut him short.

"What's being done for the people of Ethiopia?" I said. "Is aid on the way?"

"Why are you concerned with a problem that's not yours?" He was curt.

"Not mine? Whose problem is it? It doesn't seem to be yours. When was the last time you were back in your homeland?"

"A sharp tongue on someone young, inexperienced and white is preposterous," he said. "We're taking care of our people."

"What's my race got to do with it? We're all human."

"You're German."

"No, I'm not."

"I thought you were. Please, excuse me."

I was left standing with a bright red face.

What could I possibly do to be accepted and trusted by my chosen race? Why was it so hard to have my feelings recognized as genuine? I was not like other whites who lived unconcerned about injustices on a different continent thousands of miles away. I was impatient and wanted to find a way to implement change. Wasn't my black offspring testimony enough of my commitment?

In Germany my son would be called a Mischling, a mixed breed. I hoped his black brothers and sisters would not hold the same prejudice against him and that his white mother would not turn out to be a liability for him. Was it naïve of me to have such an all-embracing view of the world that did not recognize the color of people's skin?

*

Ambassador Thomas Kanza spoke often of one African leader whom he revered as a Congolese martyr. Thomas had worked with and for Patrice Lumumba. "His ideas were new and compelling and they inspired my people," Thomas said, handing me Lumumba's eulogy. "This is what our beloved Patrice wrote before his brutal and senseless murder."

"We ask for our country the right to an honorable existence, to an immaculate dignity, to independence without restrictions. The future of the Congo is a bright one and the future expects of every Congolese the accomplishment of the sacred task of reconstructing our independence and our sovereignty. For without dignity there is no liberty, without justice there is no dignity, and without independence there are no free men."

*

Lumumba who had once been a humble postal worker spent six months in a Belgian prison where he was ridiculed as a pretentious baboon. He eventually became a member of the All African Peoples Conference and president of the Congolese National Movement. After independence was won from Belgium, he was the first and only Premier of the Congo to be

233

democratically elected.

There was an African saying: "A man who suffers much knows much." Both Lumumba and Mandela suffered great indignities yet emerged stronger as a result. At the end, Lumumba paid dearly with his life.

He knew too much about corruption and his powerful enemies were ruthless. They were the Congo's former colonialists in Belgium and the CIA, which hid its direct involvement in a great and charismatic man's murder behind support for his political enemies. Lumumba's biggest foe was his fellow Congolese, Moishe Tschombe.

*

The indignities Hugh Scotland had suffered could in no way compare. He had spent one night in jail at Her Majesty's pleasure, but nevertheless considered himself a man baptized by fire and injustice. What sort of "injustice" he had suffered and the reason for it he didn't want anyone to know about, especially not his new benefactor the ambassador.

Hugh spent most of his days in the embassy now and only returned to Shaftesbury Avenue late at night. The baby and I often accompanied him. I made myself useful planning social events as Thomas' secretary. Miss Gloria was part of the past and out of our consciousness.

One night we had a shocking surprise. The locks of our flat had been changed and a notice of eviction was stuck to the door. The landlord had found out about Miss Gloria's illegal activities in his building, cancelled our lease and kept the apartment's content in lieu of our outstanding rent.

It was Bayswater again for the time being. We found a hotel efficiency room and paid a week's rent in advance. Our fortunes kept changing in less than no time, but the difference was that now we had the backing of Thomas, an important man in Knightsbridge.

We were back in Bayswater for just a few weeks when the shrill ring of the phone woke me just before dawn. I answered in the dark. "Thomas here, where's Hugh?"

From the tone in his voice I realized this was an emergency. Hugh confirmed it moments later: Kasabuvu, the Congo's president, had recalled Moishe Tschombe from exile in Spain. Tschombe was back in Leopoldville as Prime Minister.

Patrice Lumumba

Chapter 41

Thomas

A WORRIED THOMAS opened the door of the embassy himself an hour later. His staff was not up yet, and they were still unaware. An official telegram had arrived from Leopoldville and summoned Thomas back home within the week. The Queen was informed at the same time that Thomas no longer represented the sovereign nation of the Congo.

All three of us knew what this meant. If Thomas was foolish enough to return home, he would be considered a threat and killed like Lumumba. He had to stay in England for now.

"Hugh, my study," Thomas pointed the way. "I must talk to you."

"I'll make breakfast," I said.

The two men consulted for a while and were weary when they emerged. Our family's support and survival was now completely linked to Thomas Kanza, the African.

Hugh had given up on show business and abandoned the office on Shaftesbury Avenue. Thomas paid well for Hugh's advice and therefore Hugh's business had become African politics and the wealthy Congo. He hoped to make his name and fortune with both.

"Tschombe's return to power in the Congo makes my blood boil," I said over breakfast at the service table in the huge embassy kitchen.

"Right. Mine too. Most Congolese loathe the man," Thomas said.

"Sure, he's dishonest and corrupt," Hugh said.

"And the killer of our beloved Lumumba."

"If the Congolese didn't vote for him, how did he get back into power?" I was curious.

"Belgium. Not by democratic elections but help from Brussels," Thomas informed us.

I had heard enough about Tschombe to know that he embodied everything we wanted to overcome. Thomas had told us again and again that Tschombe was the archenemy of the struggles for freedom and democracy in the Congo. "He drags us back to a colonial time we thought was gone forever after independence was achieved," Thomas said.

Tschombe had ruled the enormously mineral rich Katanga province and amassed huge fortunes for himself that were hidden in bank accounts all over Europe.

"Can't you ask for help from the United Nations?" Hugh said.

"I don't trust the United Nations." Thomas shook his head. "They were part of Lumumba's betrayal."

"Why? Can you tell us more," I said.

"Lumumba was not allowed to form a government of his choice and that caused riots and civil war. Then they blamed him for not being able to maintain law and order. All along they had set him up to fail so they could declare that the Congo was not ready for self-rule."

238

"The United Nations participated in something so devious? If you can't trust the United Nations, who can you trust?"

"Thomas can trust us, Liza," Hugh said. "He and I just discussed that I'm going to fly out to Kinshasa tomorrow."

Thomas looked at me to see if I had any objections. I wasn't sure.

"Hugh has agreed to go," Thomas said. "His face is unknown in Africa which is to our advantage."

"What will Hugh do?" I wondered how this had transpired so quickly. Only a few weeks ago my husband's thoughts had been bogged down with complaints that he was not Caucasian. He had dismissed my fiery pleas for justice in Africa as mumbo jumbo.

Now he was sent on an important mission that would affect many lives. I had no idea what Hugh's motives were and I did not trust that he had such a complete, sudden change of heart and turnaround in belief, but I really didn't know for sure.

*

I had no fear of the "Dark Continent" and longed to experience it firsthand. I considered myself to be a better and more genuine choice than Hugh to do work in Africa, but there was a secret understanding between the two men from which I was excluded. I was not sure if it was because I was a woman, because I was white, or both. I felt a sting of jealousy at my handicaps.

"Hugh's mission isn't dangerous," Thomas said.

"What's he going to do?"

"He will only act as courier. Don't worry. Things will

239

turn around soon."

"How?"

"Our forces are almost ready."

During the next week, after Hugh's clandestine departure, I helped Thomas vacate the embassy and settle in a spacious Mayfair penthouse on Green Street. Only a couple of his staff remained with him. One of them, Jeannette, a petite Congolese woman, helped me with Hugh, Jr.

Thomas no longer received any official salary and he had emptied his bank account to pay for the flat. The former ambassador was now very happy that I was able to make a large pot of nourishing, inexpensive stew, renamed from West Indian to African stew.

After a few days Hugh returned to London and money flowed freely again. "Here, look at this." He showed me a packet of raw, uncut diamonds. "For Thomas! Easily turns into cash on the underground market."

"What's being done about Tschombe?" I said.

Hugh was evasive. I resorted to eavesdropping and overheard Hugh and Thomas' plan was in the works to take control of Stanleyville, the Congo's second largest city.

"Things might get dangerous." Thomas was very serious. "All information between us has to be in strictest confidence."

"You can count on me."

"Liza, don't have a false sense of safety. Make sure you're not followed."

"Followed?"

"Tschombe has his henchmen everywhere, even in London."

"I'm not afraid and can't wait for the just fight for the Congo's freedom to begin," I said. Thomas smiled, pleased.

*

Hugh made a few more trips to the Congo. He never gave me a clear understanding whom he met, but from what I could gather diamonds were exchanged for guns and ammunition for the rebel forces, as well as currency for Thomas' living expenses.

"I'm impatient," I told Thomas. "Innocent blood is being shed every day. Talk and diplomacy goes nowhere with a man like Tschombe. Don't you think we are wasting time and lives?"

"Those are strong views," he replied.

"Yes, I have strong opinions. Don't you think I'm right? What can I do?"

He smiled. "You're young and white."

"Stop saying that. Don't you trust me?"

*

The reports of atrocities Hugh brought back clouded Thomas' face with fury. It was sheer savagery committed by hired mercenaries. They slaughtered women and children and burned villages to the ground. Tschome's soldiers did their evil in the darkness of night. The stories of mass murder were endless and horrific.

Yet, Hugh managed to keep his involvement detached and self-involved. He did a job for Thomas Kanza for which he

241

expected handsome pay. At the same time, he could prove to me that he was able to provide for our family. "You and my son are all I care about," he said. "I want Hugh, Jr. to have the best of everything."

"I want freedom for the Congolese."

"In a few days I am going to return with more wealth than you can imagine. The Congo is still the richest country in Africa. When I come back you can keep a large diamond for yourself."

"That's nice, Hugh. You don't know me at all, do you?"

I didn't care about diamonds and let Hugh's promises go in one ear and out the other. True to my expectations this pledge of wealth and a precious gem remained unfulfilled.

Chapter 42

Promised Land

HUGH WAS OUT of the country never longer than a week. During that time he didn't communicate, and we were never sure when he would show up again. My feelings swayed between enjoying the freedom it gave me and concern that some harm might befall the father of my son and we would find ourselves abandoned.

When Hugh didn't return after a couple of weeks, Thomas tried to communicate with his African sources without success. No revenue was coming in and messages were no longer going back and forth.

"It's time to leave London and return home to Africa," he said. "I have to find out what happened to Hugh."

"What about Tschombe?" I asked.

"That too. It's urgent that I get involved in the struggle to depose him."

"You'll be in danger."

"I want you and Hugh Jr. to move in here. Use my bedroom." We sat up all night in his penthouse on Green Street before his departure the next day. Jeannette cried.

"The rent has been paid for a month in advance." Thomas gave me an envelope. "Here's some money for your upkeep. Liza, I'm entrusting this small household to you."

"It has become small, hasn't it?"

Thomas' elaborate parties, influential people from all over the world who had pandered to him and danced at the embassy in Knightsbridge were no more. He was left with just the four of us: Jeannette, the sweet young woman from a tiny Congolese village who spoke little English; Robert, a thirty-year-old Congolese man who spoke no English and who had been his chauffeur; my infant son; and me, a twenty-three-old German escapee who wanted to be Congolese. Not a formidable collection of allies to be leaving behind in Thomas' London base.

"I know," Thomas said. "Never mind, people are fickle and disloyal."

"You're breaking my heart."

"Don't be sad. Things will get back to normal."

"I doubt it."

Thomas' departure for Africa left me heavy-hearted. I had already learned the lesson which had just now come as a surprise to the young diplomat: we are forever alone, and our fortunes and destiny can change in the twinkle of an eye.

*

It took several weeks before Thomas called with a bad telephone connection. "Hello, Liza. Are you there?"

"Yes, tell me what's happening."

"Sorry, Tschombe has arrested Hugh."

The line went dead before I could ask for details. I was stunned. As soon as it sunk in that Hugh had been unlucky once again, this time caught in a life-and-death situation, I had to do something to help. The first thing was to inform the British Foreign Office. Hugh was a British subject.

"What is Mr. Scotland's business in the Congo?"

"My husband is a journalist and independent observer." I wiped my brow and congratulated myself that I came up with this lie in a hurry.

"Perfect. The right thing to tell a government official," Thomas said when he called back. "I'm proud of you. Foresight and secrecy, keep that up."

"Why was Hugh arrested?" I said. "How did he get connected to the rebel cause?"

"Can't talk about it on the telephone?"

"I want to come to Africa, Thomas, as soon as possible. I want to confront Tschombe, and I want to help you and your cause."

"Let me think about it. You are my eyes and ears in London, be patient."

"I can be ready to travel tomorrow."

"It is dangerous work and you are a mother. What about your son?"

"Jeannette. I have complete trust in her."

*

The Foreign Office confirmed that Hugh was held in a Leopoldville prison. The charge was treason and the punishment death. I knew how immediate such a sentence could be carried out by Tschombe's kangaroo court.

I had never met Moishe Tschombe, but my instinct told me that two things would probably matter to him: adverse publicity in London and the opinion of other African leaders.

"Thomas, Tschombe is desperately looking to gain legitimacy. I can use it to help Hugh."

"Okay," Thomas finally agreed. "I'll arrange for your ticket to Kenya, that's where we'll meet."

"Good bye, my sweet boy," I kissed Hugh Jr. and placed him in Jeanette's arms. "As soon as you're older I'll take you to Africa with me."

*

The first plane trip of my life took me to Rome and back to the European continent I had left four years earlier on the train. A lot had changed in that time. I had made a big personal transformation and was now a wife and mother. And I had a longing to become a strong, independent woman.

Although the aircraft of the East African Airline was old and rickety for the nine-hour trip from Rome to Nairobi, I didn't mind the bumpy ride. Even though I was on a mission to save my husband's life by manipulating a world political figure, my heart pounded for a more personal reason. I would soon set foot in Africa--my dream come true.

The moment I stepped off the plane onto the rich, brown earth of Kenya I was a prodigal daughter of Africa who had entered her promised land.

Chapter 43

Metamorphosis

AFTER MORE THAN one hundred years of British colonial rule and massive struggles on both sides, Kenya had become an independent and free nation in 1963.

The Mau Mau movement began among the Kikuyu tribe protesting vast stretches of Kikuyu land being taken for use by European settlers. The tribesmen regularly presented their grievances to the governments in Nairobi and London and they received nothing but empty promises. At the same time white settlers pressed for independence under minority rule.

African lives and labor had been freely given on behalf of the British Kingdom in two world wars. Now it was time for justice. Members of the Kikuyu, Emlu, Meru and Kamba tribes swore an oath to fight and if necessary die for their rights.

The Mau Mau was banned in 1950 and their leaders imprisoned. Many African civilians were detained in concentration camps. Finally, due to pressure by the British public during the Lancaster House Conference in London a schedule for independence was set. Tom Mboya who was a great leader headed the Kenyan delegation.

Jomo Kenyatta (Mzee) was released from prison in August of 1961. He became President of the Kenyan African National Union (KANU). On June 1, 1963 Mzee Kenyatta, a true son of Africa whose grandfather was a medicine man, became the first Prime Minister of a self-governing Kenya. Five months later during an exuberant celebration the world's leaders mingled with tribal people as Kenya's flag was unfurled.

A new nation was born, a new republic within the Commonwealth. Kenyatta, not long ago considered a criminal, became President.

He was a visionary who enjoyed worldwide respect. During his leadership Kenya achieved political stability, or so it seemed from the outside looking in. The truth was that internal tribalism and senseless political violence did continue. Tom Mboya, Kenyatta's rival, was assassinated. Mboya had a dream for Pan-Africanism, a single unified African Nation, but that dream never came to pass.

*

I was on the outside looking in and what I saw were advances being made toward economic progress as well as education. "Kenya is an example of possibilities for other African nations," I said to anyone who would listen. "Only the right black leadership has to get elected. And for the Congo that's Thomas Kanza."

During the last years I had devoted much of my energy to the fight against South Africa's apartheid system. I hoped that Kenyatta's success foreshadowed victory for Mandela.

The South African author Alan Paton's book *Cry the Beloved Country* had just won the Nobel Peace Prize. The book depicted an interracial love relationship for which the punishment was death. I was very proud that I had married a black man--any black man--had given birth to a black child and

248

was a living protest against such inhuman laws.

Now I was in Kenya, on African soil, and would soon be in the presence of Kenyatta himself. His private secretary Nanette picked me up at the airport; she was a proud intelligent woman educated at Oxford University. We formed an instant sisterhood in the back of the limousine that delivered us to the presidential residence.

Nanette knew all about Hugh's arrest in the Congo from her boss who was in touch with Thomas Kanza. "I'm thrilled to pass through your country on my way to Tschombe and the Congo," I said.

"We'll see. Tell me why did Hugh come to Africa?"

I was not sure how to answer. There would be no help from Kenya's president if he knew the real Hugh Scotland.

"My husband and I are deeply involved in the just fight for the Congo's freedom. Hugh did important, undercover work for Thomas."

"Thomas assured us that he knows you well. We can trust you."

"That makes me happy." Thomas had never expressed this to me. I felt elated.

When we arrived at Kenyatta's home on the outskirts of Nairobi, it was midmorning and a festival was in progress. The clear blue sky and lush grounds hurt my eyes and the heat was humid and sticky. A colorful collection of tribes in their garb performed music and dance. The President, seated with his family on the mansion's veranda, clearly enjoyed the gay spectacle.

"It's Baba Wa Taifa's birthday," Nanette said.

"Baba Wa ....?"

"Baba Wa Taifa means Father of the Nation. You tired?"

"Not a bit."

"Let's join in."

"I feel out of place in this London business suit. I didn't bring anything suitable to wear."

"Relax." Nanette took me to her suite of offices and handed me one of her crisp batik outfits. "It's handmade in Gatundu, Jomo's hometown. Colors look good on you, try it on."

"Now I'm real," I said, dressed in my African costume.

"Muendelee na moyo huo huo."

"Moyo huo," I replied. "I don't know what it means but I would love to learn Swahili."

"It means that you got the spirit."

*

Kenyatta was very tall and distinguished. In his mid sixties, his hair was gray; his skin was shiny and smooth. I was drawn to his kind, intelligent eyes and told myself that he knows much because he has suffered. His clothing was casual, white trousers, short-sleeved blue shirt open at the neck and sandals.

"He looks European," I said to Nanette.

"And you look African." We laughed. Kenyatta carried a large white, flowing fly whisk in his right hand which he swung around with exuberance.

"Baba, Mrs. Scotland," Nanette introduced me to the President.

"I see. Welcome to Kenya. Let's go inside. You must be hot."

"Baba, Baba," the crowd shouted and waved. Kenyatta waved back. Nanette and I followed him into the cool residence. Over lunch, just the three of us, he came straight to the point.

"Thomas and I talked."

"Is Thomas in Nairobi?"

"Your husband's predicament is difficult."

"That is why I am here."

"You can count on my help, Mrs. Scotland."

"Thank you, Mr. President. May I ask where Thomas is? When will I see him?"

"The Congo's problems are huge, especially now with my friend Tschombe back in power."

"Friend?"

Kenyatta laughed. "You have children?"

"A son, Thomas is his godfather."

"Let's see. You are smart and well-informed."

"What's your advice, Mr. President?"

"Get world-wide attention. The press will love it. Beautiful, young white woman fights Moishe Tschombe, the ugliest black bully in Africa."

Nanette looked as surprised as I was.

"That's quite a contrast," she said.

"Right," Kenyatta chuckled.

I was beginning to feel uneasy. "I need to consult with Thomas."

"First things first, you need to rest," Nanette said. "Jomo, I'm taking Liza over to my house!"

*

When I woke up jet-lagged, many conflicting thoughts were in my head. I wasn't sure what plans were being hatched for me. During the day my proposed mission became clearer. Nanette explained: "First get and then keep your husband's imprisonment in the public eye."

"How?"

"Become a focal point for the International press."

"Me?"

"Tschombe's dictatorship, attest to it."

"That's no problem!"

"If Hugh disappears overnight Tschombe looks worse."

"I could say Hugh's an innocent impresario from England."

"Isn't that what he is?"

"There's more to it."

"Journalist, family man, show business, stick with it."

"Show business in the Congo?" We both laughed.

*

252

In Kenya different races seemed to have learned to live in harmony. Kenyatta, now married to an African, was married before to an English woman and he had white advisors. International journalists and embassy staff were stationed in Nairobi and affluent white tourists enjoyed safaris through the Serengeti National Park and Game Reserve.

After several days I still had not been contacted by Thomas and meanwhile I was eager to leave the Nairobi metropolis and travel inland.

"Unspoiled Africa, Nanette. That's what I would like to experience. I'm not a tourist."

"There's still a lot of poverty. I will get the driver to take us for a trip," Nanette said.

We traveled for hours over expansive land and visited a number of small villages and hamlets. My white face was a rarity. Naked, big-bellied children only ventured from behind their mothers to touch me after Nanette spoke to them in their native tongue. I felt connection and deep love.

"Infant mortality's rampant in these parts," Nanette said.

"Why?'

"Why? Big businesses! You know Cow and Gate?"

"Yes, of course. The largest British Baby food manufacturer, what are they doing to help?"

"Help? They sure found their way into this remote bush."

"Good."

"Not good, wolves in sheep's clothing. African mothers stop breast feeding their infants. Bottles with formula instead of mother's milk which has all the antibodies against disease."

"That's outrageous. I breastfed my son."

"The promises were bigger and healthier children. Now the babies are dead."

"Feeding bottles need to be sterilized."

"Right, that compounded the problem."

*

Now I was eager and impatient to become a spokesperson. I had not come to Africa to enjoy myself. There was work for me and I was just waiting for final instructions from Thomas. "Are you sure Thomas knows I'm here?" I asked Nanette again.

"He knows."

"When will I see him?"

"Soon, maybe even today."

When he walked into the kitchen I was dressed in my African caftan cooking Masai tribal food. But was that him? I looked twice.

The man in front of me was out of breath, haggard and dressed in a stained tee shirt and jeans. "Thomas?" I threw myself into his arms. "What happened to your Bond Street suits?"

"You have acclimatized, I see. Nanette's twin, ha?"

"Dinner's ready."

"Smells great, haven't eaten all day." Thomas sounded the same, but he was no longer the composed ex-ambassador who had left England just a few weeks before. I could feel his nervousness. He looked around and then he pinned his eyes on the door.

"Excuse me," Nanette said. "You two have to talk. I'll be back later."

Thomas and I sat opposite each other in Nanette's kitchen. I served him a steaming plate of rice and fish stew.

"You are not hungry, Liza?"

"Remember I made you stew in London?"

"Those were the days, your famous stew. Africa's a different world."

"Are you glad to be home?"

"Home's the Congo." His face darkened.

"You're safe here."

"Nowhere am I safe anymore."

"It's the waiting and inactivity that's driving me crazy. I'm eager to do what it takes to help the Congo and Hugh," I said.

"In that order?"

"Okay, Hugh and the Congo. Take me there."

Thomas smiled. "I have something else in mind for you."

He outlined the plan. I was to speak out in public and get press attention for Hugh and Thomas' cause, which was to overthrow Tschombe. Thomas did not say as much, but Hugh was an unfortunate minor player. In the scheme of fast moving African politics, he might have been forgotten and abandoned. He would never be African and one of their own. Thomas did

255

not have to spell it out and on this same evening, after dinner, he disappeared again.

There was now a link to be made between millions of empty bellies, a plundered nation and the black Englishman who languished in a Leopoldville jail. I was that link and needed to string it together into one and the same web of injustices committed by the same man.

I was tongue-tied at the beginning of my first radio broadcast, but as the studio interview in Nairobi progressed I became more articulate. My short answers to questions turned into longer explanations and ended with passionate commentary from my heart: "The Congo's leader Moische Tschombe has millions of victims. Patrice Lumumba. My husband, a black businessman, is completely innocent. Tschombe himself is the criminal and murderer. He committed treason and is a puppet of Belgian imperialists. Stand and fight to depose Tschombe."

When I was finished I held the microphone and raised my voice: "Long live a free Congo! Long live a free Africa!"

The interviewer looked at Nanette, who waited in the wings. What had happened to me? What had I said? I was unaccustomed to public speaking. And my accent? I loathed the way I spoke. When I got excited my voice got away and seemed to play tricks on me by getting more German. My telltale Germanic accent! I hated myself when I spoke that way.

"Great fiery speech." Nanette put my mind at ease. "Let's see what happens next."

Again we had lunch with Kenyatta and he too praised my effort. "Call me Jomo, Liza," he said.

A couple of press interviews were arranged for

international journalists, after which Thomas showed up again and told me to return to London and duplicate my media efforts in England.

"Tschombe knows about you now. Makes Hugh more secure and you less safe," he said. But I didn't fear danger and the threat of Tschombe's possible revenge somehow excited me.

When I arrived back in London, family friend George Browne picked me up at Heathrow airport. His genuine concern seemed stronger than the concern I had for myself.

After a quick, precious reunion with my son I got to work with media interviews.

The more I opened myself to speak to newspapers, radio and television the easier it became. I knew my cause was just and not self-serving. Tschombe was in the way of the Congo's independence. Hugh's imprisonment was political, and the fact he was accused of treason worked in our favor. I pointed out that it was an act of vengeance against Thomas Kanza who was our friend and the most capable person for new Congo leadership.

I also learned quickly that reporters from different newspapers slanted my words to suit their own agendas. This was dangerous and infuriated me. A single word could be misconstrued and harm our cause.

Although generally I found the British media to be fair, I developed special relationships with certain reporters, who captured my fervent words the best and seemed to care the most and who were best informed about the urgency of the African struggle.

I was unrelenting and time and time again I mentioned

257

the murder of Patrice Lumumba and identified Tschombe as his killer.

Chapter 44

No Time to Waste

IN GERMANY REPORTS of my political activities reached the people I had left behind. Fritz called to say Mother and the rest of the family were concerned. My picture had appeared in the *Bildzeitung*, a German tabloid. The headlines read: "White woman fights like a tigress for her black husband."

"True," I said. That is what I am doing and a whole lot more."

"Mother grieves for you. You know how old she is. And your safety! Don't you think it's time to come back to Germany?"

"Germany? Why? I've long given up being German."

"I can't help you. Sister, you're on your own." The line went dead.

*

A few days later a letter from Wolfgang arrived. The envelope showed he was now Dr. Wolfgang Ligges, Attorney-at-Law. My heart pounded. I opened it slowly and read: "My Beloved." His words were gracious and forgiving. He still thought of me and missed me which was a comfort.

259

I had managed to live without romantic love for some time now. I loved my son and I loved the African people. The feelings Wolfgang and I had shared could no longer reach me, and I was not sure if they had ever been the right and enduring kind. For now I couldn't allow them to stand in the way of what my focus needed to be.

Wolfgang's understanding, however, was important to me. Maybe destiny would one day prove that our bond had not been fleeting and shallow. He was in the past and maybe in the future, but it was the present I had to be concerned with.

I wrote him back a letter that I hoped would hold the door open for a continuing relationship:

"My first and not forgotten Love! Your letter meant the world to me. So much has happened since Heidelberg. I am grateful you found it in your heart to forgive me. I have not had an easy time and live a life of constant worry. A never-ending stream of unfortunate events has me wonder if I will ever find peace. I can't turn back. I must explore where my path will lead. I have a son now, a beautiful boy who is my life. The time we had together was too short and our caresses did not encompass what is in our hearts and thoughts. I don't know the viewpoints you hold dear regarding the world and our country. You may not agree with my fundamental convictions in which case we would not have had a future together anyway. By leaving I may have saved us both a lot of sorrow. My son is black, as is his father, who is now a prisoner in the Congo. I work hard to help set him free. I have also fallen in love with the African continent and its people. They have become my people and there is a lot of work to be done to set them free. Tomorrow I'll return to Nairobi and you will be in my thoughts. Congratulations, Herr Doctor Ligges. I am sure your

260

future will be bright, successful and happy. Is there someone new and special in your life? Let's not bemoan the past, but look forward to a lifelong friendship and please let me hear from you as often as possible. Your letters are a great comfort. I will keep you informed about the outcome of my mission in the Congo. With much Love, Liza (My name is now Liza Scotland. I have outgrown Liesel which is a small and silly name and should only be given to cows with bells around their necks.)"

At the airport I mailed the letter. Thomas had just called me back to Nairobi after only a week. My son received tender competent care from Jeanette, who carried him like an African child on her back wrapped in a Congolese shawl and the sight delighted me.

*

Africa consumed my thoughts day and night. I found it hard to be objective. Everything African seemed to be better, more beautiful and for the world to emulate: respect of elders and ancestors; families living together in harmony without jealousies; children cared for by the entire community; art, music, culture. It all was so exciting.

I opposed any kind of missionary work. The white man had no right to force his religion and culture on anyone. White religion was not better than the beliefs held in the African bush. And I despised leaders like Tschombe who had sold out their people.

Thomas, who met me again in Kenya, had been appointed foreign minister of the insurgent forces in the Congo. The rebels were led by a man called Christophe Gbenye.

Since very little was known about these rebels, Thomas

261

made it my job to get the word out that they were legitimate, on the right track and gaining support and strength.

I took notes and on my return to London repeated to the media word for word what Thomas had told me.

More reporters started to besiege me and I held press conferences in our living room on Green Street. There was much uncaring ignorance about that part of Africa and the reason for the civil war waged in the Congo. Even in Nairobi I encountered journalists who regretted independence. "Kenya has done better under the British."

I spoke to reporters from my heart and with passion. Several times my picture and quotes were on the front pages of London newspapers. The message got out and that was important.

Hugh was alive though not well. A British reporter had been allowed to check on his grim condition in his Leopoldville prison cell.

Thomas informed me on the phone that the United Nations were now backing Tschombe.

"No time to waste," he said. "There will be a massive rebel attack for control of Stanleyville. The world needs to understand that we have our people's support."

"So your forces are ready to fight? What can I do?"

"Keep representing our case. We trust you, the only white as a matter of fact."

"Thanks."

"Intensify your efforts."

"Can I come and see what's going on? Help me

262

understand, Thomas."

*

Thomas agreed and a couple of days later I would be on my way again. However, I had a sudden premonition of impending disaster. What would happen to my child if I didn't return and Hugh also perished? Would my brother Fritz step forward to claim his nephew? I called him.

"Fritz, please, can you meet me tomorrow at Frankfurt airport? I have a couple hours layover and an urgent matter to discuss with you."

"What's going on? You just gave me the brush-off."

"It's really important. Please!"

"I'll see what I can do."

The moment I entered the terminal I heard the loudspeaker announcement: "Mrs. Scotland, passenger in transit for Nairobi, please proceed through passport control to the domestic lounge where your party is waiting."

Chapter 45

Heart of Stone

I RUSHED TO greet my older brother. He still cared about me and he would agree to love and care for his nephew if something should happen to me.

Wrong, it was Mother, not Fritz, who waited for me. I spotted her right away. Her eyesight was poor; she didn't see me yet. I stopped dead in my tracks.

She had aged a lot. Her hair was now snow-white, covered by a familiar dark green felt hat with a feather at the back. Under her open, moss green Lodenmantel she wore a two-piece suit I remembered. Far from new it was meticulously well kept as was the silk scarf around her neck and the polished-to-a-shine leather purse on her arm. This was the same outfit she had worn when I was fourteen and she saw me off to boarding school. Mother didn't discard anything that had good wear left in it and she was oblivious to fashion trends.

Just to see her made me feel anxious and uncomfortable. She must have left Wallmerod at dawn and traveled for hours by train and bus to meet my plane on time. How could Fritz do this to me? I should turn on my heels and disappear back into the secured part of the airport, but it was too late. She saw me and waved.

"There is my daughter, the world traveler!" She said

loudly.

Everyone around us heard her and looked at me. I felt obligated to embrace my mother who had not seen her daughter in years. I was a mother myself now. But what was wrong with me? I stiffened when she hugged me and was unable to show any kind of warmth to match her excitement at this mother-daughter reunion. To me it was unexpected and unwelcome.

I felt hot and torn, embarrassed at myself. I denied the person who gave birth to me, had dearly wanted, loved and nurtured me as her Wunschkind through childhood and sacrificed for me during a time of war. Deep inside I knew my reaction was abnormal and should not be what it was.

But the hard shell around me was for my protection and allowed me to hide. Mother had committed the unforgivable. She had never shown remorse. To show her any kind of affection would be to condone who she was. I had not forgotten nor forgiven. Many years before I had vowed never to call her Mother again. I had not faltered.

This unfortunate, public airport encounter had to be brought to an end as soon as possible. I looked at my watch. "Hello, you shouldn't have come. My plane leaves shortly. I can't miss it. I've important work in Africa."

"A few minutes with your mother after all this time is not important?" A single tear trickled down her cheek which she wiped quickly with her white handkerchief.

"Can you give me just a minute, Liebling?"

She took hold of my arm and led me to an empty spot on a bench where we seated ourselves and faced each other. I sat on the edge, prepared to jump up at any moment. She opened her purse and took out a small package.

"I want my grandson to have this from his grandmother. What's his name?"

"Hugh." I felt myself soften and smile at the mention of my son.

"Hag....? What kind of name is that?"

There it was again; her criticism of me for something as simple as my child's name.

I spelled it out for her. "H U G H. Happens to be a distinguished English name."

"For H-u-g-h, hard to pronounce, sorry, I don't speak English."

I held the small box on my lap and stared at the wrapper. I contemplated for a moment what the meaning of this gift might be. Was it acceptance of her black grandson? Acceptance of my path?

I felt the urge to hug her and call her Mother again, but the moment passed. All I managed was cold formality.

"Thank you. This wasn't necessary. My son has everything he needs."

"He doesn't have this. It's your silver baby spoon with your name engraved in it. You were such a precious child. I'm sure he is too."

"My son is beautiful. Thank you." I did not look at her. "Please take care of yourself," I said and stood up.

"And you too."

She rose and after a brief, awkward moment we turned away from each other. I walked fast, back to my plane that

266

would take me far away from this place of sorrow.

By the time I landed at the now familiar Nairobi airport and plunged back into the hurly-burly of Africa, the quiet elderly German lady was far from my mind.

Chapter 46

The African

Two men escorted me to a small twin-engine propeller plane. Thomas was already on board, and as soon as I was strapped into my seat we took off.

"Finally," I said. "Finally, I'm worthy of seeing the Congo. I can hardly wait."

Thomas smiled.

After we landed I was no longer joking or smiling.

"Oh, my God," I said. "Look at them."

Thousands of warriors emerged silently from the forests that bordered the Congo River. Bands of children, not even ten. Others were wide-eyed teenagers with warrior tribal markings on their faces and bodies. A few of them had ill-fitting uniforms and looked like scarecrows. Most wore nothing more than a loincloth. They carried spears, machetes, some guns and a few automatic rifles.

"That's a badly equipped army," I said, trembling. "Thomas, they have barely begun life and now you are asking them to face death?"

"Be positive," Thomas said. "I'm very proud of their determination. We will win and they will be the heroes."

"They're boys."

Thomas shook his head and signaled dismissal. As silently as the fighters had appeared they vanished back into the jungle. Thomas changed the subject. He pointed to thatched huts across the river.

"Look, a medical compound run by missionaries. Our eyes are on it."

"Why?"

"Mostly whites, an American doctor Carlson is in charge. They look to be harmless."

"American? Are you sure? So close to your forces?"

"Look who's talking," Thomas said.

"That's different. I'm one of you, and I hope you'll never forget."

"You won't let me."

"Right."

*

During my short stay I did not have a chance to see Gbenye who Thomas said had taken on the mantle of Lumumba. "He's elusive and careful to the extreme. Even I don't know where he is right now."

"I hope to meet him when I come back," I said.

"Yes, hopefully soon," Thomas replied.

*

After I returned to London two days later I woke up to newspaper headlines: "Hostages in the Congo!"

The pathetic rebel forces had managed to gain control of Stanleyville. They had taken hostage all the whites from the medical compound of the American doctor. I was dumbfounded.

Soon the phone began to ring off the hook. Every newspaper in England wanted my comments. Who were these rebels? I was their spokesperson. What did they want? The tone of the reporters was accusatory.

"Tschombe has U.N. backing," a reporter from the *Daily Telegraph* said. "The world's outraged. Immediate international help for the doctor and the other Americans has been called for."

I was out of my depth. "Exaggeration," I said. "I just saw Thomas Kanza. He showed no ill will towards the doctor. No one will be harmed." After that I stopped answering the phone and I told Jeanette to take messages.

"You want this call," she said. She handed me the receiver during the first chaotic morning. "It's Thomas." I grabbed the phone.

"Stay calm," was the first thing he said.

"Stay calm? How can anyone stay calm? You have no idea how the press is hounding me."

"I'm sorry you had to get involved."

"Sorry? How can you justify hostage taking?" For the first time I was angry with the man. Until today I had blindly supported him.

"We finally have the world's attention," he said. "Don't we, Liza?"

"Wrong attention."

"No one wanted to deal with us. We pleaded long enough."

"You lose credibility."

"Liza, you know what Tschombe has done and keeps on doing every day. Why are thousands of African lives less worth fighting for than a few American lives?"

"Thomas, you know that's not what I believe."

"Well, if you're still committed to our cause you need to get it over to the press. Don't give up on us now, Liza. We need you more than ever."

"You promise Dr. Carlson and his people will not be harmed?"

"No harm will come to them as long as we are not attacked. No American paratroopers! No outside interference!"

*

Jeanette called all the London papers to schedule a press conference for that evening, once again in our living room. Every paper showed up. I faced the reporters and cameras alone in defense of a cause that had become dangerous and messy.

The media questions came fast and furious: "How can you condone hostage taking? Who's responsible if the hostages are killed? Are you aware that Dr. Carlson was on a humanitarian mission to help the very people who are now threatening his life?"

My answers were simple and honest. "No, I don't condone hostage taking. Opportunities were missed which could have avoided this. Thomas is a cultured, nonviolent man who has been forced into this desperate position to help his suffering nation. It's a struggle for freedom of the Congolese people."

"The Congo has black leadership."

"Tschombe was not democratically elected. He employs mercenaries--soldiers for hire--pays them fifty pounds a week, men like the ruthless Irishman "Mad Mike.""

There had already been reports written about Major Michael Hoare, notorious for his cruelty. He had been seen with human heads hanging as trophies on his vehicles.

"Does Europe and America condone Mad Mike? Do we expect a caring man like Thomas Kanza to stand idly by? My message from Thomas Kanza is this: no harm will come to the hostages as long as no paratroopers land in Stanleyville. There is no need for a rescue mission. Negotiations are in progress with President Kenyatta as mediator."

The rebels led by Gbenye who turned out to be a fanatic and Thomas Kanza, a diplomat with no fighting experience had no real chance against the well-equipped, ruthless enemy. Tschombe had unlimited resources as well as backing from abroad.

Africa was waking from its slumber and violence was pervasive. Why was it so unthinkable to have a band of rebels use the same strategy that had kept them down? It had worked for their oppressors.

*

Belgian and American troops launched their massive attack on Stanleyville on November 24, 1964 and named it Red

272

Dragon.

There was no warning and the assault descended from the sky at dusk--deafening sounds of aircraft followed by an onslaught of paratroopers. Many of the boy rebels ran back into the bush. Eyewitness reports spoke of utter chaos and no resistance. People, white and black alike, dashed for shelter from bullets and hand grenades. Hostages and their captors all ran together for their lives.

In the chaos no one knew who shot Dr. Paul Carlson. He was killed in the crossfire and so were most of the other hostages. Piles of bodies lay in Lumumba Square, too many to count.

Tschombe took control of Stanleyville and the rest of the Congo, which had been his goal all along.

I had been a naïve pawn. I never again heard from my son's godfather, the man who loved his country more than his life, Thomas Kanza, and I presumed he was killed.

Chapter 47

Stone for his Pillow

TOO MANY INNOCENT lives had been lost. What should I do now with my own? Self incriminating questions robbed me of sleep. Had it been right to support the Congolese rebels? Should I have begged Thomas to wait for a peaceful solution? He would not have listened. The massacre had been a betrayal of my faith in Thomas who had promised me that the hostages would not be harmed.

My paradigm changed. Violence did not solve anything. I could not decide which side had been right. Would the outcome have been different if Thomas had not taken such desperate measures? Had America acted before all other options were explored? In the end everyone but Tschombe lost and evil seemed to have triumphed.

To make me feel worse I received another letter from Wolfgang. He had gotten married. His wife's name was Brigitte and she was a teacher. I reasoned that I could not have expected a different outcome, but my heart still felt disappointment. Our love connection was now forever gone. I managed to send him congratulations and good wishes.

*

There was still my responsibility to my own husband. Hugh had been part of the big picture. He was one of many held prisoner in the Congo. I had been ineffective in my efforts to help save the nation from a dictator. Now I was running out of time trying to save one man.

New hope came through the influential human rights organization, Amnesty International. They had experience at freeing political prisoners, and when they contacted me I was grateful for their help. I also appreciated that the British press had not abandoned me.

Tschombe was on his way to England and Germany where he would meet the Rhein Ruhr Club, a group of steel and coal millionaires, to secure a loan for the Congo. I was sure these German millionaires, for whom I felt disdain, were not prepared to loan money for altruistic reasons. Crooks deserved each other as far as I was concerned.

I had befriended a reporter from the London *Daily Express*. In exchange for an exclusive cover story his paper offered to set up and pay for my travel to force a confrontation between Tschombe and myself.

I knew that Hugh was now held at the Binza maximum-security prison outside Leopoldville and that he had been beaten. The press confirmed that he would soon be executed for treason.

Whenever and wherever Tschombe landed in Europe, Amnesty International and I were there to demonstrate. I was happy to be part of a grass root effort again and I stood at Heathrow with my sign: "Tschombe murdered Lumumba." My fellow demonstrators shouted: "Free Hugh Scotland."

When Tschombe spent one night at the Savoy Hotel in London, I tried to speak with him, but I was sent away by his bodyguards.

The *Daily Express* booked me on the same Lufthansa flight as Tschombe the next day. He and his entourage occupied the whole first Class section. The reporter and I sat in coach. Via the stewardess I sent a note. "Hugh Scotland is innocent. Please talk to me about his release."

The reply was short. "Come to the Congo. We can talk there." I figured this was a trap, but I also didn't dismiss the possibility that I might take him up on it.

Amnesty International and I held more loud demonstrations in Bonn and Berlin. I showed up in the lobbies of every hotel where he stayed and created unfavorable publicity for him. We made a mighty noise, but the bully was a coward. He remained adamant that he would only speak to me in Leopoldville.

His loan was denied. German industrialists did not want to be seen in association with a dictator. They had become sensitive to world opinion. Our demonstrations made them aware that Tschombe could turn to be a liability. Grassroots efforts could be powerful and they worked.

*

Hugh's old client, George Browne, was still my good friend. He was genuine and cared about Hugh, my son and me. After I returned from my trip I reported to him that I had Tschombe's invitation to the Congo.

"What do you think? Is it a trap to silence me?"

I looked to George for an answer. Besides his talents as an entertainer he was a student of many different religions and philosophies like Zen Buddhism and the Tao. I was interested to hear if he considered it my responsibility to give in to a man who had power over Hugh's life.

George had never married. He was in a longstanding relationship with a former English fashion model whom he had met in Paris. We had never discussed our personal feelings.

"You're a very special person," he said. His face was serious. "And you have an unusual sense of responsibility."

"I have to do everything I can for Hugh. He is my son's father, and I owe him a great deal. If it helps, I'll be the pawn."

"Don't go to the Congo. I don't want you to." He looked at me, and I stared back into his eyes. What I saw there was something I had never expected from a man who seemed to be more of the spirit than of the flesh--the longing that came from passionate love.

He stretched out his hand to me and I took it. Then he opened his arms, and I fell into them. He offered his lips, and when they met mine, nothing else in the world mattered.

Unbeknownst to me a true love had waited patiently, but could now no longer remain in chains. True love was bigger than the two of us. It could not be held back by thoughts of convention, feelings of responsibility or guilt. True love was unchained in this instance and had to be free.

*

The next few days were utter bliss. For the first time I felt the warmth and intimacy of unconditional love. It gave my life new meaning and direction. I could not get enough of George's words that told me I was loved. For a few days we did not think of anything else, but each other.

The fate of Hugh Scotland still loomed like a huge cloud over our happiness. George was a moral man. Hugh was his friend, and his friend's life was at stake. Together now we increased our efforts to get Hugh released, especially through the British Foreign Office.

Tschombe did not want to lose face and give Hugh his freedom outright. During a visit from the Red Cross his guards turned a blind eye, and Hugh was spirited away by a couple of British agents. At night they crossed the border into Rwanda. Hugh was free and after a debriefing would be back in London in a matter of days.

George and I did not communicate to each other our discomfort that we would have to discontinue our love relationship. It had become so vital to both of us, but was inappropriate and selfish in the light of Hugh's homecoming. Hugh had just been snatched from death's door.

George provided me his limousine service to pick Hugh up from Heathrow, and then he went out of town. The press had gathered at the airport in force, and we waited for Hugh's exit through immigration to welcome him home.

He looked different. His hair was curly, and he was a lot thinner, which was not a bad thing. I thought of what he had been through and felt my heart go out to him. The crowd cheered when we embraced. Hugh was startled at first by the commotion. I thanked the press for their unwavering support.

Then something came over Hugh. "Do you all see this spot on my jacket? Do you realize what that is? It's dried blood. They beat the hell out of me and tortured me and made me sleep on the floor with nothing but a stone for my pillow."

I wanted to sink into a hole. Hugh focused with self-pity on his suffering rather than on his salvation.

The reporters, one by one, closed down their microphones and disappeared. The television evening news only mentioned briefly that Hugh Scotland was now free.

I remembered an African proverb: "A bitter heart devours its owner."

The wheels of justice and love turn slowly. Many years later when my boy was a man he made contact with his father. The dreamer and opportunist Hugh Senior had found his way into the United Nations where he worked for many years at I don't know what. When son and father encountered each other there was a feeling of mutual discomfort.

Afflicted with dementia Hugh died in the 1980s. He spent his last years destitute and institutionalized in New York City and still held on to a faded picture of a tall, blond woman who he insisted would one day come back to him.

*

The press had kept an eye on mercenary "Mad Mike" Hoare and he had no peace when he returned to Ireland. He was eventually put on trial in The Hague and I gave damning testimony against him to the Belgian attorneys who represented the people of Zaire, the former Congo.

Moishe Tschombe's days of glory were numbered and justice caught up with him in an unusual way. He fled the Congo and his plane was forced to land in Morocco, just as Lumumba's plane had been forced down from the sky by Tschombe's men.

In Morocco Tschombe was held in jail while he awaited extradition to whichever country wanted to put him on trial for crimes against humanity. He used his ill-gotten wealth stashed in European banks to have food delivered to his cell. He so gorged himself and swelled to enormous proportions until he ate himself to death.

Chapter 48

Respectability

IN THE NEXT twenty years I became a respectable mother, housewife and entrepreneur.

I had divorced Hugh and in London the interracial union between George and me was no longer controversial. We mixed in affluent circles and life in a tree-lined suburb of London was satisfying and comfortable. The intense struggles of my younger years gave way to settling down.

I still cared about South Africa since apartheid had not been abolished, but I watched from my armchair in my designer living room how things took care of themselves and did not need me. Majority rule was eventually won not by violence, but by something more powerful--the strength of soul stirring music.

The proponents of apartheid were scared stiff in their white skins when they could not escape the beat of drums and the chanting from dawn to dusk. A long suffering nation raised their voices in unison until Mandela was free and could lead his people in the direction of self-rule and dignity.

I took my son to his school, swimming lessons and soccer games. I made gourmet pizzas and let the dough rise twice just as it said in the recipe. I presided as hostess over elegant dinner parties. A fashion model, doctors, lawyers and a judge as well as educators and an Anglican minister who had himself married a charming black woman were regular guests.

I smiled to myself at the realization that I had almost become like Mother in spite of myself.

In 1970 our daughter Annette Liesel was born. Romance still bloomed and George recorded a song for me: "Put a ring around your finger, put a chain around your heart. Our love will live and linger, Darling, we will never part."

My husband was successful with his unique style of calypso music as well as his own compositions. He performed with greats like Cleo Lane, John Dankworth and Elizabeth Welch and joined The National Theater at the "Old Vic." We owned a three-storey Victorian house with five spacious bedrooms. I had changed my name back to Liesel at George's request. He thought it sounded more melodic, and I was now known as Liesel Browne.

George was my best friend, lover and confidant. I shared many things with him. Never though did I reach deep enough to bring back my hidden secrets. Every once in a while I would relate the story of how my hero father had opposed Hitler and saved a Jewish neighbor's son. As a family we befriended people from around the world, but no Jews.

*

During these years I decided to reestablish some kind of truth with Germany. Dr. Wolfgang Ligges was not forgotten and I found him through the Lawyer's Association. We visited the Ligges country home and he, his wife and two lovely daughters came to stay with us in England. Wolfgang and I both knew how to keep secrets and it was an unspoken agreement between us that our lover's past would never be

281

brought up. His wife Brigitte was a better wife than I could ever have been for the man I had once loved and almost married.

George, the children and I, vacationed all over Europe, North Africa and Hawaii. A few times we briefly stopped to see the children's grandmother, who always welcomed us. However, my relationship with my mother remained cold and painful to both of us. My homeland did not seem to have changed and I never stayed long enough to investigate. My mind was made up. Germany was the most sinister place in the world; I was always relieved to depart.

Ingrid Neul had settled down with a banker husband, had no children and none were planned. She spoiled her dachshund.

Fritz and I were always distant, in miles as well as in spirit. He was a man who had been old enough to know the Nazi era and had fought a war that represented the opposite of everything I held dear. He was wrong and I was right, so there could be no common ground between us. I had forgotten the times when Fritz had argued with Father and listened to the BBC and that I really had no evidence of how much of a Nazi he really was. All I thought about was that he did not defend me or the Jewish neighbor who came to our house in 1951. Therefore my brother remained an enigma.

Fritz never returned to his love, the sea. He retired on a government pension which met his needs, and after he divorced Anna found a soul mate to share his later days.

I had been burnt in Africa. Respectability and prosperity was what mattered to me now, and I had found both in my chosen country, the great Great Britain.

My little daughter Annette was a ray of sunshine with her stand-up-comic sense of humor. Even when she was diagnosed with a life threatening kidney disease, her fighting spirit and joyful nature prevailed and she recovered from major surgery in no time.

Of the two children, Hugh Jr. was lighter skinned and could be mistaken for Mediterranean. Annette was blessed with her father's DNA and darker skin although her eyes were green, which added to her special beauty.

My children's growing years were unencumbered by problems. Only once was I made aware of the hurt which can be caused to a child by prejudice based on the color of one's skin.

During her first year in school Annette's heart was set on playing an angel in the Christmas Nativity show. We called her our little angel, but her teacher said "angels are white and blond. You'll be a shepherd instead."

This unfortunate typecasting of first graders was never forgotten--not by Annette and not by me. It left a wound with a thin scab that could be made to bleed and fester at any time.

*

I contributed to our family's financial success and taught English to foreign students for a while. In 1977, at age 36, I ventured into opening a business of my own. We called our health food restaurant on Welbeck Street in the heart of London, "Liesel's Apple."

Many hours of hard work were required. Mother had sent me to boarding school, and I did the same with my daughter. The reasons may have been different, but we were both mothers who wanted the best for our daughters. I remembered the problems I caused my mother. Annette was still sweet and there was no reason to foresee difficulties in the future.

Hugh Jr., who was 16, would soon choose a profession that would take him to his own prosperity and success. George's creativity earned him an excellent income and there were composition royalties and a book of West Indian stories. We worked hard and reaped the rewards.

*

I should have been satisfied to spend the rest of my days in England's green and pleasant land, gathered outside Buckingham Palace for the Queen's birthday celebrations every June, one of her loyal and grateful subjects. I would have had the security of home ownership, a generous British pension, good friends, neighbors and eventually grandchildren's visits.

Why do we humans get restless when things go well? Why do we fathom disconnecting ourselves from the security of the known in exchange for the ruinous whims of an unknown fate? Only our souls know, and if we find the answer, we are fortunate enough to have found ourselves.

Chapter 49

Wanderlust

SINCE MY DAYS of African involvement and the killings in Stanleyville I did not hold the United States in particularly high regard. None of us did. Britain seemed much more humanitarian, manageable and quaint. America, the all powerful, was regarded as a bully.

It was the weather at first. "Oh, if we could only move to a sunnier climate." Then the annoying parking fines which filled the boot (trunk) of my Volvo. Every day when I unloaded supplies for the restaurant and double parked just for a second, a meter maid sprang out from nowhere and slapped a ticket on my car. I was convinced she had it in for me.

The congestion of central London, the stress of the business, the fog and grime all began to wear on me. We were in a rut, and I looked to do something about it in a big and permanent way.

We explored a move to sunny Spain where we had been on holiday many times, but we dismissed the idea because of the language barrier.

Our restaurant catered to a lunchtime crowd of business people, and one regular was a solicitor who showed up with a gorgeous tan one day. "Where did you vacation?" I asked.

He had not been to one of the conventional holiday

spots for British people--the Greek islands, Italy, Majorca, Spain, but to a more wondrous location, less common and farther a field.

"My wife and I just returned from Palm Beach, Florida. We love it there and have purchased a home."

The next day he brought in brochures and photographs to show off. What I saw I wanted for myself and my family. Sprawling homes with Mediterranean-style swimming pools, a sky and ocean as clear and blue as the senses could imagine, palms and sandy beaches, in one word--paradise.

I could no longer rest. My psyche had embraced a picture of heaven and I had to find a way to lead my family out of darkness into the abundant light and stunning beauty of the place where we truly belonged, Palm Beach, Florida.

I knew nothing about that part of the world, except what I had just learned from a fellow Englishman. He liked it there, and if I could see it myself and agree, I would move heaven and earth to acquire our own home under the same sunny sky.

*

A few weeks later, in the summer of 1980, I took a Pan American jet for an exploratory trip. George stayed behind in London to take care of the restaurant.

My eyes confirmed what I had imagined and much more. I had always loved the sea. This was not the windswept, frigid water of the North Sea or the familiar Mediterranean which had become congested with high-rise real estate. The air was balmy and fragrant and the Atlantic Ocean took my breath away with turquoise waters and white crested waves.

I knew I had arrived at my final destination--Shangri-la,

my promised land. To search elsewhere would be a mistake. This was where I needed to be. This was where I could forget the past and reward myself and my family with everlasting beauty. This was where we would come to rest and find a true and permanent home.

As far as I was concerned the planet belonged to everyone equally. Our wandering spirits should be allowed to settle wherever we came ashore from our nomadic homelessness. In other words, I considered living in Palm Beach our birthright.

I had no idea that this right had been claimed long ago by the richest and most socially exclusive members of a tight, genteel society and I might as well have tried to break into a medieval fortress.

George was no fool. When I returned full of promise for a better life, he said, "I don't see anything wrong with the old. America holds no special appeal."

"Wait and see," I said.

"I remember what happened to Paul Robeson and the Soledad Brothers, Florida's in the Deep South."

"How deep can the South be? It's 1980." Even if there was a remnant of the past, we were a family as normal and traditional as a slice of apple pie. No one would think twice about welcoming us as neighbors and useful contributing members of the community.

"Darling, stop living in the past," I argued my case. "The days you remember are long gone. We have nothing but a prosperous future ahead of us. And it's a better climate for Annette and her kidney problems."

I knew the issue of our daughter's health and well-being would be my trump card.

"I will think about it," George promised.

Over the next few weeks, he brought out all his objections, American education, drugs in schools and moving costs. How could we abandon our friends and the life we knew and loved?

I had a convincing answer for all of it on the tip of my tongue, until he brought out his trump card, immigration. There was no way to move to the United States, at least not anytime in the near future. Each country had quotas and only allowed a certain number of immigrants. We could go on a waiting list, but that would take an indefinite number of years. That was that, good-bye to my dream, farewell Florida.

"We'll take a vacation," George said.

Chapter 50

Good Fortune

THE *DAILY TELEGRAPH* ran a small classified ad: "Invitation - Free U.S. Immigration Seminar." The facilitator was a Palm Beach lawyer by the name of Michael Blank.

Our solicitor customer was about to relocate his family to Palm Beach with Mr. Blank's help. "Hear what Michael has to say," he said. "He can help you with immigration."

Everything fell into place without much effort irrespective of George. Palm Beach was meant to be.

I had a private consultation with attorney Michael Blank at his Regent Hotel room that same afternoon.

"Please come in," he said. I expected an older man, but took in with delight his trim figure and golden tan. He was exceptionably well attired and groomed, with black hair and a glistening smile. The phone rang and he excused himself.

"Yes, I'm going to be free shortly. Please come to the Regent Hotel, room 624. Yes. No problem, I can help you."

It was obvious that I was not the only one in need of help and advice from this handsome man with his Gucci belt and shoes to match. I shopped on Bond Street and had made purchases on Worth Avenue, Palm Beach's exclusive stretch of designer boutiques, and I knew the price tags. Everyone in

Palm Beach was beautiful and looked just like this man whose law practice had to be very successful.

The lawyer's time was valuable, so I got straight to the point. "My family and I would like to live in the United States. I have been to Palm Beach and would like to settle there."

"Excellent, you've come to the right person to make your wish come true."

He handed me his business card and told me immigration was his sole field of legal expertise. If a specific branch of advocacy existed just for immigration, there had to be many families like us.

"My law practice provides total service to settle folks into their happy new life in the Palm Beaches."

What a nice man. That's all I needed to hear.

"What about waiting lists?"

His confident smile got even brighter.

"It only takes as long as you need to be ready. No waiting lists."

"Wonderful."

"Tell me about your financial holdings, businesses, real estate, antiques, anything you may want to dispose of."

I hesitated for a moment. What if we didn't qualify? I ran through the list.

"We can sell our home and business. I recently purchased three rental properties at auction. We have some nice antique pieces, art and furniture."

"You're well qualified and have no problem."

Those were magical words.

"It's best to sell everything and bring only cash to the United States," the lawyer said. "How much money, in your estimation, will your liquidated assets produce?"

I had no idea and was not sure if it was better to understate or overestimate. I settled on a round figure. "Roughly 200,000 pounds…yes, at least that much if we sell everything."

He did some calculations. "Around 350,000 dollars, not a large amount, but we can work with it, not a problem."

I felt a bit intimidated. "What are your fees?" I asked.

"Very reasonable," he said. "$3,500 for all immigration work up to your green cards, which will give you the right to permanent residency."

"That's very reasonable," I said.

Attorney Blank nodded. "I have a 100% success rate. Once you're in the United States I guarantee to keep you there."

All the right answers and everything I needed to hear. There were no waiting lists and no delays in realizing my dream. We qualified for the American way of life.

The knock on the door signaled the arrival of his next client. He issued his final instructions for the day: "You're bringing your daughter, so it's best to arrive during the school holidays. The week before departure call my Palm Beach office. I'll tell you what to say to the INS at your port of entry in Miami. Don't worry and don't lose my business card."

*

291

I had just hired our American legal counsel, a qualified man who would become our trusted family guardian. Problems and adjustments lay ahead, but with a good lawyer we could avoid pitfalls.

George's stumbling block was now removed and the road was clear. He saw it on my face the moment I walked through the door.

"You worried for nothing, darling. We have no problem getting into America. We have an attorney now who has told me what to do."

I knew how to follow instructions and moved fast. The whole process from original idea to liquidating our assets to packing for Florida took a total of four months.

I had left Germany with sixty borrowed marks. How different this was. We had a substantial amount of money and I was not alone. Our wealth, though not enormous, was acquired honestly, neither inherited nor earned at the expense of others.

The move to America was for the good of our entire family, I reasoned. More time to spend together, a healthier climate and more attention to our daughter, the growing Annette. Hugh Jr. would remain in England for now, since he had started his profession as the apprentice of a famous chef. As soon as we were settled, he would join us. Our reasons were solid. "You're going to have a place in the sun anytime you want to visit," we told our friends.

*

Family didn't include my mother. I knew she would be hurt that I placed a bigger ocean and another three thousand miles of distance between us. "She's tiny now," Fritz said. "In pain all the time riddled with osteoporosis."

The Dietrich Bonhoefer Home for the Aged in Luedenscheid, Sauerland where she resided was named after the remarkable Protestant pastor and author who had sacrificed his life by resisting the Nazis. The home was inhabited by elderly Germans whose crime had been at least silence, if not more. In the case of Else Steffens it was active support of Hitler and his "Final Solution."

Was an attempt made to redeem these souls in their final days? Could one man's goodness wash away the sins of his compatriots? Was wrongdoing ever acknowledged by any of these men and women now under one roof and so close to their graves? I had my doubts and wondered about the significance and symbolism of the Bonhoefer name.

Mother had long given up asking me to come home. When I called and told her we were now headed to America, she held back her tears.

"Now I'm going to die and never see you again."

"Are you not well taken care of?" I still did not have it in me to call her Mother. "You can phone or write if you need something." I knew my mother didn't have material needs, which was all I was prepared to offer. Again, I felt a moment of sadness that passed.

Part Three

Golden Door

Chapter 51

The Beauty and The Blank

THE DAY WAS bitter cold with heaps of snow when on December 12, 1980 George, Annette and I took a taxicab to Heathrow. We boarded the British Airways flight for my second emigration and I crossed a much bigger body of water to my new destination. This time we did not travel light; each of us had a large suitcase and oversized bag. The flight was uneventful and we felt adventurous, even cheerful.

We produced our tourist visas to the INS on arrival in Miami, and the friendly officer welcomed us and wished us a wonderful winter vacation in Florida. We had no problem; everything went just as Michael Blank promised when I had called him the week before.

In London it was easy to get around by public transport or taxicabs, but I had gotten a driver's license when we moved to the suburbs. I drove north on Interstate 95 in our rental car. George and Annette looked out of the window while I kept my eyes on the road and adjusted myself to driving on the right. The traffic was heavy. From the vantage point of the busy highway my family could not imagine why I had raved about this place. "Wait until we get to Palm Beach," I said. "Then you will be amazed."

They were. We shed our traveling clothes and spent the

rest of the day pool-side and in the spa before a scrumptious dinner at the Wellington Country Club.

"Good decision. Well done," George said. He was happy, Annette was happy and I was over the moon when we fell asleep in our new home.

The next morning, jet lag aside, we wasted no time and crossed the Intercostal Waterways via the Okeechobee Bridge on to the island of Palm Beach proper. First things first, and that was to check in with our legal advisor Michael Blank.

My family got a foretaste of what was in store for us: stucco homes, magnificent architecture, manicured lawns and spectacular gardens. Our eyes couldn't take it all in fast enough.

The attorney's office was easy to find at the Palm Beach Towers and occupied the whole right side of the lower floor. We had arrived at the door of the one man who was the anointed conductor of our affairs. He would put all the different pieces of the orchestra together, and our future lives in America would be a symphony.

We sensed the moment we walked in that this was a well- run, refined and highly successful legal practice. The smile of Mr. Blank's secretary was as winning as his. I turned to my husband and gave him my "I told you so" look.

George and I declined the offer of refreshments, we were nervous, but Annette was not intimidated and accepted a cool glass of soda. We waited in the outer office for "our" man to finish what he was doing and attend to us.

When he came out from behind his huge, mahogany desk, I saw for a fleeting moment a look of surprise, if not shock, on his face when he saw George and Annette.

296

Of course, he had only seen me, the blond, snow-white specimen of our family and seemed to be taken unawares that our family was interracial. I never thought of mentioning it to him in London. Not a big deal. He would get to know and love us, as would everyone else. Only our looks deceived. We were a regular family in pursuit of a beautiful, non-confrontational way of life on the island of our dreams, Palm Beach.

"Greetings and welcome to America," Michael Blank said. We felt welcomed. On the credenza behind him were several photographs close and dear to his heart, Michael Blank with a lovely woman, Michael Blank in front of oceanfront property, Michael Blank with people who looked important, although I didn't recognize them. No words had to spell it out; he was influential and rich.

"Thank you very much for taking our case," I said. We sat down in front of his desk. "What are the steps we need to take to get our immigration status changed?"

"Did you liquidate in the UK and bring a check? " I nodded. "First you open a bank account. You don't have social security numbers and therefore you need me."

He buzzed his secretary on the intercom. "Please be so kind and make an appointment for the Brownes with the manager of The First National Bank."

He looked at me. "May I see your check?" I put the small piece of paper on his desk. It represented almost all our worldly possessions, our home and all its furnishings--nice things bought at Harrods and sold as part of the quick real estate deal--a car and business.

He picked up the cashier's check. Again I sensed some disappointment, but maybe I was too sensitive. He said all the

297

right things: "Very good. You're going to take this over to the bank and after you open your account come back and leave my retainer with the secretary up front. Have a nice day, and remember don't do anything without consulting me first."

"We wouldn't even buy a safety pin without you," I said. He smiled and we were on our way.

At the bank, the female who received our check beamed with friendliness. Our attorney had clout and opened doors.

"Since you're Michael's clients, we will take the best care of you." 'Michael's clients' was a good and safe thing to be.

*

Back at our hotel in Wellington was a message from a Harry Silton, a fellow Brit who was already settled in the Palm Beaches. He offered to help us. "I'll come to welcome you this afternoon," he said. He represented a company called Island Investments. Everyone was so accommodating and went out of their way for us.

Harry had a slight limp in his left leg which was endearing, as was his familiar British accent. Already aware that things were done differently in America we were glad our fellow countryman could ease our culture shock. We could trust him to guide our entry into the Palm Beach way of life.

Harry convinced us that it was essential to purchase a home without delay. Prices rose every day. Palm Beach not only included the island itself, but surrounding areas that were all under the umbrella of The Palm Beaches.

We stayed in Wellington, west and inland. "An up-and-coming area," Harry said. "Prince Charles comes to play polo

298

and many English folks have already snapped up beautiful homes."

We were tired, but to disappoint Harry wouldn't be right. We let him chauffeur us around and show us real estate that more than met our needs. Everything we saw appealed to us.

After a couple of days we signed on the dotted line for a brand new house on Lake Wellington. Harry shook his head when George attempted to make an offer less than the full asking price. "Prices are set," he said. I glared at George and shook my head, "please be quiet and don't embarrass us."

Harry's Island Investment office was in the same building as Michael Blank's law office which was a fortunate coincidence. "Michael paves everyone's way to success with the INS. He has hundreds of clients from all over the world," Harry said.

"We know," I said. "How lucky for us."

"And don't worry. I figured you wanted Michael to see your real estate contract. I've already walked it over to him. He's delighted with your wonderful decision."

Thank God for Michael. Because we had no legal status yet, he arranged for a direct mortgage with the developer and builder at an interest rate of 18% with a 20% down payment.

"The interest rate seems a little high," I said.

"Don't worry. It ends up to your advantage. House prices go sky high and in no time you're going to have enough equity to pay the mortgage off. If you rent you throw away your money." Great financial advice! Everyone had our interest at heart which felt good.

"Don't forget our immigration," I reminded Michael. The only cloud on the horizon we could foresee.

"You've no problem. I'll apply to change your status to treaty investor. All you need to do is invest in a business. Why don't you let Harry show you what's for sale around town? Your social security cards should arrive any day."

We were not planning on a business so soon and looked forward to relaxation for a while, but if it was required to legalize our status we would comply and relax later.

The Treaty Investor's agreement between the United Kingdom and the United States allowed people with money to come in and invest in the American economy. We had a successful restaurant in London.

"That would be an excellent business venture in the Palm Beaches too. Lots of wealthy patrons who never cook," Michael said. "Harry's a business broker and he's the right man to help you."

With our home purchase out of the way Harry went into action to show us the many restaurants that were for sale. He also took us to a car dealership where his nice salesman friend helped us into a special deal car just because Harry was with us.

What could be better than our new Florida life? It was December and we thought about our shivering, cold friends back in England.

To my delight Annette had no problem adjusting herself. By early January I saw her off on the yellow school bus for her first day at an American public school. Another milestone in getting settled.

Harry showed us three restaurants before he took us to La Crepe de Pampole on the island's Chilean Avenue.

"Not quite sure if the owners want to sell this profitable business but let's have a look at it anyway," he said.

This was it, the perfect location and a family enterprise, not big, just fifty seats. But would the French owners agree to sell? I already started to see the new sign, "Liesel's Apple," above the entrance door.

While Harry was involved in a serious discussion with the owners we waited outside and looked around. We were just one block from the world famous Worth Avenue. The restaurant's fare was country French and specialized in savory and desert crepes with forty different fillings. We looked at Harry with anticipation when he emerged.

"I am not sure yet, but maybe, just maybe, I can swing this for you. They have a daughter in California and want to relocate."

"Please do your best, Harry. This is the restaurant we want. We're going to come back for dinner tonight."

"Don't breathe a word to the owners. They speak only French, and I don't want them to know you're interested. All negotiations have to go through me."

That was a fair and reasonable request. We had dinner and liked it. The owners and waiters gave us special attention and a carafe of free wine. "A votre sante!" What a lovely place. We couldn't wait for Harry to come back with a verdict in our favor.

Ten o'clock Monday morning we got the call. The deal was on. We were ecstatic. "Come straight to the office and put

301

down your deposit. I don't want them to change their minds."

George turned into the prudent businessman. "Can we see the financial reports?"

"After the deposit is paid; a restaurant in America is what we call a cash business." We knew that meant not all earnings went through the books. George frowned.

Harry expanded on what we could expect. "The present owners made a ton of money and purchased a lovely home with a pool. It's all paid off."

When the books of our prospective business showed a financial loss over the past few years we went to Michael Blank's office for advice. Michael also explained the principle of "cash under the table," and told us it was up to us how we wanted to do business. There was plenty of revenue coming in. "Take my word for it. I frequent the restaurant myself."

George fidgeted with his pen which irritated me.

"And with the two of you it will be even better," Michael said.

"George is a wonderful entertainer," I said. "And we always pay our taxes."

"That's right," George agreed. "In light of the red in the books the asking price should be reduced."

I cringed when Harry went for the door, the limp in his leg more pronounced than before. What if the owners changed their minds and no longer wanted to sell?

"Harry, come back." George was ready to give in. A quick closing date was set for the end of January.

"You don't want to miss out on the season," Harry and

Michael said. We paid no particular attention. What did we know about seasons? Florida didn't have any; it was always warm and tropical.

*

The business lease only showed up at the closing table. No wonder it had taken time to prepare the mountain of paperwork. The sellers had arrived early in Michael's office with a smile and cheerful "Bon jour" and sat meekly opposite us in the conference room. Could we read through all this now? George shook his head.

Michael saw we were overwhelmed and came to the rescue. He stood behind me, looked over my shoulder and handed me his gold Mount Blanc fountain pen.

"Just sign this, Baby. I've checked everything. There's no problem." His tone of voice was kind, almost fatherly. He called me 'Baby,' which signaled to everyone in the room our special closeness and that he was the one who took care of us.

My signature was first. I passed the many document pages around the conference table to the other principals, George to my right and then Madame and Monsieur Digion. Michael's secretary who was a notary sealed our deal right then and there.

Chapter 52

American Business

AFTER OUR ACQUISITION of an American investment business for immigration purposes we went straight to work twelve-hour shifts. The sellers' English turned out to be much better than expected. They took us through the labyrinth of things to do and watch for. The equipment was old and had special quirks. Marguerite, French expatriate and the tight keeper of the secret recipe for crepes was delicate and menopaused.

"Don't make Marguerite cry," the sellers said. We had no intention of making anyone cry including ourselves. We split the work. I was in charge of finances, bookkeeping and the front of the house, while George ordered supplies, compiled the weekly payroll and soon began to entertain our guests.

This was a new thing we tried and hoped it would go over well. We also put out a call to Hugh Jr. to pack up in England and come out to lend a hand as chef in our new family venture.

All six members of the staff talked French, right down to the Haitian busboy-cleaner-prep cook, who spoke pidgin French. Our head waitress, Teresa, was an attractive and assertive French import. Since she had been with the sellers for some time, the regular customers knew her. She appointed herself spokesperson for all the staff and demanded raises.

"Plenty of better jobs in Palm Beach," she said which scared us. All the staff made us uncomfortable. We asked Teresa what was needed to have everyone stay. George and I consulted and reached an agreement to settle our first labor dispute with what we thought was quite a big increase in hourly pay for everyone.

I watched Teresa from then on for signs of further dissatisfaction. I often saw her huddled with the patrons. Teresa had power over our success.

By the end of the first month I had the inkling we were doomed. Bills came in left and right. Demand for town, county, state and federal taxes, licenses, sales taxes, employment and unemployment taxes, taxes here there and everywhere. The rent was due and way over the amount we had budgeted.

I took a careful look at our complicated lease with its riders, clauses, exclusions, increases and page after page of legalese. There were discrepancies only Michael Blank could explain, but he was no longer available when I called and I didn't tell George.

I poured over the numbers. Fifty seats had to produce revenue to cover our expense. Even if we charged twice as much for a plate of food and filled every seat at lunch and dinner, that wasn't going to happen. The Florida sun no longer shone so bright. I couldn't let it set on us and our future and I had to figure out a way to stay afloat. Our very lives were at stake and I was responsible for putting us in jeopardy.

Hugh's arrival from England didn't improve the situation much, although he made a valiant effort to take charge of the kitchen. To work with the moody Marguerite was no easy task.

It became us--the Browne family--against them, the French, and very soon it was us against the world. The truth of our situation was slow to filter into my mind at first, but it was not long before a grim picture emerged. We had been had, and although we were not the only ones, our situation was more unique and dire.

We were shackled to a struggling business on the Island of Palm Beach, a place of rare and perplexing peculiarities. We walked, breathed and worked on the sacred ground of the extravagant and overindulged. We were imposters and had no entitlement to set foot on such hallowed territory.

The most serious infraction was George, entertainer extraordinaire and exceptional human being. His blackness was anathema, undesirable to the extreme and elicited racist opinions, gestures and wordings straight out of the *Uncle Tom's Cabin* of my childhood.

I was judged to be equal if not worse. I was the excommunicated. Between entre nous--they all spoke and loved anything French, in the strictest confidence, I was "that" woman. I had done the unforgivable and married a black man which was in very bad taste. The milieu would never be the same if our infringement on Palm Beach was allowed to continue.

People of color did enter the island, but they were expected to leave when their work was done. They were servants with written permits issued by the owners and givers of their daily bread and they could be revoked at any time and at will. We had paid money and were business owners, so therefore this law didn't apply to us. Our interracial family was an awkward dilemma in the 1980s for a town which tried to hold on to its privileged past.

My father's daughter found herself in a situation of unjust discrimination based on the color of her husband's skin. The father's sins were visited upon the daughter. George had told me this would happen and he was right.

George did not allow the town to define who he was or should be. His denial of the insurmountable problem had a huge impact on me. The problem was insurmountable because it was ingrained in the hearts and minds of the people whom we now depended on for our survival.

The community declared war on us. It didn't take much effort to come up with a way to deter us from staying in their midst. The stratagem could be used in many different ways and the end result would always spell victory.

Ordinances, the town issued ordinances. We were in constant noncompliance. Some of them were so esoteric that there was no way we could or should have known about them.

The sign, "Liesel's Apple," was a violation--$500 worth for every day it stayed up. It turned out that the French owner's sign was grandfathered, an expression I had never heard before. Ours was the same size and built to specification by the town's official sign scribe, but it was still in violation. "Sorry, you are violating an important ordinance," the town manager said. "It has to come down."

Our trash violated another ordinance because it smelled. During trash pickup days our garbage was overlooked or spilled. I called the sanitation department and was told by a polite female voice, "Sorry, we can't pick up your garbage due to its odor."

I explained that restaurant trash was bound to smell when it sat in the sun uncollected. "We don't produce unusual, smelly garbage," I said.

"Sorry, you are in violation. Please bag and remove your own waste as soon as possible," the woman on the telephone instructed. .

One lunch time three large, official looking men came in and disrupted our business. Their faces were extra serious. "All your doors open in the wrong direction," they said. "This violation threatens life and limb of your patrons. You're negligent."

We stood stunned. The restaurant emptied out of guests and the men stormed out, leaving a citation and a demand for payment of another large fine.

Almost every day brought an unhappy surprise. Whatever we did violated something while surrounding Palm Beach-approved businesses took advantage of us. They filled our parking lot with their cars and made it unavailable for our guests.

All this stress and confusion needed an understanding ear. Who better than the legal mind of our attorney who had promised total service and involvement in our American settlement. Michael Blank did meet with me a couple of times, but his demeanor had changed from very accommodating to, "don't bother me with things I can't do anything about. It was your choice to come to Palm Beach."

That fact I could not deny and I had overwhelming guilt. When I spoke with Harry Silton to see if we could dispose of the restaurant and retrieve some of our finances I became aware of several disturbing realities.

Michael Blank was his boss and the owner/broker of Island Investments, although Michael Blank's name was not on the door as required by real estate law. Our landlord lived in the same building and Michael Blank knew him. Our lease was indeed "special." It had huge increases. The seller's rental agreement had run out. They had planned to close the unprofitable restaurant when we came along and bought it instead and signed an even more expensive lease.

Michael Blank collected fees and commissions on all real estate transactions. From us, from the landlord, from the developer of our home and from the sellers. Michael Blank sat pretty, while we were at risk of losing everything we had.

One more thing Harry, our fellow Englishman, clarified. Michael Blank had known from the moment he laid eyes on George that we would fail. He knew Palm Beach. It was his town.

Chapter 53

Lucky old Sun

I RAGED AGAINST Michael Blank, the man who had betrayed our trust. I was not yet aware of the many lessons in store for me, lessons we can only learn when we are stripped of what we think matters most. The plundered are not blameless in being robbed. Long before I came to America I had become a consumer, a collector of material possessions--meaningless things to enhance body and home. They helped me forget the past and made me feel I was somebody who demanded respect. In the process I had lost my spirit and my essence.

Michael Blank was my facilitator, although at the time I saw the young man only as an unwelcome intruder into our lives, somebody who had snatched away our success.

More and more George and I fought battles against each other as well as the deceitful world around us. He had an outlet in his music. At night he picked up his guitar and came out from hiding among the storeroom boxes where he had banished himself during the day ever since a middle-aged female lunch customer declared: "When I look up from my food I don't want to look at a nigger."

George overheard the remark, but he never spoke about what it did to him. In the evenings he sang the Blues, haunting melodies of America's past that now had a special meaning for him: *"Old Man River,"* *"Summertime,"* *"That Lucky Old Sun."* People took notice and looked up from their entrees in the small eatery. They heard such outstanding performances from the quiet man who sat in the corner. He was no longer black and undesirable, but an artist who could touch their hearts. This was how George Browne dealt with the town of Palm Beach.

I did what I knew how to do when I was in trouble and needed help. I went to the press. A reporter from the Fort Lauderdale *Sun Sentinel* wrote a feature about our predicament. It did some good in that the town manager paid us a visit and sent a sanitation truck to pick up our trash.

The *Palm Beach Post* also wrote an article which praised the quality of our food and George's entertainment, but that turned into a double-edged sword. On the one hand it brought as much business as we could handle mostly from across the bridge in West Palm Beach. It also brought a letter from the town's ordinance committee that informed us that we did not possess a nightclub license and were therefore not allowed to entertain anyone. And, dread of all dreads, a letter came from the INS--application for change of status from tourist to treaty investor--DENIED.

"Your application was not received on time. You are NOT allowed to work in your investment. It is an investment only and you must employ only American workers."

Michael Blank, our immigration attorney, had not filed timely paperwork on our behalf.

*

311

Some aspects of our plight were shared by other British families who slaved like us in doomed businesses. These enterprises had been designed for sale to eager treaty investors in search of the sun, but were not profitable enough to be operated for any length of time.

The idea was for the investors to fail and after investing and profits had been made on commissions by realtors, business brokers and attorneys, to go back home. Some of these enterprises were restaurants, but a lot were dry cleaners and Laundromats. The joke among us British was, "we've been taken to the cleaners."

We all lived in overpriced homes in Wellington, and one by one these ruined families did return back to England to the life they knew and trusted. Things looked very bleak. Michael Blank even seemed to be in cahoots with the INS. Rumor had it British nationals were picked up by the feared INS and deported.

Chapter 54

The Friend

IT WAS TOWARDS the end of lunchtime one day when a man walked into the restaurant. "Would you mind staying open a little longer? My wife just had therapy after her stroke and we would like to have lunch."

"Of course not, we don't mind," I said, "and we'll be glad to accommodate any special dietary needs you might have."

The man was grateful and the next week he returned at the same time with his wife and her caretaker.

He was a kind man and after a few weeks of regular visits he said, "Can I help you in any way?"

"You surely have enough to worry about," I said. But there was something genuine about him that made me want to open my heart to him. No other patrons seemed to care about us.

"Please have a seat," he said. "I'm Jerry Kassel from New York, my wife's Norma. We spend winters here in our Florida home." As it turned out for the first time in my life I sat opposite a Jew.

He was a member of the mysterious group of people I knew nothing about. Deep-rooted feelings of shame came back.

Didn't he hear from my accent I was German? I hoped he wouldn't't ask.

"We're from England," I said. "It's beautiful here, but we're having a hard time with all the ordinances. There're so many."

He laughed. "Palm Beach's a quirky town. Don't take it personal."

"I know it's personal," I said and went to the back and fetched George. "This is my husband and business partner."

"You do have a problem," Mr. Kassel said. "That's why I live across the Intercoastal."

Mr. Kassel's kindness, wit and sympathetic ear made all the difference in the world. I found out it was not just blacks who were undesirable in Palm Beach, but Jews as well. Even unlimited wealth did not assure entry into certain country clubs if you were a Jew.

Jerry Kassel was a businessman with a law degree. He pointed out the illegality of Michael Blank's actions. "You should take the matter to court and prevent other families from falling into the same trap."

I began to educate myself at the West Palm Beach law library, where I researched immigration and real estate law. Michael Blank had a conflict of interest which was illegal in Florida.

Jerry Kassel whom we now considered a friend, did remarkable things for us. One day he walked through Palm Beach to his barber shop with his arm around George. "What's going on?" The barber said. "Why are you with him?"

"Why not? We're here for a hair cut."

Jerry even offered us money for the business, but we turned that down. Then he encouraged all his Jewish friends to patronize our restaurant. We were very grateful, but I also felt I didn't deserve his generosity.

Since by then he knew I was German, I found it necessary one day to tell him the usual lie which I believed myself. "My father fought against the Nazis and saved a Jewish neighbor's son."

"Your father was very brave. You must miss him a lot." I nodded. Family was very important to Jerry, and I wanted him to think it was important to me too.

To think that my people had justified the extermination of Jews like my friend Jerry. What a horrifying thought. Hitler's hideous words came back to me, words I had read in my teenage years. "Only now did I become acquainted with the seducer of our people (Jews). I didn't know what to be more amazed at: the agility of their tongues or their virtuosity at lying....if the Jew is victorious over the other peoples of the world, his crown will be the funeral wreath of humanity."

It was ironic that it was me who had the agility of a lying tongue, a daughter of the Reich. I lied about my Nazi father to a friend.

With Jerry's unwavering support we managed to hold on to our investment for two winter seasons and one summer. By May the town emptied out and everyone migrated to their summer homes up north. When the second May approached we realized that we could not spend another off-season in Palm Beach.

"We have to go back to England," George said.

"That's out of the question."

I searched and found a law firm to take our case against Michael Blank on a contingency basis. Our immigration status was changed from tourist to treaty investor through the efforts of our new attorney. But the moment we handed the restaurant back to the previous owners we were out of status again. Our Wellington house sold at a loss. We were without financial resources or work and had disintegrated on all fronts.

I no longer trusted my decisions. It was my fault we were back where we started twenty years before. Only now we had less. Twenty years ago we were younger. We sailed on wings of our love and overcoming obstacles was a breeze.

George seemed to have shriveled under the pressure of Palm Beach's disdain for him. He no longer made me feel safe and his blind acceptance of our fate irritated me. The magic of an adoring life partner was gone.

Hugh's chef talents were in demand and he easily found a well paying job in Palm Beach.

Our daughter Annette was thirteen when the dream life which had never materialized for us in Palm Beach ended and our decision was to go west.

Chapter 55

California

WE MEANDERED WESTWARD via Denver, Colorado, and Reno, Nevada, without any particular time frame and without a final destination in mind. After we reached the California coast north of San Francisco, we turned south. We lingered a while in the city and tried to get a feel for it. It was cosmopolitan, but could we find housing and work? Would there be prejudice against us? We had adopted a dog at the Palm Beach shelter. Did landlords accept pets? After a couple of weeks nothing fell into place and we went on our way south along the Pacific.

I drove without blemish, observed every traffic sign and speed limit to avoid attention to the car with its three ex-treaty investors and their dog. We had no green cards and feared the powerful INS. The mountain cliffs and crashing seas we passed were reflections of our inner turmoil.

When we reached Los Angeles, a monthly "relocation special" at the Holiday Inn in Glendale was inexpensive and our dog was no problem. The sprawling city with many illegal immigrants seemed to be a good place for us to get lost.

After we moved into a Woodland Hills townhouse in the San Fernando Valley I returned by plane to Florida for our household items and drove a 24–foot U Haul truck back to LA in four days.

California was our second American home and we had no choice, but to settle in. If only George could find work, some of his self-esteem might be restored.

We had little money left. We knew no one and had no welfare system to fall back on, just our wits. George explored the entertainment field, but without an agent to hype his artistry he was unsuccessful in a town full of vibrant, young talent. Already a dispirited shadow of his former self he became more moody and withdrawn. Solutions and survival had to come from me.

Before I became an entrepreneur I had worked in retail. I was hired on the spot as cosmetic's manager in a Glendale department store, and I took a chance with the employment applications with regard to my immigration status. Responsibility to put food on my family's table and pay rent had to prevail and I left all citizenship questions blank.

The cosmetics industry crosses national boundaries and serves women and men in all countries. I was on familiar ground and could not fail. It was more pleasant than selling shoe polish which my brother Fritz had to do after the war.

I had entertained loftier aspirations for myself, but now I could keep body and soul together by nothing more than recommending skin-deep remedies. It was a breeze. I arrived early and stayed late. My sales volume exceeded everyone's expectations, and the income derived from hard work was enough to pay for our upkeep. I manifested my survival skills in America and fought back against defeat.

The INS could overthrow my efforts at any moment and I felt a constant, gnawing element of uncertainty.

My business proficiency was replaced at home by a sense of failure and conflict with my family. At work I was enthusiastic, spontaneous and tireless, but at home I had no energy left to do anything positive. I was a harried bundle of nerves. The external life that provided our sustenance was more important than the crumbling family situation I felt powerless to do anything about.

Annette had matured and was no longer the cheerful girl we could count on to make us laugh. A lonely child myself after the age of nine, I had not leaned on my mother and was self-reliant. I was unaware that I had forced my daughter into the same kind of aloneness and saw no danger in allowing her the same freedom I had taken for myself.

She saw my fallibility and frailty too early in her life. The certainty she would always be safe with her family was replaced by the realization that nothing was certain anymore. Our fate was cast with the weather and a hurricane could come by and blow us into different directions at any time.

"Why are your clothes all over the place, Annette? You're old enough to look after yourself." My nagging was constant.

George couldn't do anything right either. "What did you do all day while I worked?" My rhetorical questions rubbed only salt into his wounds. "You do nothing all day while I work and when I come home I have to clean and cook as well."

He spent his time with spiritual books which infuriated me and I don't know why.

Only Snowball, my first non-human family member, did not irritate me. The once forsaken, flea bitten creature at the pound was now beauty-parlored, well nourished and snow-white. Her doghood brought me much joy.

The wife and mother I had become was not a person I wanted to be, yet I was trapped. My soul was pretty much dead. I felt confined in a long, dark tunnel with no light at the end.

Annette was on constant edge. George was sporadic at disciplining her and the school principal left recorded messages that she was truant from her classes. When we asked her about it her answers were vague. Soon she was expelled from school. I realized that we had lost control of our daughter and so had the educational system.

One evening the situation came to a head. After a bitter fight between George and Annette all three of us realized that to cling to each other no longer served us well. The time had arrived to break the chains around our hearts and set each other free. Only as individuals, unburdened with responsibility for each other, could we begin to repair our lives and fulfill our unique and separate destinies. My heart told me the time was now.

At first George could not fathom the thought of separation. Where was our love and grace? Our love had been special and we believed our vows were eternal. We had gotten to know each other over 20 years, had overcome adversity together and had enjoyed a large measure of happiness.

I vacillated: Should I act on my need to be by myself? Figure out alone the purpose of my life and how I should live the rest of it? Or should I give in to my fear that I would be without a steady companion whose love I could always count on?

As long as George was near my focus would continue to be on him as it had been on Wolfgang, Hugh and before that on my mother and father and the guilt I felt for what they had done.

Hugh Jr. was well off. He worked hard and owned a nice house in Florida. Although he had female friends, no lady had yet crossed his path special enough to be considered for marriage.

"Why don't you have Dad live with me until a decision can be made?" My son's big heart went out to his stepfather who needed his help.

I drove George to the airport, numb and beyond sad. Neither one of us spoke. My first marriage was bound to fail, but why this one too? Why could I not hold on to love? What did I expect from a partner that I had not found yet?

After George's departure, Annette and I created a new life for ourselves. We moved into a smaller apartment and started to enjoy each other's company as two friends and roommates.

*

During the two years George lived with Hugh I realized that I had to go on alone and stay in the United States. I filed for divorce. Michael Blank settled out of court which gave George the funds to return to his beloved England where he still lives today.

Chapter 56

Single Life

"MOM, WHY DON'T you go out on a date?" Annette was the nagger now. "You're still good-looking."

"You want to get rid of me?" I couldn't see myself in the company of a man again, although sometimes I did feel lonely. The man I was married to for 21 years had now set me free. On my most recent birthday George sent a card: "You always had that spark of God. Be happy and free."

I tried going out with single girl friends. Younger, California-tanned men were attracted to me which was a pleasant surprise and brought out my playful spirit. I was curious about where a new romantic relationship might take me.

Our roles as mother and daughter were now often reversed. Annette checked on me and waited up for my return from an outing. I avoided bringing men home. None of these relationships seemed serious enough. I didn't want to expose my daughter to a stream of males I had no emotional attachment to.

My mother had not prepared me for sex, and like her I put off addressing the subject with my daughter. It didn't seem appropriate. My child was a homebody, bookish and serious and, although she was mature, I just couldn't imagine her in a sexually active way. When I returned from work or a date she was curled up, reading on the sofa.

Los Angeles was a place full of people with problems. Solutions could be found in a variety of ways-- from therapy if you had the money, to self-help groups and twelve step programs if you didn't. Even in churches and temples of every denomination psychological counseling was freely available.

As far I was concerned I didn't need any outside guidance. There was nothing wrong with me. I was strong and could provide for myself and my child through every adverse condition. I worked and never missed a beat. Which one of these problem-solving institutions could I fit into anyway?

I became an expert with other people's problems. Not far from work was a gathering place, an Austrian restaurant and bar where an African-American pianist played jazz a few times a week. It reminded me of long gone times in London when George and his band entertained enthusiastic crowds and I was romanced in music and songs. How prophetic the words of the *September Song* sounded now--"the few precious years I spent with you."

The Austrian owner of the establishment and his wife Greta spoke German, a language I was not comfortable with, but once in a while I allowed myself to be drawn into speaking in my mother tongue. My sentences often started off in German, but to translate in my mind was cumbersome and I was soon back into English.

Greta started to confide in me about her marital problems. "I became my husband's possession when I was sixteen."

"His possession, are you serious?" I began to think of

ways to liberate this sweet woman. After all, I considered myself an expert at leaving men.

"You should just get up one day, take your two daughters and walk out." I said.

"Leave and go where? I have no profession, no means of support."

"If I can support myself, so can you." I hatched a plan to come to her rescue. Soon I had a job for Greta as my assistant at the store. Her means of support was in place and I hired a moving truck to relocate her and the daughters to a temporary safe place.

In a very short time Greta blossomed into a confident and very attractive woman who was ready for a new partner. I was delighted for her when Sebastian, a handsome, soft-spoken and kind man came into her life. He was an attorney and a devout Jew--the second Jew I was able to befriend and experience in a very positive way.

My friend's happiness and second chance made me doubly aware of my own singleness. If only I could get another chance. This time, I hoped that I would be wise enough to hold on to love if it ever came my way again.

*

My first encounter with the blessings of a twelve-step program came thanks to a colleague from work. She took me to an open Alcoholics Anonymous meeting. I couldn't relate to the terrible disease of alcoholism, but the open way it was dealt with was nothing short of miraculous. Everyone was welcomed and offered unconditional love and encouragement to look inward and identify faults not in others, but in oneself.

This fellowship was on to several fundamental truths. If only it could apply to me. I sometimes drank too much, but I was not an alcoholic with the deadly addiction they described.

Yet many of the feelings were the same. Like them I was looking for "us," a way out of loneliness and my self-imposed separateness from the human race which had been a painful part of me since childhood.

I returned for a second AA meeting by myself at a different location in the Valley.

Chapter 57

Craig

THE MOMENT HE sat down next to me his presence was intense. I didn't look to see who he was or what he looked like. He remained silent during the program. When it was over we formed a circle and held hands with our heads bowed while the Lord's Prayer was recited. He held on to my hand a little longer.

"Haven't seen you before. First time here?" I looked at a tall, conservatively well-dressed man who was about my age.

"Yes, it is."

After we exchanged a few more polite words he handed me his business card.

"Call me. I would like to hear from you."

After he departed I looked at his name and credentials: "Craig Sloniker. Quality Control Manager."

He didn't have my name and there was no way he could contact me. Over the next few days I thought about him. It was up to me to call if I wanted to see him again.

When his secretary put me through to him I felt awkward, but he was friendly. "What day is good for dinner?" He said.

I got ready for our first date with special care. When we sat down to eat he didn't take his eyes off me. Right away there was chemistry between us that made our stomachs feel full before we ate.

He had a great sense of humor and we made each other laugh as if we were old friends. After our enchanting first date, we spent more time together and discussed more serious subjects.

"AA saved my life," he said. "I would be dead without the program."

"What made you start to drink in the first place?"

"My first wife died of cancer just after she gave birth to our son."

"How tragic." My heart went out to him.

"You should have seen me in my second marriage," he said with a laugh.

"What happened?"

"A beautiful heiress for a wife, a new daughter and membership at the country club. Can you imagine how I wrecked that?"

I had no idea and shook my head. His smile was infectious and I expected something funny and outrageous.

"I'm quiet a handyman and had a workshop on our estate. I worked while I drank. One day, just as my wife came through the door, the ceiling collapsed and a mountain of empty whiskey bottles rained down on us from above."

"What did your wife say?"

"It's not what she said, she looked daggers. Then she turned and ran. That was it for her. Too many broken promises! She called her attorney and filed for divorce."

"She didn't want to help you?"

"No, I was a hopeless alcoholic. I lost everything and reached rock bottom before I turned my life around."

"You have most certainly done that and you must be very proud of your achievements."

"Enough of me, I want to hear about you, Liesel. What brought you to AA?"

I could make up a story about heavy drinking. That would give us something in common. But I couldn't come up with a convincing scenario.

"I'm not an alcoholic, but the meetings are beneficial to anyone."

He looked surprised and disappointed.

"What I told you about myself must have come as a shock. As a non-alcoholic you'll not be able to relate to such depravity. I should have known, you're too beautiful and pure inside and out."

I shook my head. "Oh no," I said. "I understand and feel for you and I'm far from pure. I continue to make mistakes."

He weighed my words.

"Are you aware that I've got to work on my recovery daily? There's no cure."

"Why's that?" Unlucky in love, I reasoned. Two lost wives, no wonder he's an alcoholic.

He changed the subject away from himself and his disease. "Let me hear about you. Where did you grow up in Germany? What are your secrets? People don't just show up at a meeting without good reason."

"My life's an open book."

A no-problem, uncomplicated personality would impress him and give him assurance that I didn't need to be analyzed or change. I was the daughter of Nazis and I would never talk about that. I wanted to focus on him and his need to stay healthy. Still, I had to say something about myself.

"My marriage to a nice man ended without bitterness. We just fell out of love one day and went our separate ways. Like you, I have two children who are no problem." I sounded like Michael Blank.

*

We had met in October and by the middle of November we were head over heels in love. I felt well respected, and he told me how happy I made him.

"I may not come home tonight, all right?" I said to Annette one Saturday evening.

"Of course, you look happy, Mom, have fun and don't worry about me."

Craig lived in an apartment not far from us in Encino. Our friendship had gone so well that we ended several evenings with passionate kisses which left both of us wanting more. Tonight was the night. He knew how to build up tension and desire between us when he looked into my eyes.

"You're so pure and wonderful," he said. I felt virginal. Here was another chance. The past didn't matter anymore. I was a young girl again about to begin her first love affair. Only this time I was blessed with the right man who respected me for who I was. I had found redemption with a man who was even a few years younger than me.

When I entered his spotless and stylish home for the first time, I was surprised. "Not like a bachelor pad," I said.

"What did you expect? We're like each other."

"How do I deserve to be so lucky?"

He kissed me gently. "Look in the bedroom," he said. Candles emanated fragrance and on the pillow were a long stemmed red rose and an envelope. I looked at him with adoration.

"Go and open it. Who do you think it's for?"

"No idea," I said. The moment was magical. He had written a poem for me in calligraphy and tied it with ribbon to the rose. My heart soared with love and wonderment and I fought back tears of joy.

"Come on, kitten," he said. "Don't cry." He held me close and stroked my back. Our passion was intense, but he didn't rush. We were meant for each other and our moment of bliss would continue for the rest of our lives.

He took off his jacket and hung it neatly on the valet in the corner. I wore a tight, black dress which I knew showed off my trim figure. It also covered me modestly to the neck in keeping with his image of me. He unzipped me at the back. I felt impatient, but he continued to take his time. He folded my garment over a chair with care.

"Oh, Kitten," he sighed as he began to unbutton his stiffly starched, white shirt. I was tempted to help him, but he was more comfortable doing it himself. I stood in my lacy lingerie and trembled with anticipation.

He excused himself and went to the adjoining bathroom. I took of my stockings, bra and panties and slipped under the crisp covers which smelled of lavender. Then I closed my eyes and waited in a state of rapture.

When I heard the water run in the bathroom sink I glanced through the door and saw he had finished washing his hands. He wiped the sink dry with his towel and then threw the towel into a hamper.

Where had I seen such extensive hygiene and cleanliness before? I wasn't sure, but I had a fleeting feeling of déjàvu.

At last he was beside me under the covers and I was tight and secure in his arms. Then we made love through most of the night with a passion that knew no bounds.

The next morning when I wanted to get up and make him breakfast, he said, "Stay in bed and let me take care of you." Soon he arrived with a tray which not only held French toast but also a bud vase with my rose.

"Good morning, my love," he said. "Thank you for an amazing night."

This was what life with the right partner was supposed to be all about. It was Sunday. I suggested finding a church and attend services. I had a need to thank my Creator who had brought me to this point of happiness. Craig agreed that the force they call the "Higher Power" in his program was responsible. "God has redeemed and rewarded me with your presence in my life," he said.

331

Before we left for church he made sure everything was tidy and in place. His color-coded shirts were lined up on identical hangers, equal distance from each other, as were his collection of polished shoes. He emptied the clothes dryer and allowed me to place his shorts in their designated drawer.

"Please make sure the washed ones end up on the bottom for equal wear and tear." I thought he was joking, but he looked serious.

He stripped the bed sheets to be washed, at which point I had a go at teasing him.

"They were good for a repeat performance, don't you think?"

He took it in good humor, but was adamant. "I have a system, keeps me sober." This keeping sober through order began to look slightly weird when I saw that he had folded my underwear on the dresser.

*

That Christmas Eve he spent with us at my place. Annette and I prepared dinner, and the Christmas tree was lit. It took three trips to his car to get all the packages he had brought for us. He showered Annette and me with an abundance of thoughtful gifts, from an expensive raincoat and several sweaters to jewelry, books and even gear for Snowball.

We were overwhelmed and embarrassed at how little we had gotten for him. They were just token things. I wanted to keep it simple. The greatest gift was our love for each other and, as a symbol, I wore my black leotard with a red bow around my waist. I was my gift to him.

Annette danced around in her new boots. He had

remembered her size. Only Snowball was not impressed with the elaborate Holiday celebration. She remained wary of Craig and growled at him whenever he as much as looked at her.

On Christmas morning Craig asked me to marry him. He knelt in front of me and proposed on his knees like I had seen men do in movies. I felt like a character in a fairy tale. This couldn't be me.

"Kitten, will you marry me? I never want to face another day without you."

I heard violins, put my head against his shoulder and purred like a cat. Of course, my answer was a resounding: "Yes!"

Chapter 58

Family

FOR THE FIRST time in my life I was about to marry a man who was so normal and formal that he proposed in a conventional way. He also was part of a conventional, much desired by me, American family from Kalamazoo, Michigan.

I couldn't wait to meet my future in-laws, his parents and older sister, and wondered what it would feel and sound like to call someone "Mom." I was ready, and there was only a brief thought of my own mother whom I kept out of the picture as far as Craig was concerned.

Craig wanted our wedding to remain a secret for now. "It'll be a delightful surprise to my folks when they come for their annual California visit in May." It was April already.

"They are going to be thrilled with you as their new daughter." Music to my ears; he was in charge and made all the decisions which was a first for me and meant I didn't have to worry about any details of our life together. I could relax and concentrate on what made him happy.

Even though I had learned to live with my illegal immigration status and no longer worried about it on a day-to-day basis the INS problem would now be solved. As Craig's wife Annette and I would be eligible for our green cards and so would the still unmarried Hugh in Florida.

Craig had introduced himself to my son on the phone and the two of them got on great. He took care of things the right and proper way.

His job for a plumbing conglomerate paid well. He was their quality control manager. Who would be better suited to control and manage the quality of anything than my most capable fiancé?

"What do you think of marrying me in Santa Barbara?" He said one day.

"I love it, the perfect spot for two hopeless romantics. All your ideas are great."

*

His parents had booked their vacation in the beautiful seaside town of Santa Barbara for the whole month of May. To include them our wedding ceremony would take place in the middle of their stay. None of my family and friends were going to be invited. "Too far for them to travel," Craig said. "Let's keep it small."

We spent a weekend in Santa Barbara and met the minister of the small Unity Church on the hill where we would exchange vows. The church had a beautiful view through olive groves down to the Pacific Ocean. Neither one of us had religious affiliations and "unity" sounded good.

One small detail of our nuptials I kept to myself as a surprise for him--my ivory lace wedding dress. With golden thread embroidered in the seams was the name "Craig." No one would see it, only he when I took it off. The calf length dress was layered over a satin petticoat and was gorgeous without being formal.

Our honeymoon would follow the ceremony. We planned to travel up the Pacific Coast to Carmel, the same coastline I had journeyed down with George in an uncertain and pathetic frame of mind. How things had turned around.

*

We agreed that to buy a house was a good idea. I had the down payment from my settled lawsuit and with our combined incomes a mortgage was soon in place. We found a house in Canoga Park, just the right layout and close to his AA meetings.

Homemaking and decorating had always been my forte, so it felt strange to have a man so interested and involved in every aspect, color scheme and design of our new home. He was very handy, and I knew I would never have to hold a hammer in my hand again.

I liked more earthy tones, but the deep blue he preferred for the den was lovely too. To keep him happy and sober was what mattered. He was my center of gravity. From him, through him, to him everything flowed with ease and certainty.

*

If only his relationship with Annette hadn't lost some of its beginning charm. He didn't want to be around the "know-it-all teenager." That's what he called her, in fact he didn't care for children in general, his own or other people's. He was proud of his vasectomy and adamant: "No more kids."

"Don't worry, darling, no more for me either."

Annette had found a job and was about to share her older girlfriend's house. Craig said "she's a smart kid."

I promised myself that when Craig and I were settled my daughter would be part of our married life.

Only the reluctant Snowball would move with me to our new house. Craig had not made any headway with her, but that too was bound to change.

*

At the beginning of May we picked his parents up at the quaint regional Santa Barbara airport. They showed great warmth and acceptance of me. When Craig told them over dinner of our wedding plans they expressed genuine joy.

"Welcome to our family, Liesel. We're delighted our son is no longer alone," his mother said.

"Thank you, Mrs. Sloniker."

"Please call me, Mom."

I wasn't so sure if I could. It felt strange, since I had not used the word "Mother" after the age of nine, but I was touched by her request and very happy.

Only a few things needed to be done before the big day. We had already bought matching rings. The marriage license and the move into our joint property still remained.

Craig was always punctual. I worried something had happened to him when he didn't show up at the Van Nuys' town hall at the appointed time. Eventually he rushed in breathless and half an hour late.

"Sweetheart, what's wrong?"

He held his arm and looked in pain. A blood test was needed to get our license which was no big deal for me, but he was hurt.

"The nurse was rough and couldn't find my vein," he said.

"Sorry, darling, let's get this over. I'm going to take you to lunch and kiss you better."

When we emerged outside fully licensed by the State of California to be married Craig said: "I've got to lie down."

I spent the afternoon finalizing our moving arrangements.

Chapter 59

The Move

I WAS AN expert in relocation. It had taken some convincing, but Craig had agreed to my suggestion: Each one of us would pack our own belongings and he would drive the U-Haul truck. To help carry the heavy pieces, I had hired a couple of Mexicans, who were thrilled with a day's pay.

The morning started well, as we planned it and on schedule. We cleared out my place first. At Craig's apartment he was nervous and observed every move our two helpers made. There was a language barrier, but he tried to tell them in Spanish to be extra careful.

I kept the situation on a cheerful keel and rewarded the men with smiles and refreshments to offset the building tension. With every piece of his furniture he issued instructions--how to lift it, turn it, and carry it down the stairs. The two men nodded and worked to the best of their ability.

Then disaster struck. Craig's antique roll top desk, his prized possession, banged into the cement wall as it was moved downstairs by the Mexicans. We examined the damage which was a scratch and a kink in the wood.

"Don't worry, that's no problem to fix," I said and looked at Craig with an encouraging smile.

The men's profuse apologies fell on Craig's deaf ears.

The rage I saw on his face instantly frightened me. We were outside the building when he grabbed my arm and pulled me up the stairs back into his apartment. He kicked the door shut. He grabbed my shoulders and my body went limp and then he hit me. With every punch he hurled words that I could barely make out.

"Stupid.... no respect.... moving company.... no English, Mexicans....your fault....don't ever bring...."

I fell on the floor and covered my head. All I thought was...it's happening again. My mother punishes me. It's not right or just, but I can't do anything about it. It's 1951. Our Jewish neighbor has come and gone. I'm alone and left behind to suffer my mother's fury. Craig has become my mother.

Chapter 60

In Vino Veritas

WHEN HIS RAGE was over he tried to help me up. I was disorientated and didn't want to return to this foreign place with a strange man I didn't understand. I wanted to be back in Bottrop, Germany, so I could explain to Mother about our neighbor. Start my life over again. "What did he do that was so terrible?" I would ask her. "What did he do?"

Craig took my limp body into his arms and stroked my hair. "Please forgive me. I'm so sorry. I can't believe what I did to you, kitten." I was not angry with him, just brokenhearted.

We got through the rest of the day somehow. I was zombie like. My body functioned and continued to move boxes, but my soul was no longer present. After I picked Snowball up from the beauty parlor where she had spent the day out of harm's way, I went to bed.

"I'll return the truck and go straight to a meeting," Craig said. "Rest, sleep and don't worry about me. Someone will drive me home."

I woke before dawn and felt my way to the bathroom in unfamiliar surroundings. I didn't want to put the bedside light on and wake Craig. Something traumatic had happened, but I couldn't remember what. My body ached which was to be expected after a day of heavy moving, but why, when I looked

341

into the mirror, why was my face so swollen and why were there bruises on my arms?

I returned to the bedroom to find Craig, but his side of the bed had not been slept on. Maybe he had fallen asleep on the sofa in the den. I searched from room to room, but he was nowhere to be found. Now I was anxious. He hadn't come home. It was too early to make phone calls, so I sat in the den by the unlit fireplace and waited. Snowball curled up on my lap and ever so often licked my hand.

"Here we are girl, just you and me in our new home…we'll be all right, you'll see." The dog listened and kept licking.

At nine a.m. I called Craig's AA sponsor. "Have you seen Craig? We moved yesterday and he went to a meeting, but hasn't returned."

"Craig is fine and will be there soon."

"What a relief. Thank you."

When he walked through the door he looked normal and not tired like I had expected him to look. He was distant and avoided touching me.

"How about breakfast?" I said.

"No, thanks, I just stopped by to get a few things. I'm on my way to Santa Barbara to see my parents." It was the Sunday before our wedding which was to take place the following Saturday.

"Has there been a change in plans?" My heart beat fast. It was urgent that we discuss the trauma of the previous day. He remained aloof and packed and before I had the strength to raise objections he was out the door, and I watched his car pull away.

I was alone and as the hours turned into days I thought about what happened and I came out guilty. I was responsible and had wrecked another chance at happiness which I should have know I didn't deserve in the first place.

I had no fellowship like Craig. Who was interested in me? My friends would ask questions if they saw my bruises. I couldn't allow that to happen, it wasn't his fault. I couldn't burden Annette, she was too young.

I knew I had made Craig happy. He would come to his senses and return home. I just needed another chance to prove my love.

The phone didn't ring. I called in sick at work. This desolation was unlike any other I had felt before. I could not shake or overcome it like I had so many other obstacles in the past. I was stuck in a pitiful state with no one to pity me.

*

He called on Friday evening, the day before we were to be married and came to the house. "We need to talk," he said as he walked in. He looked unshaven and tired, less put together than he usual did.

"That's an understatement. Where have you been the last few days?" I sat upright in an armchair, and he sat frozen opposite me.

"You are a stranger to me," he said.

"I wasn't until a few days ago," I replied, but then I stopped. I realized it would be best to listen and not say anything else.

"I don't know who you are, and you don't know me. We made our commitment too quickly. There is a wall around you, you say and do all the right things, but I don't know what's behind the wall. It frightens me, and I can't take that chance."

Where in the world was he going with this? What wall?

"Isn't love supposed to overcome....?"

"Let me finish what I have to say. I know what I did to you was unforgivable and very wrong."

"It was nothing. I have already forgotten it."

"I can't forget. I came very close to drinking again. It's not wise to get married now, Liesel, maybe after time and therapy."

When the front door closed behind him the pain in my chest was unbearable. I doubled over in agony. My life had no purpose; I was not wanted or needed by anyone. I had brought nothing but destruction and pain to others. The world would be better off without me.

In a daze I managed to drive to the corner store where I purchased a gallon jug of white wine. I returned to the house and emptied my supply of prescription sleeping pills into a paper towel on the night stand. I dressed in a white cotton nightshirt with long sleeves and buttons to the neck and got a large drinking glass from the kitchen.

My mind was so off balance, bent on permanent disappearance into the void of nothingness, that not even the fate of my beloved Snowball entered my head. I wallowed in the past, in the dim recesses of my memory where too many things had been left undone. I had to blot out consciousness of my wretched life. I would prove to Craig that he had turned his

344

back on one of his own, a fellow alcoholic.

I uncorked the bottle, filled the glass and forced myself to take large gulps of wine followed by a mouthful of pills which I repeated several times. Then I leaned back on the pillow and was still.

Whatever might be on the other side could in no way compare to the inexpressible pain of my repugnant life among the living.

Chapter 61

The Pit

"I'M HURTING. Leave me alone." Who was shaking me? There were voices some distance away, faint and out of reach. Heavy head, cold wetness, vomit smell, painful shaking again.

When I was lifted from horizontal to vertical my head spun in ever increasing and widening revolutions till it felt like it would fly off and burst. A warm, wet towel wiped my face. I was helpless like a baby. Where was I? I couldn't shake a sense of ensnarement and aloneness.

Then there was a faint recognition of Craig's familiar voice. A female sound above me, "Help me hold her up." A loose garment was slipped over my head. I suddenly felt weightless as I was lifted and transported by the strong lover's arms of Craig. He carried me away from the bed and put my shivering body into an armchair by the fireplace. I wanted to open my eyes, but I could not. I wanted to utter his name, but I could not articulate a word.

More strangers' voices by the entrance; Craig's hush-hush explanations: "overdose...sleeping pills...wine...insanity, institution."

A man took charge: "Ambulance at the back."

Another man's voice: "Her medical records?"

My fate was discussed. I had no input and it did not matter in the least. I was observing someone else.

I was horizontal again secured with straps and wheels were under me. Outside a ray of sun hit my face. "She looks like a ghost," someone said. "What a tragedy, she and her husband just moved in."

Craig was beside me, everyone else was a stranger. He would not leave me now. He was in charge of my life, my husband to be.

"Why don't you sit up front," one of the men said. "Pomona's 80 miles away."

"Pomona? Why?" I thought.

Craig's voice. "Here's her purse with her credit cards. I'm not coming. Take good care of her. She means a lot to me."

The ambulance doors slammed shut. I was claustrophobic, my first time inside an ambulance. Medical smell, the engine started. I was moved away to somewhere, sick and hopeless.

Time didn't matter. I lay motionless; once in a while I picked up a word from the two paramedics who drove in and out of traffic along the congested freeways. "Poor woman, you think her husband would have come along."

I wanted to defend him. He did nothing wrong. He needed to protect his sobriety. To be alone was nothing new to me. I had always been alone and misunderstood for as long as I could remember.

The ambulance came to an abrupt halt.

"Sorry dear, we've broken down." I thought how funny

and symbolic this was. My whole life had broken down, and now even the vehicle which transported me to a destination unknown was a disabled wreck at the side of the Ventura Freeway. The rest of the world sped by, unconcerned.

The men had lunch, a coke and hamburgers while they radioed for help. A repair truck couldn't fix the problem. I was reloaded, still stretched out on the gurney and now had a four-man escort. After we drove a lot longer we pulled up outside a dark-brown stone building. I was not lucid enough to wonder why I was in front of this foreboding institution so far from home.

I was wheeled inside and placed next to the reception desk. There I remained unnoticed for quite some time with my arms strapped down and my large leather purse on my stomach. My instinct told me this was not a place I wanted to be.

It was early evening before I was processed by the nurse who had been busy until then. An unsmiling, silent orderly in white garb unlocked double doors to several long corridors, pushed me through and locked up behind us.

No way out of here, I thought. As we made our way deeper into the building I heard moans and groans from different directions. Who did they belong to?

When we arrived at a windowless room with two beds, a night stand, armchair and sink, the attendant unstrapped me and motioned me to the bed on the right. Why didn't anyone speak to me?

The bed was unmade with crumpled sheets. No one cared about me and I didn't deserve special attention, but I wasn't about to occupy another person's bed. I placed myself on the chair. The attendant left. I had not uttered a word all day--just my internal dialogues and observations.

A nurse, who arrived with a sleeveless garment, helped me out of the dress Craig had put me in many hours before.

"My God, look at your arms, dear," she said. I glanced down at my body and saw black and blue bruises, but I couldn't remember where I'd gotten them. I wanted to get into bed. When the sheets were changed I pulled the covers over my head and escaped back into fretful unconsciousness.

When I awoke someone's breath was on my face; a pale eerie woman with uncombed, stringy hair leaned over me. I made no sound. Her hands were around my gold chain necklace with the diamond and ruby heart that Craig had given me for Christmas. She snapped it off and broke the chain.

"You're not allowed to keep it, they'll take everything." She spoke as if she wanted to warn a conspirator.

"He's not allowed to see you if he's been in jail." She scurried away with my possession clenched in her fist. Our room door was open. She was the occupant of the second bed. I did nothing, said nothing and just closed my eyes again.

My thoughts were free and carried me away from this strange place to wherever I wanted to go. I walked with my father in the forests of my childhood with my tiny hand in his. He smiled at me. "Musche Pusche, you are our Wunschkind, the child we longed for all these years."

It was a good place to be. I wanted to stay and hear more soothing words of endearment from the only man I had ever trusted.

Another voice close to my face brought me back. "Mom, you awake? It's Annette."

It must be a trick. Annette didn't know where I was. Besides I wouldn't want her to see me in this condition and place. When I opened my eyes just a slit I saw my daughter look at my arms.

"How in the world could you let him do this to you?" She went on to denounce my almost husband. "I never liked him. There was always something creepy about him. The name Craig means cave-dweller."

My mouth felt dry and my voice was hoarse. "What are you doing here? Who told you?"

"He did. The cave-dweller himself."

"Is he here?"

"Oh Mom, you sound like you're expecting him. Forget him. He's bad news for you."

"How did you get here? It's a long way."

"I've friends and got a ride. Mom, you're a complete mess. You belong in a hospital."

"Isn't this a hospital?"

"It's a nuthouse, Mom! Yeah, your man loves you so much he and his AA buddies sent you to a nuthouse, an insane asylum, and not even a nice one. I've got to get you out right away. Isn't there anyone around here to talk to?"

Annette glanced at my roommate who stared into space. We looked at each other and suppressed a chuckle.

"Right back, Mom."

I felt my spirit lift a little. My daughter had come for me. She was remarkable, strong and in charge. I had lost control of my life, and here was family who had stepped in to help me get back on my feet.

Chapter 62

Rachel

MY BRUISES FADED, but my memory of Craig remained vivid. We disposed of the house at a loss and I moved again. Craig was not in touch in person, but handled our joint affairs through a realtor. I took a one-bedroom apartment in Van Nuys that allowed pets. After work I looked forward to solitary time when I could think and write just as I had in my childhood seated at my father's desk after his death.

Slowly I recovered and began to get a clearer aim on how I wanted to be and how I wanted to feel which was serene with my world weariness gone forever.

As I wrote my thoughts I expressed gratitude for the many blessings in my life. I assumed myself to be happy and well, in an unshakable place and condition where I was safe and no longer on the edge of disaster. I still shut out my German past. Instead I thought of myself at peace with my identity as a citizen of the world who gathered blossoms of knowledge and understanding on her chosen path.

The road map I drew for myself gave purpose to the life I had not been allowed to leave. I knew now that entrance into the world beyond could not be forced or demanded. I was left to stand in darkness at the gate. When my time came to leave this world of bondage it would not be on my terms. I envisioned my spirit light and free and ascending the mountain top to fly with birds of paradise to an eternal home.

When a brochure arrived in the mail for a seminar on "Emotional Healing and Transformation," it caught my eye. On the spur of the moment I signed up for the weekend event.

To drop Craig from my mind and heart was easier said than done. I had not heard from him and I presumed that he had moved on with his life. I wanted to do the same.

At the seminar in Santa Monica we were about 100 men and women. Some couples came to work on their relationships. Others, like me, had a romantic breakup or some other emotional problem.

I had no idea what to expect. Since childhood I had kept my own counsel. I felt out of place in the gathering which lasted from Friday to Sunday night. How typically Californian, everyone wore their emotions on their sleeves and was ready to cry.

Not me. This was foreign to my nature. I sat in the back as an observer and regretted the wasted money.

During his farewell speech Craig said I had a wall around me. Even if there was one, it was my wall of protection. What I hid, my family's Nazi past, needed to be hidden. I felt tired and felt an urge to slip out through the back door of the warehouse-like building, but the door was locked. Tomorrow I would not return to this charade.

But somehow I did and I got caught up in the spirit of looking for solutions within myself. Problems were human. To tap into the value of one's own wisdom and truth could be learned. We were responsible for one life only, our own.

353

The Commandment said: "Thou shalt love thy neighbor as thyself." We were commanded to love ourselves as well as others. To be able to do so we had to find our own unique worth, not our parents', spouse's or children's values, but our own rightful path towards serenity and truth.

*

On the evening of the second day of the seminar a woman named Rachel stood on the podium and spoke about herself. She had come to Los Angeles to pursue an acting career. She was young and beautiful, in her early thirties, with delicate, pale skin and a mass of wavy, shoulder length hair. Her dark eyes were clouded with sadness.

"I have wonderful parents. I'm an only child and my mother and father are very protective of me." Everyone in the room smiled and could relate.

"Too protective; you see, both my parents survived Auschwitz."

We hung on to every one of her words. I wanted to disappear. I sat on the edge of my seat.

"All the time that's what I hear, we're survivors, don't you ever forget. How could I? They drummed it into me day and night. 'Rachel, it's your responsibility to never forget and forgive what was done to us in the camps.' How could I feel good about anything after what they went through? All my relationships with men end in shambles. My life is a mess because of what the Nazis did to my parents."

Here it was. The embodiment of my worse fear was a woman like me and she was accusing me. I had not expected this to happen in Santa Monica, in a time and place so distant and different from the dark land of my birth. The wall around my past crumbled and fell at my feet.

I felt an irresistible need to reply. I stood up and in a trance like state moved to the front. All eyes in the room were on me. There was no time to plan a speech or explanations.

"My parents were Nazis," I said from the podium with my eyes downcast.

A collective sigh. No one heard me and I needed to clarify. "I was born as a gift to Adolf Hitler and dedicated to him at two weeks old."

Thirty-seven years after the end of World War II there was I, my father's daughter, his blond, blue-eyed Wunschkind, face to face with her true legacy.

Rachel made the next move. She glared at me and stormed off the stage, sat down and faced me with hatefulness. The facilitator of the seminar, Dr. Barbara De Angelis, came to stand next to me. Did I need protection from the group's wrath? I braced myself.

But after moments of stunned silence something else happened. Men and women rose to their feet. And it was not anger that motivated them. They rushed and embraced me and lines formed from people who poured out their hearts to me with understanding and love.

This is what I heard over and over: "We need to re-examine a mutual wound and take away lessons. We also need to discard what no longer serves us."

"How can we let bygones be bygones?" I said. "It will never be possible."

"Indiscriminate guilt and blame between Germans and Jews no longer serves us. You and Rachel must learn to work

355

together if you both want to be happy and free in your future."

Again and again I shook my head. I saw a circle had formed around Rachel at the opposite corner of the large room.

"I hate to be German and I don't deserve this amount of focus. Rachel does." The attention I got embarrassed me.

"Like father, like daughter," I said.

I was an apple from the same tree and had no right not to be painted with the same brush. I was German and didn't deserve to be coddled. "You need to focus on Rachel. She deserves compassion. Please leave me alone."

I wanted to run.

Chapter 63

My Neighbor's Hand

IT AMAZED ME how many arms around me were from Jews as I soon discovered. Where did this generosity come from? Surely, I represented an enemy of such magnitude and my kind had brought such death and destruction to the Jewish people that nothing could bridge the divide.

Only one day remained before this weekend journey into the past would come to a close. How insignificant Craig had become. It was Rachel whom I had been forced to face instead. And my neighbor who had walked swiftly away on the fateful spring day of 1951. Could there ever be healing with them?

When I got home I couldn't begin to think of sleep. I was feverish with burning urgency. One day remained for me to explain to Rachel that I was not like my parents and other Germans. I wanted to convince her that I was on her side and that I had denounced my people and family at the age of nine. In my soul I had taken my neighbor's hand and walked away with him.

*

The photographs and few small mementoes I had from Germany were in the metal box that had traveled with me forever. I had often been tempted to throw it away, but it was still hidden in my closet. I had not opened it since I put it together hastily in my mother's house before I fled to England.

I undid the string. The lid had rusted, but the content was unharmed and I emptied it on my bed. There was my childhood diary, family photographs and a couple of letters from my mother, also the black and white photo of my name-giving ceremony and dedication to the Fuehrer and the Nazi cause. My father had orchestrated it with pride under the large portrait of Adolph Hitler. The photograph which showed our family of four was in pristine condition. I studied my mother's face. What went through her mind at that moment?

There was another picture of Mother and me with my doll Maritzebelle. I had been such a nurtured and happy child and part of a loving family, yet I had ended up alone and far away from home.

"Why?" I cried. "Where has my family gone? Why Papa?" I cried until dawn.

*

Rachel arrived the next day with the same dark circles around her eyes. Our paired predicament became the focus for the rest of the seminar. I spoke from the podium about my neighbor and told about my confusion and hate when I learned the truth about my parents. I addressed the group, but I only wanted to reach one heart--Rachel's.

We ran into each other in the bathroom and were cordial.

"Let's start a dialogue," we said and after the seminar was over we did. Our predicament and relationship was complicated. It remained that way and she stopped calling me after a few months. However, I was besieged with requests to stay in touch from many other Jewish seminar participants.

"Keep on telling your story," they said.

The more I spoke the truth the easier it got. I found a bridge to lead me out of my isolation. When our veils are lifted and we stand in the light of vulnerability and redemption others who see us may be moved to discard their own muteness and stand in the radiant light with us. I realized that when I brought my innermost fears to light they dissipated and I began to help others to do the same.

I could sympathize with every man and woman of the Jewish faith who had such a heavy burden of the past to bear and I still condemned my own people.

It was through the love of insightful Jews and my encounter with them that I began to realize that I needed to look back not with anger against a past I could do nothing about. I had to learn to accept and change the only thing I could change which was me and my feelings towards my people.

Maybe to turn my back on my family for so many years had not been just, though understandable. I had felt betrayed and believed the guilty needed to be cast off. I had severed my physical and emotional ties to avoid being contaminated myself.

But were we not supposed to love and honor our parents? Had I broken one of the Ten Commandments? Was it up to me to judge my parents? Was it my own self-righteous doing or grace that led me to take a path different from them?

My mother held some of the answers.

Chapter 64

Mother

JEWISH FRIENDS FROM the seminar kept checking on me and they urged: "Go to Germany and visit your mother. Look at her again with new eyes. What actually did she do?" I was not sure any more.

"You have changed. Could your mother have changed too?" I heard again and again.

After all my moving, Mother and I were completely out of touch. She had no way to find me if she ever needed to get hold of me. I had her number and when I found the courage to make the call, I was shocked at the frailty in her voice.

"Ja, hier ist Frau Steffens. Wer ist am Telephone bitte?

"It's me, your daughter Liesel, calling from America. How are you?" I still couldn't bring myself to say "Mother."

"Where's Liesel? Is she coming home to see me?" She sounded excited and hopeful.

"I'm coming to see you very soon. Are you strong and healthy?"

"I will die before I see my daughter again." My mother's words pierced my heart.

"No, you're not going to die. I've been busy, but now I'll come to see you. We go out somewhere and talk. Many things I want to tell you."

"What things?" She sounded tired.

"Nice things. We'll have a Kaffeeklatsch, just you and me. I'll tell you about your wonderful grandchildren Hugh and Annette." Her hearing was poor.

"Am I going to see my daughter Liesel again before I die?"

"I'm right here on the telephone. This is Liesel speaking to you."

"I want to see my daughter again before I die. She was always a good person, she was our Wunschkind."

Now I was in tears. I had not been a "good person" to her. I had failed my duties as a daughter in every possible way. Was she forgiving me? Did she remember the day the neighbor came to our house and she was unjust and had punished me?

These matters could not be discussed long distance. I promised again to make arrangements for a trip to Germany soon. Maybe I would bring Annette for a three-generation reunion, three very different women, part of the same family.

After I hung up the phone, I thought about our relationship. I had dismissed Else Steffens for so long, but she held the key to healing the past and was much more important to my future than I wanted to believe. I also realized that I missed my mother's love.

I pictured her sitting in the retirement home, struck by age and crippled by osteoporosis, the once tall, vibrant woman now stooped towards the ground. I knew I had to see her one more time before the earth claimed her mortal bones and she joined my father in the unreachable place beyond the horizon.

Annette, Snowball, Hugh,
Jessica & Liesel

Jessica L. Browne

Tyler L. Browne

Liesel & Ingrid Neul

Chapter 65

Sunset

FATHER HAD DIED in 1950 by the sea. I pictured death like a ship that sailed quietly away towards a shining beacon and thousands of lanterns beckoned "come homeward" to the harbor of your soul.

Although I was still procrastinating I sent Fritz a note with my phone number and address. I asked how our mother was doing and told him I planned a visit soon.

My brother called a few days later. "Sorry to inform you, Mother died last night. Nothing could be done. She was comatose the last couple of weeks."

Two weeks since our final conversation. "I'm devastated," I said.

"We're both orphans now," Fritz said who was in his 60s.

I thought his remark was odd and touching at the same time. Our mother had meant a great deal to him. I wanted to comfort my brother, but could not find the right words. We all die alone, but our mother had left the earth more alone because of me.

Fritz said she was at the funeral home in Luedenscheid. "She wanted her head to rest on a certain cushion, and we followed her wishes. Remember you made mother a pillow?"

I felt shamed. I remembered it well, the pillow with the large red rose I had stitched as a little girl. Mother had preserved and cherished my effort and taken it to her deathbed.

"When's the funeral?" I said.

"Planning to attend?"

"I...I...don't know," I mumbled. "I'm not sure."

"We figured that. Don't worry. I am going to take care of everything. She wanted to be cremated."

We hung up. I didn't get the chance to tell Fritz that I wasn't worthy since I had abandoned Mother when she was alive.

My mother died alone, and I now mourned alone. I mourned for all those lost and lonely years and I mourned for my mother and my motherless self.

*

Longing to connect to a person of my mother's age I found a Jewish retirement home in Encino and walked in with a bouquet of flowers. I asked the receptionist, "you have a female resident who gets no family visits?"

"Sure, we do. Esther, room 25 down the hall. Esther doesn't have anyone."

I went to her room and opened the door. Esther was in bed, a frail woman in her late 80s.

"Hello," I said cheerfully. "I've come to talk to you. I brought you these flowers."

"Please have a seat," she said. She was surprised and

obviously delighted with my visit. After I arranged the flowers in a vase I sat next to her bed.

"Your name?" Esther said.

"Sorry, I should have introduced myself. My name is Liesel."

"Lovely name, are you Jewish?"

"No, I'm German."

"Never mind, I like you anyway."

Esther's statement put me at ease and we talked for the rest of the afternoon. She was sharp and witty and I promised to return on a regular basis.

Esther became a surrogate mother to whom I could offer my attention and love. It helped me deal with my guilt about abandoning my own mother at the end of her life.

Chapter 66

New Life

"MOM, I"M pregnant," Annette said one day out of the blue.

"Don't joke."

"No joke. And no I'm not getting married if that's what you were thinking."

I stared at my daughter's stomach. "How did this happen? Who's the father?"

"Gone with the Santa Ana winds! I want to have the baby and I can do it alone."

We discussed the medical implications and decided it was best for Annette to return to England. Her doctors and kidney surgeon were there and knew her medical history. They would be better equipped to monitor her and the baby's health.

My beautiful granddaughter, Jessica, was born on June 21, 1989. Like Annette's, her middle name was Liesel. When I learned about her safe arrival, I was elated. There was a future for our family. Part of my mother, me and Annette would carry on for another generation. We had another opportunity to redeem ourselves as a family if we continued to follow the right path together.

When Jessica was four months old Annette returned

with her to the United States. We now rented a roomy Beverly Hills apartment. Annette was a remarkable and selfless mother with a natural talent for nurturing.

Chapter 67

The Way of Religion

I HAD RUN from any organized religion and I avoided any group that was interested in the way my soul progressed. The nuns in Limburg had been wise and never tried to indoctrinate me with Catholicism. I had always appreciated their tolerance.

The one thing my father taught me that I retained and practiced consistently was to examine what I was told by others. I had not always listened to my inner voice that urged me to be more cautious as in the case of my involvement in African politics and my Palm Beach naïveté.

I had learned my lesson. My aversion in allowing myself to be influenced by anyone was strong and blind faith in authority was something I had never been able to fathom. After all, my father had been inspired by a man who had led him and his subjects to death and destruction on a massive scale. What good was faith unless it brought peace and justice?

I was not without spirituality and a belief in an almighty power, the Creator of the universe, and my spirit had gathered pearls of wisdom from many sources and faiths, the tribes of the African bush, as well as world religions like Hinduism, Buddhism, Islam and Christianity. They all seemed to have a fundamental oneness and I considered them built on basically the same principles and understandings. There could only be one God, so believers throughout the world worshiped one and the same divine being now and throughout the ages.

To my understanding at the time Judaism did not seem to fit into this group of universal spirituality. Being German was not a religion, but a Jew had a special faith as well as ethnicity. My father would never have been able to comprehend that a German might be a Jew or a Jew a German.

Being Jewish was inherited and could not be understood by outsiders. Since by now I had met many special human beings of the Jewish faith I wondered what this unique faith was. The elusive mystique of Judaism began to fascinate me.

I wrote an article about my childhood encounter with my Jewish neighbor called "The Awakening," which the *Los Angeles Times* published as a large feature on the front page of their "View" section. Early in the morning on the day of publication I received a phone call which turned out to be the first of many.

"This is Rabbi Asa."

I was shocked. A rabbi called ME? He explained that a member of his flock had read the piece and had rushed over to the Rabbi's house in tears.

"Would you be so kind and come to the synagogue to address our congregation during a Friday night service?" I had never spoken to a rabbi before, much less been inside a synagogue.

By now I accepted that with my family secret out in the open came new responsibility. My life had a mission and if a rabbi made a request I felt obliged to comply no matter what the outcome and consequences might be.

No one in my family had ever set foot in a synagogue. Would I not be desecrating such a temple of worship just by my presence? I had many conflicting feelings and thoughts in my head and heart. There was also fear of facing single-handedly a large group of Jews, not in a social setting, but in the sanctity of their own consecrated place of worship and in front of their ancestor's God.

I agreed to meet the Rabbi and his congregants, but I soon got cold feet. However, every excuse I came up with to cancel seemed lame. I had no more time for evasion and falsehood; I needed to overcome my fear.

Rabbi Asa had called back and invited me to his home for dinner before the service. He called it Shabbat. The very word intimidated me. I had no idea what it meant, but I felt a great honor was bestowed on me.

That was confirmed when I sat down with his family. The formal, white tablecloth and china setting brought back memories of the way my mother had set the table for festive occasions. Everything had a special place and order. I told the Rabbi's wife how overwhelmed and honored I felt at my first Shabbat dinner in an orthodox Jewish home.

The Rabbi was kind enough to explain a few principles before the dinner started. I heard the greeting "Shabbat Shalom" for the first time. Every detail was deeply meaningful even to an outsider like me.

I discovered Shabbat happened every week at sunset and had five components; I hung on every one of the Rabbi's words and explanations. My soul started to sing and shout on the inside, "Truth, I am hearing eternal truth."

The five purposes of this weekly feast were: awareness of the world, marvel at the universe and the beauty of creation, freedom from slavery, not just for Jews, but for all people in bondage, identity and fellowship with the Jewish people, enhancement of one's person through joy, rest and holiness, and dedication to peace.

These were not abstract values, but cardinal truths I had always believed in except for the third part about identity. That evening I realized that Jews were diverse and different just like the people of Africa were different in their customs, but nevertheless, there was oneness in their fundamental principles that mattered. A good Jew who followed his scriptures would live his life with the same righteousness as a devout Moslem, Buddhist or Christian.

There were many firsts for me on that Friday night. My entrance into the synagogue had me literally shaking in my shoes. I sat in a place of honor; they called it Bima, and I faced the congregation. A prayer book, *Gates of Prayer,* was put into my hands. I tried to follow the service, but I got caught up in verses which astonished me:

"Let there be love and understanding amongst us; let peace and friendship be our shelter from life's storms. Eternal God, help us to walk with good companions, to live with hope in our hearts and eternity in our thoughts, that we may lie down in peace and rise up to find our hearts waiting to do Your will."

"May this vision never fade: let us continue to work for the day when the nations will be one and at peace. Then shall we sing with one accord, as Israel sang at the shores of the Red Sea."

*

374

When it came my time to speak, I was again hit with strong feelings of unworthiness. What right did I have to be here? I was very conscious of my German accent and it seemed to weigh down my tongue like a rock. But I saw that the assembly of people wanted to hear what I had to say and that it mattered to them.

And then I took heart. I, the German, daughter of Nazis, had not come alone. I was accompanied by my neighbor. My neighbor, the defamed and forgotten stranger of Bottrop was not a stranger here. These were his people, his fellow Jews. It was as if my neighbor had taken my hand again and spoken to me gently:

"Liesel, meet my people. See what my people, your neighbors are like. See with your own eyes and hear with your own ears what you and your people were so afraid of. It was your prejudices and fears that told you we were different. Differences and bigotry only exist because of your fears, judgments and suspicions."

Chapter 68

His Name

AFTER MY FIRST invitation to speak publicly in front of a large group many others followed and not just from Jewish organizations. I spoke to Christian congregations and asked them to seek out Jewish counterparts in their neighborhoods. I encouraged pastors to speak to rabbis and find commonality. As I traveled around the country, I encountered many wonderful people who nourished my soul.

I met Jews who had never spoken to a German and never imagined themselves sharing a common grief. I encountered Germans who felt shame like I did, and who had always believed they were alone with their desolate feelings. Whenever and wherever I was called to share my story and that of my neighbor's, I felt compelled to bare my heart and soul.

*

My neighbor and his family were now so real that I began to wonder what their names were. The only person I could ask was my brother Fritz who no longer lived in Bottrop. I was careful how I asked my questions. After all, on the day of my encounter with this neighbor I was ostracized and no one had ever mentioned him again.

"Hello, Fritz, how are you?" My brother was pleased by my call and we conversed for a while about superficialities.

"Still happy in the United States," I said. "Coming to visit?"

"Maybe one day I will take you up on it."

"That would be nice." I itched to get to the purpose for my call.

"Fritz, do you by chance remember a man who came down Gladbecker Strasse when...." I didn't have to finish.

"That was Willi Meyer." My brother had the neighbor's name on the tip of his tongue as if he had been as preoccupied with his existence as I was. Now I had the name. I wrote it down.

"Is that Meyer with an "e" or "a?"

"With an "e." They really ruffed him up," Fritz said. "Quite a shame!"

I restrained myself from asking who "they" were. "Do you know where the Meyer family is now?"

"No, I don't, but the Witkes might. They had a visit from Willi once. They still live in the same house. Why do you want to know?"

"Just curious." I chatted some more then said goodbye. We promised to keep in touch.

As soon as I hung up I got the Witke's phone number from international information.

A man answered and I identified myself as an interested party from America. "I'm looking for a man who has lived in Bottrop--Willi Meyer," I said. Again, there was no hesitation about name recognition.

"Yes, Willi Meyer was here once for a short time. He also visited a friend."

"Who's the friend?"

"Her name's Johanna Banner. She knows more about the Meyers."

In minutes I had the number for Johanna Banner on Sterkrader Strasse. How easy it was! Why had I not made these calls long ago?

"Mrs. Banner, please excuse my call, but I am trying to find a family by the name of Meyer."

"Why? Who are you?" She sounded elderly and suspicious.

"Mrs. Banner, I met and spoke to Willi Meyer once many years ago when I was a child and lived on Gladbecker Strasse with my family. Willi told me he looked for a man who had saved his son." My German sounded foreign to me.

She was silent.

"I already spoke to Mr. Witke. He told me you are a friend of the Meyers and know where they are. It means a great deal to me to find them." Still silence on the other end. I could not give up now.

"At the time I thought the person who saved the boy was my father, but this turned out not to be the case. Do you by chance know who the man was who did save my neighbor's son?"

More silence.

Then she said his name. I took the receiver from my ear and put my head on my knees. She didn't know me, but she heard how I sobbed.

"That can't be true," I said after I pulled myself together.

She spoke again. "It's true! I was the Meyers' nanny, you know."

"You were the one who hid the boy?"

"Yes, I was. There was no one else in Bottrop who would have done such a thing. I was just 19. The Meyers had no one else."

I was overwhelmed. These were soul shattering revelations.

*

In the darkness of Bottrop there had been at least two shining lights endowed with enough compassion to save a precious life even though it endangered their own. One was Johanna Banner and the other was...Friedrich Sommer.

Mother's pervert!

I could still see the overweight Herr Sommer. I saw him wave to me to come inside his Kino.

And now I imagined his bulky body rushing through the night with a child in his arms.

Chapter 69

The Search

AT THE END of our conversation Mrs. Banner reflected on her own life and how different it was from mine. She regretted that she never had the opportunity to leave Bottrop.

"You were lucky you got away. People never forgave me. I have remained an outcast to this day."

My heart raged against my hometown and went out to this brave, lonely woman who had to bear such injustice for so long.

Willi Meyer and his son had been back to see her several times from Israel, but she believed Willi had passed away. "Look for his son. If I remembered right he's an attorney in the United States somewhere."

I had much to think about and a lot to do. I made many fruitless phone calls to Israel and searched for attorneys by the name of Meyer listed with the American Bar Association, all to no avail. I never gave up.

There was someone else I needed to find out about.

My Father!

I don't know if it was my secret hope that one day in spite of Mother I would hear an eyewitness say "that man was your Papa." Now I knew for sure that would never be. The hero of Bottrop had a different identity.

I thought much about Herr Sommer. Oh, if only I could see and speak to him now and give him the praise he deserved.

The man who was my father, who held my small hand and showed me the wonders of the forest was also the other man; the man who had a role in the fate of our neighbors.

For too long I had not wanted to think about my father at all, good or bad. His duality bewildered and frightened me. I had adored him and cradled him at the moment of his death. He had talked to me about values, of how I should live my life. Yet all was meaningless since it came from a man who did not live by what he preached. It came from a man who was a hard-core Nazi.

*

The Simon Wiesenthal Center in Los Angeles was helpful and had resources in Berlin where the Holocaust records were kept. Later on they were moved to Washington, DC. The information on my father's participation in Poland was sparse. Investigations were abandoned due to his natural death in 1950. Prosecution did not extend to the next generation.

There was a mountain of evidence against Koch and the mass murder he had orchestrated against Jewish and Polish civilians. I knew my father had been in charge of the children.

*

As far as my father's time in Bottrop was concerned he had not sat at home idly and read his books and walked in the woods. He was the local Blockwart, a particularly nasty, deceitful individual and nuisance for his neighbors who snooped around and turned them in for the slightest infraction against the Nazi Reich.

Now I saw why Mother was so terrified when I brought Willi Meyer home. She believed he had come to get revenge.

Willi Meyer, our neighbor the Jew, had suffered much at our hands but I had looked into his eyes and not seen a hint of vengefulness or even animosity.

*

A couple of years had passed since I wrote my article "The Awakening." I now embraced everything Jewish. Elie Wiesel's book *Night* had a profound affect on me. It depicted the Jewish faith as so strong that it sustained believers through the concentration camps.

I enrolled in a Judaic Studies course at the University Synagogue on Sunset Boulevard in Los Angeles and I often brought my granddaughter Jessica in her stroller. We sat in the back. The class was full of prospective converts, mostly young brides about to be married into Jewish families.

The thought of conversion and embracing the Jewish faith as my own did not come to me until my attorney Chuck Hurewitz brought up the subject over lunch. Chuck had taken care of my legal affairs ever since I was besieged with calls after the article in the *LA Times*.

"You must feel wonderful to be born a Jew, you have strong family roots," I said. "I don't know where I belong. I'm only sure where I don't belong, and that's Germany."

"Have you considered becoming a Jew?" He asked.

It had never crossed my mind, but now I began to think about it. When I brought the subject up with Rabbi Freehling, the senior rabbi at University Synagogue, he said, "you have met one of the requirements and have studied our faith. We would love to welcome you as one of our own."

"What does it cost to become a Jew?"

He laughed. "It's free for now, but it'll cost you plenty later." I laughed as well without knowing what he meant.

As the day of my religious conversion neared and I assimilated more and more into the Jewish community my personal life also took a turn for the better.

*

Out with a neighbor one day on an errand we got caught in traffic. He was late for his dinner appointment with an old friend from Detroit and had no time to drop me off first. The neighbor suggested I join them. When we entered the restaurant, Hugo's in Hollywood, a tall, handsome man rose to his feet to greet us.

"Hello, my name's Don Appel."

We sat down and the two men reminisced about old times. He spoke in a warm and melodic voice and said he had brought his mother to live near him during the final months of her life.

What a nice man, I thought. He wore no wedding band. When we got up to leave I said "would you like to attend my conversion to Judaism ceremony in two weeks?"

"How did you know I'm Jewish?"

"I didn't."

Outside the restaurant he handed me his business card, and I promised to call with the details. On the passenger side of Don Appel's bright red MG sports car sat a huge Irish Wolfhound.

"That's Clancey, my adopted son from the shelter."

Over dinner the next night at the romantic Beau Rivage in Malibu Don and I discovered that we had a lot in common and were able to converse with ease. He seemed to be a free-spirited man, divorced for the past five years, who was very comfortable with himself. He was cultured and well read and he loved music and travel.

We shared a great love for animals and nature, and we made each other laugh. I felt safe enough to tell him about my problems with the INS and that my daughter and I might have to return to England.

The evening went so well that Don invited me to his apartment in the Hollywood Hills a couple of days later and cooked dinner for me. Clancey, the dog, took a fancy to me and pressed his huge body against mine. Don was able to catch me just before I tumbled. We laughed and kissed, and I stayed until dawn.

Our next date was lunch at a new restaurant. We enjoyed the lovely and serene garden setting. Out of the blue Don put his two fists on the table.

"Pick a hand," he said and laughed. I had no idea what surprise was in store for me.

"Go ahead."

I reached for the right. He opened his hand and revealed an antique diamond ring.

384

"We only know each other for a short time, but I would be honored if you became my wife. Will you marry me?"

"I can't think of a better way to spend the rest of my life." The ring had been his mother's engagement ring.

*

On June 1, 1990, I accepted the religion of Israel and promised to live by its principles and practices. The record showed that Liesel became Leah bat Abraham and Sarah. Leah was Jacob's wife and the mother of Joseph and Benjamin.

"Thy people shall be my people and thy God my God. (Book of Ruth)

Two months later at a sunrise ceremony that gathered our family and friends and overlooked the Pacific Ocean at the Beau Rivage, I became Mrs. Appel. A jazz band jammed and a black singer serenaded the song Don had picked for me: *What are you doing the rest of your life.*

I was my beloved's, and my beloved was mine.

A Bride Again in 1990

Don H. Appel

Chapter 70

Return to the Past

A PHONE CALL came from Wallmerod, Germany, where I had last lived with my mother. "We thought you were dead. You're invited to your Marienschule's 40th class reunion...."

My past had searched for me and I agreed to answer the call. I decided to combine my visit to the Westerwald region and the convent school with two other trips down memory lane.

When I walked along the corridors of the ancient Marienschule in Limburg I felt an unexpected sense of belonging and pride. For over 100 years this institution had educated women, many of whom had become community leaders, well-known writers and artists. Nineteen of my classmates attended, and all remembered me as the rebel of the class who sat at the back and did her own thing.

Only a few nuns still remained, and in the tradition of tolerance the school now also employed men and non-catholic teachers. I asked for permission to speak to the large assembly of former pupils that spanned the generations from graduates in 1941 to the class of 2001.

This is what I said: "I am Liesel Appel, born Steffens, teacher's training seminar of 1961. Please excuse my mistakes in German. For almost 40 years I have lived in English-speaking countries, first in the United Kingdom and today in the United States. I am honored that I was not forgotten and one of you made the effort to find me.

I remember my time in the Marienschule with fondness and love. I was not a good pupil and squandered my time here dreaming of far away places. Nevertheless, everything turned out all right. The dedicated nuns of this school gave me something special for my life, which they taught by example. I learned tolerance, to think of others and respect every human being on planet earth.

My life after school went through many ups and downs like every life. We all have our own unique life story. The profession we selected is an important one--to educate and lead young people. We lead best by our example, how we direct ourselves and what our world views are.

Please allow me to quote from Kahlil Gibran's *Prophet*. 'When a teacher asked how he should teach, the answer was: the teacher who walks in the shadow of the temple gives not of his wisdom, but rather of his faith and his lovingness. He leads you to the threshold of your own mind. The vision of one man lends not its wings to another. You are the bows from which your children as living arrows are sent forth. You may give them your love but not your thoughts for their souls dwell in the house of tomorrow.'

Sisters, I thank you for leading me to the threshold of my own thoughts and sending me into the world as a living arrow.

Our world is small. If we could shrink the world's population to a group of 100 people with the same human ratio, the world would look as follows:

58 Asians, 21 Europeans, 20 Africans,

52 women, 48 men,

70 non-white human beings, 30 white,

30 Christians, 70 non-Christians.

When we see our world from this perspective, it is clear how important tolerance and understanding is. When we are able, like today, to participate in free religious expression, we are better off than 3 billion people in the world.

When we have food in our refrigerators, clothes on our bodies and a roof over our head, we are richer than 75 percent of the rest of the world.

Today I am a Jew, as is my husband. I often address groups in the United States on our responsibilities and unity as world citizens and on the necessary healing between Germans and Jews. Let's walk gently together on this planet in sandals of love."

When I finished the room full of women rose to their feet, applauded and I received a bouquet of flowers. Unexpectedly, I had a room full of German sisters who agreed.

*

Wolfgang Ligges and his wife Brigitte were happy to hear from me and invited me to spent time at their home.

The third stop of my one-week journey into the past was Bottrop which I had only planned provisionally. I was not sure if I would go through with it when the time came.

The night in the Ligges' large house in the country started with pleasantries.

Brigitte was a wonderful hostess and prepared a lovely meal for me; I told her on the phone I was a vegetarian. Wolfgang who sported a beard and still looked great had been able to retire early from his government position and lived very comfortably with Brigitte, also retired as a teacher. We had all become grandparents and enjoyed talking about the development and progress of our children.

"Deutschland's different from when you left Liesel," Wolfgang said. He referred to Germany's prosperity. "The past has been forgotten, and rightly so. We have new opportunities and new challenges. Too many foreign workers drain our resources, and since our unification we have been inundated with problems from the former East Germany."

"I still have lingering issues with my past," I said. I could see that irritated Wolfgang and his wife. They both knew of my speeches, writings and openness regarding my family's Nazi history. I had mailed them the *LA Times* article, but not received any comments. They also knew I had converted to Judaism and married a Jew.

"It's 2001," Wolfgang said. "No one's interested in the subject you're referring to."

"It's not a question of interest," I said. I tried to remain a polite guest. "It's a matter of justice and of responsibility."

"Long completed," Brigitte said. "Jews have received generous government compensations. They have returned, collected and gone away again, satisfied. I don't know where you get your misconceptions."

The way this conversation was developing made me uncomfortable. I seriously questioned my preoccupation with the past. Maybe I was wrong and should let go.

When I talked about my father and said how wrong he had been in his beliefs and work for Koch in Poland they came to his defense.

"You're doing your father an injustice," Wolfgang, the lawyer said. "You won't be able to prove any wrongdoing. Everyone had to be a Nazi in those days, there was no choice."

"There are always choices," I said.

"That's melodramatic. You are making up stories."

"You have always exaggerated," Brigitte said.

I had no idea what she was referring to.

"Give this nonsense up."

That night when I went to bed I wondered if maybe I had been away too long and was out of touch.

Nothing was said about the subject in the morning. At breakfast I asked directions from their house to Bottrop which was about 100 kilometers away.

"You're not going to find what you're looking for," Wolfgang said. "Bottrop is a modern city. Enjoy your day, drive carefully and don't look for trouble."

*

Wolfgang was right about Bottrop. It was now a thriving city of more than 120,000 people with a modern town center, new hotels, busy restaurants and buzzing coffee houses. It was a sunny spring day, and Bottropers were out and about.

I left the town center and drove down the main thoroughfare, Gladbecker Strasse, to the suburb of Bottrop-Eigen where we had lived.

392

There time had stood still. My heart pounded in my chest. Grayness and soot of the long closed coal mines still clung to the house-facades and sorrow and ugliness still permeated the air. Progress had passed over this part of town.

What was I doing here? I wanted to turn my car around and flee. Nothing good would come from walking on this unholy pavement which had once been littered with a thousand pieces of glass. Willi Meyer had walked down this sidewalk in a hurry. He couldn't get away fast enough.

I should do the same, as quickly as possible and go as far away as possible. I should return to my new home where it was warm and life was unencumbered by guilt, grief and memories of treachery. But I had walked down hundreds of tree-lined streets and boulevards, but this street pulled me back again and again to my life-changing encounter with a Jew.

I parked the car and walked into the Witke's Kaufhaus (department store) which spanned the length of what had been three individually owned properties during my childhood: 332, our house, 333, the Sommer's Kino and 334, the former, smaller Kaufhaus. I had no plan how to proceed.

Inside the store I asked a sales assistant to speak to business owner, Herr Witke. She left and soon Guenther Witke, a good looking man in his forties came and greeted me.

"I hope I'm not imposing," I said. "My name's Liesel Steffens. I was just passing through after a class reunion. We used to live.... "

"Of course, I remember you and your family. Your brother Fritz and I get together once in a while. I tell you what, let's go upstairs and surprise Mother. Mother will be delighted to receive a visit from a member of the Steffens family."

I followed him up the stairs, outwardly calm, but I shook inside. I was about to set foot in the home of the Meyer family. If only the walls could speak. Had the Meyers just celebrated Shabbat and prayed for their neighbors when the hellish mob broke in?

It was an immaculately dressed Frau Witke who opened the door to the apartment. Although, she was in her seventies she looked great and prepared as if she had expected a visitor.

"Guten Tag, I'm Liesel Steffens. I lived next door when I was a child."

"Of course, I remember," she said. "You were a cute little girl. Your mother braided your hair."

"Not so cute anymore," I said smiling.

"She was a wonderful woman, your mother. I remember your family very well."

Guenther excused himself and went back down to the store. I followed Mrs. Witke into the sitting room where she invited me to take a seat on the sofa.

"What may I get you? We have freshly baked Apfelstollen."

How she reminded me of my mother. I declined the offer and listened to her recollections instead. She was widowed and had several successful children and grandchildren.

After her husband died, Guenther took over the running of their Kaufhaus. It was the only one in Bottrop-Eigen, and the business supplied more than adequate financial support for her whole family.

I felt my anxiety grow. I wanted to hear from her lips how she perceived the past and her ownership of the Meyer property.

"Would it be possible for me to see the part of the building which was our old house?" I asked.

"Of course, we have made improvements and taken excellent care of it." She was proud to lead the way. A new staircase connected the property on the upper floors. Below, the area which had once been the cinema now belonged to the department store. I was careful with all of my questions as she took me towards the section of the house I had lived in as a child.

There was our former living room, the kitchen, the room Oma had died in, my bedroom. The apartment seemed so much smaller than I remembered it and gloomy and it was not as nicely furnished, though very clean and neat.

Mrs. Witke told me she rented it out to one of her employees. Nothing but sad memories came back to me in these rooms. Lucky I got away. I looked for our balcony, but it was no longer there. I did not want to linger.

When we returned back to her apartment, which had been the Meyer's home, perspiration was on my forehead and I felt faint. I sat back down on the sofa.

"Anything wrong?" Frau Witke said. "Let me get you a glass of water."

When she went to the kitchen I realized I had to find a way to direct our conversation to the only subject matter that interested me so I could leave.

When she returned I took a deep breath. "Have you ever

heard of the Meyer family?"

Her reaction showed no hesitation, no trace of guilt. "Yes," she answered easily. "A man named Willi Meyer came here once, many years ago. He sat on the same spot on the sofa where you're sitting now. Trembled the whole time he was here."

Willi had trembled. I trembled now.

"He asked about this house. Thought it was his property and he deserved compensation. Can you imagine?"

She looked at me, confident I would understand his outrageous request. After all, I was a neighbor's daughter, a Steffens. I said nothing.

"We acquired this house legally," she went on. "The Meyers had no claim to it whatsoever. He pointed out how his family had been forced to abandon the property and leave Bottrop. We told him that had nothing to do with us."

I felt vindicated. I was not wrong in seeking justice. Not everyone had been compensated. Our neighbor hadn't.

Frau Witke added, "The Meyers were good people though, and very well respected. They used to give free communion dresses to the little Catholic girls who didn't have the money to purchase them."

Tears in my eyes, I had heard enough and needed to leave. I went downstairs to the store, and Guenther escorted me to my car.

"This part of Bottrop has not changed much," he said. "You should take a look at the other areas of town while you're here. We even have a Warner Brother's movie theme park like Disneyland and get visitors from all over."

I had no intention to entertain myself or to sightsee in Bottrop. I did not want to eat there nor spend the night. I had come for one reason only. My next stop was the Rathaus (town hall).

Chapter 71

The Archives

I WALKED TO the town's archives which were housed in a different building from the town hall on a close-by street.

There I approached an accommodating clerk. "How far back in history do your records go?"

"How long do you need them? We go back several hundred years."

I didn't beat around the bush.

"Do you have records of the Jews of Bottrop?"

I wondered if I might be stonewalled, but she looked at me, a fellow German and said, "that's not a request we have ever gotten before, but you're in luck. There's one person in town who knows all about the Jews of Bottrop. He is the town historian."

"How can I find him?"

"His name is Dr. Manfred Lueck. He has retired, but you're lucky. He happens to be in the building today."

She showed the way to a room filled with books.

The man who soon entered the quiet library was tall, dressed in sports coat and trousers and he looked to be in his 60s. From behind his glasses he studied me with caution and then he gestured for me to take a seat at a large conference table.

"The receptionist tells me you are looking for information. How may I help you and what is your interest in the subject?" He spoke softly and didn't mention the word "Jews."

"It's personal," I said almost in a whisper. "My name is Liesel Appel. I live in America, but I grew up in Bottrop. Have you heard the name Willi Meyer?"

He nodded. "Yes, the name is familiar." He studied me with curiosity as well as uncertainty. "Just a moment, please," he said and left.

He returned a short time later with a briefcase in which he carried several books. He took out two thin volumes with the title *Juden in Bottrop*.

He was the author and compiler of this documentary history about the Jews of Bottrop, from the first arrival of Jewish families in 1808 until their deportation in 1944. He turned pages until he found what he was looking for--a paragraph on page 87.

"Here it is! Meyer, Wilhelm (1911-1939)." Then he pointed to another entry on the opposite page and whispered "these Meyers are connected." I read, Meyer, August (1911-1936)." As it turned out the year 1911 pertained to the Meyers' arrival in town. In the case of August Meyer, Willi's father, he was born on June 10th, 1874 in Unna, and he died in Bottrop on February 21st, 1936.

Willi Meyer was born on August 3rd, 1903 in Rauxel. Therefore he was 48 years old when he met me in 1951. The short paragraph said that he ran his family's business on 334 Gladbecker Strasse after his father's death. On the night of the pogrom--November 9-10, 1938, he was incarcerated with his wife and son. The family business was abandoned and extinguished on November 24, 1938. So stated the matter of fact three-by-two inch paragraph on page 87…business abandoned and extinguished, family immigrated to Palestine.

I was not the historian, but I had some other historical information.

The Meyer's son was not incarcerated. He was thrown from the balcony at the back of the house like a piece of garbage.

"Dr.Lueck, do you know what happened to the Meyer's son?"

He was fearful now and looked around in the room. Was anyone listening?

"Please speak to me in English," he said.

I gladly complied. "Do you know that Willi Meyer's son was thrown from the balcony on Kristallnacht?" When I repeated the question, he nodded.

"Just found out about it. It was too late to include in the book. I only recently discovered there was an eyewitness. Edgar August was the baby's name. They grabbed him out of his baby carriage and you're right; they threw him off the balcony and beat his parents and grandmother into unconsciousness."

I gasped. "Who did it?"

"I don't know. All records were destroyed. I could not uncover a thing about anyone who participated and I only came to Bottrop as an historian in the 1970s."

"You're looking at the daughter of one of the guilty, Herr Doktor Lueck. Edgar August is my neighbor's son. We owned the building next door, number 332, and my parents were ardent Nazis."

This chance meeting had turned up revelations for both of us, but the atmosphere became so intense that I could only ask a few more questions.

"How many Jews lived in Bottrop?"

"About 200."

"What happened to them?"

"They all perished."

"Are there Jews in Bottrop now?"

"No."

We were both spent, and I was ready to leave. Then I realized that he might not have known what happened to the Meyer baby.

"Did you know the baby did not perish?" I said.

Dr. Lueck shook his head, surprised.

"He was caught and saved by the arms of a man called Friedrich Sommer. A young woman, Johanna Banner, hid the boy till he was smuggled to England on a Kindertransport. Edgar August may still be alive and I live for the day when I will find him. Dr. Lueck, you should know that there once lived two heroes in the town of Bottrop."

I forgot to tell him that I now was a Jew.

My Plea

Edgar August Meyer, born September 1937 in Essen, Germany, son of Wilhelm and Fajga Dobra Meyer – you are my beloved neighbor's son. Are you still living on this earth? Where are you? Do you have children?

If any member of the Meyer family of Bottrop reads this or anyone knows their whereabouts, please kindly contact me via email at ankhapp@aol.com or visit my website www.theneighborsson.com.

*

The young girl Willi Meyer spoke to in 1951 became a woman who never forgot and never will.

We all need forgiveness just as we need to forgive. I will always be a seeker of truth.

Epilogue

THE CLERGYMAN AT my brother's funeral in 2001 said that he saw Fritz as a lone protestor in the town square of Hemer, Germany, with a placard that read: "PEACE."

Fritz left several letters one of them was for me. It contained family data and a few sparse explanations on how he felt or wanted the world to know he thought and felt about our father:

"Our father was an honest and upright German civil servant. His great love for nature was the driving force in his life. Besides his occupation as teacher he was employed as official consultant in matters of mycology with his own department for flora and fungus research.

His membership in the National Socialist Party was the result of his naïveté and political inexperience, not in the least because at the time it was unthinkable for an educator not to be politically affiliated. It would have been professional suicide not to be. Later, after the war, he admitted to have been too politically inexperienced and that his conduct and his support of the national leadership was an error. At his trial, which was unjustly brought against him, he was classified as a Mitlaufer (reluctant follower)."

*

Fritz never faced the truth, at least not openly. But his actions spoke louder than his words. He was in fact a deserter

403

from the German navy and orders had been given to shoot him on sight if he was caught in the arctic region in the winter of 1945.

Fritz knew, as did I, that our father was not a reluctant follower, but a passionate Nazi. Unlike me, until the end of his days, my brother felt the need to close ranks and defend our parents. Maybe he wanted to lift my burden and make me feel better. It was our mother who could more accurately be described as a follower.

*

After the bustle of Los Angeles and Florida's flat and humid beauty, I once again live in a small picturesque town, a North Carolina town very much like Klingenberg am Main where I was born. People know each other and care about their neighbors, and that means a lot to me.

There's the beauty of hills and meadows and the majesty of the Smokey and Blue Ridge Mountain Ranges, as well as a scenic river and vineyards that produce some excellent wines.

I take joy in watching the bright red cardinal, chickadees and the family of doves who wait patiently on my balcony for their breakfast of sunflower seeds, fruits and nuts. I drink in the vibrancy of the changing seasons--blooming dogwoods in spring, a summer's hike through mountain wilderness, autumn's hope that every fallen leaf will be replaced by a bud in spring and the stillness of a stark winter's night with a cozy fire lit and one of the cats purring on my lap.

No longer do I try to swim upstream or wonder what might have been. Yet I often reflect on the people from my past. My parents, who gave me life, but were not part of the way I lived it. My brother, whose humanity I did not see until I attended his funeral and it was too late to exchange thoughts. They are my dead and part of me, as I was always part of them. I will never be able to let them go.

I believed that I was free of prejudice and bigotry of any kind when in fact I was imprisoned by the most terrible kind, hatred against my own family and people.

My story is not unique. There are countless women and men, who also left our homeland at the time I did and probably for the same reason. We settled all over the world and tried to deny our Germanness, to ourselves as well as to the people we encountered along the way. I wandered to England, Africa and the United States, in search of an identity that would be better than my own. I became African and Jew and always fell short.

Heimat is more than just home and homeland. It cannot be translated into any one word and contains components of the spirit, feelings of well being and belonging. We all have to belong somewhere.

Yet we hoped that if we distanced ourselves physically from that most beautiful stretch of land in the heart of Europe we once called Heimat, we could free ourselves from its stigma. We wanted to move forward and seek different seas, rivers, mountains and cities. Eventually, we had to come home to piece together and realize who we are, where we came from and who we have become.

*

In 2001 I finally became a citizen of the United States and I believe that this remarkable nation has a special role to bring peace, unity and justice to the rest of the world.

*

Willi Meyer came back to the place of his torment soon after the war and offered us a heart filled with gratitude for the man who saved his son and the woman who hid him. Had he been received differently and his suffering been acknowledged, the process of forgiveness and healing might have started right then and there on the fateful spring day of 1951.

But we were not able to receive a person of such generous spirit, because he was a Jew. Could it be because we felt we did not deserve to be in the presence of such a man? Or was it plain hatred of Jews and the fear of retribution?

Today we are desensitized to pain and suffering. We listen to and watch great horrors from every part of the world. Perhaps what happened to the 200 Bottrop Jews many years ago does not seem so unusual and important from the perspective of current events. Yet, it is part of the greatest inhumanity ever committed, and it is an indelible part of my own personal history.

We must remain vigilant and dedicated and preserve the truth of the Shoah. We must learn from it and make sure nothing like it ever happens again. Firsthand testimony will soon be gone, but our work must continue for as long as we live and beyond through our children and our children's children.

*

I hope one day I will be able to tell Edgar August Meyer that I, as the only remaining member of the original Steffens family of four, accept responsibility. It was my family and others like it who turned away from them. They were our neighbors, and we betrayed them. We stole their livelihood, their property, their memories, their Heimat.

Like the Meyers, I am also a voiceless stranger in the country of my birth. I have no influence with anyone in Bottrop, but I would dearly like to see the Meyers and the other Jews of Bottrop receive some justice at least and at last.

I call the now thriving Bottrop and any other town "where the shoe fits" to look back into its past and reach out to the special human beings who were once part of its life, by establishing permanent Jewish memorials and by compensating the Meyers and the other families for what was so cruelly stolen from them.

Liesel Steffens Appel 2005

Acknowledgements

My appreciation goes to two great New York literary agents, Richard Pine of "Inkwell Management," and Adam Chromy of "Artists and Artisans. They both believed in the story of *The Neighbor's Son*. Much gratitude to Chuck Hurewitz, my California attorney, for his steadfastness and protecting me, and to attorney Dr. Aaron Bovshow and his wife Herta for their friendship. Thank you to my editor, Dr. Charles Patterson, for pushing me to reach deeper into my consciousness. Thanks to "my" Rabbi, Allan Freehling, Patricia Haynie and the Jupiter, Florida and Asheville, North Carolina Bahai'i communities for their spiritual guidance. I have always believed: "The world is but one country and mankind it's citizens." Credit goes to Robert E. Kelley and the Tuesday Night Gipsy Moon writer's gang, Drs. Brian and Anna Marie Clement, my buddies at Hippocrates Health Institute and the Biltmore Estate and my neighbors at Belvedere. My many non-human companions, past and present, are never forgotten. They brought so much joy into my life. (That's EB Longoria with me on the cover.) I hold dear my children, Hugh K. Scotland and Annette L. Browne. My grandchildren, Jessica and Tyler Browne; you are our hope for the future as are the Appel children Kasey and Sofia. Christine Longoria, I cherish you my friend extraordinaire. And most of all, Don Appel, husband of my heart. What are you doing the rest of your life?

CPSIA information can be obtained
at www.ICGtesting.com
Printed in the USA
LVOW13s1023020217
522993LV00016B/458/P